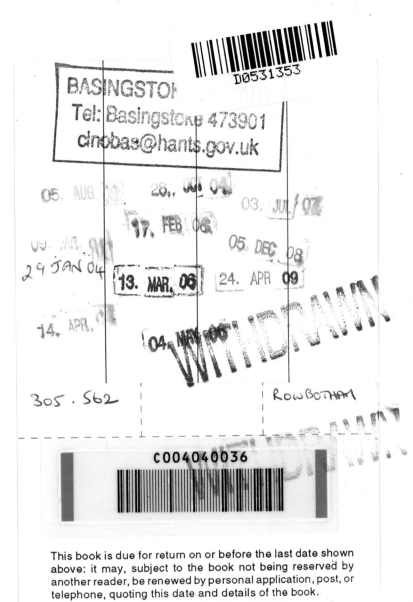
This book is due for return on or before the last date shown above: it may, subject to the book not being reserved by another reader, be renewed by personal application, post, or telephone, quoting this date and details of the book.

HAMPSHIRE COUNTY COUNCIL
County Library

100% recycled paper

Looking at Class

Film, Television and the Working Class in Britain

Edited by
Sheila Rowbotham
and
Huw Beynon

Rivers Oram Press / London New York Sydney

First published in 2001 by
Rivers Oram Press
144 Hemingford Road
London N1 1DE

Distributed in the USA by
New York University Press
838 Broadway
New York
NY 10003-4812

Distributed in Australia by UNIReps
University of New South Wales
Sydney
NSW 2052

Set in Helvetica by NJ Design Associates
and printed in Great Britain by TJ (International) Ltd,
Padstow, Cornwall

Front cover photograph by Sirkka-Liisa Konttinen/
Amber Associates

British Library Cataloguing in Publication Data
A catalogue record for this book is available from
the British Library

ISBN (cloth) 1 85489 120 0
ISBN (paper) 1 85489 121 9

Contents

Acknowledgements

Thanks to all the contributors for giving their time and for their support in the long process of editing. We are grateful to Sonia Lane, Ann Oluwole and Sandra Bonney for typing the transcripts of the conference and the interviews; also Sandra Bonney and Anne Morrow provided crucial administrative back-up. Thanks also to Tony Garnett, Ken Loach, Parallax Films, Lynne Ramsay, Skreba World Productions, Amber Films, Berwick Street Film Collective, Faction Films, Zero One, Lusia Films and Kalina Owczarek for help in tracking down visuals; Humphrey Trevelyan, Lusia Films, Hermione Harris and Jonathan Collinson who provided information on the dating of Marc Karlin's films and to Ken Loach and *Red Pepper* for permission to reprint 'The Subversive Who Surprises'. We thank the Lipmann-Miliband trust for a grant which enabled Kerry William Purcell to do the picture research. Thanks to Helen Armitage for laborious and exhaustive editing. Finally thanks to Will Atkinson whose love of the movies was infectious.

Stills and photographs are courtesy of Amber Films, BBC, Berwick Street Film Collective, Channel 4, Paul Chedlow, Steve Conlan, Faction Films, Sunil Gupta, Sirkka-Liisa Konttinen, Lusia Films, Parallax, Pathé, Skreba, Southall Black Sisters, World Productions and Zero One. Every effort has been made to contact all copyright holders. The publishers will be pleased to make good in future editions any errors or omissions brought to their attention.

Marc Karlin, who died on 19 January 1999, was a vital inspirational force behind both the conference 'Images of Labour' held at Manchester University in 1997 and the decision to put this collection together. *Looking at Class* is dedicated to his memory.

WHATEVER HAPPENED TO THE WORKING CLASS?

Sheila Rowbotham and Huw Beynon

Looking at Class originated in 'Images of Labour: A Conference on Films and the Working Class in Britain, 1957–97', which we organised with Paul Kelemen through the International Centre for Labour Studies at Manchester University in March 1997. It was jointly sponsored by the Cornerhouse Cinema and Frontline Books, which ran an accompanying programme of films and a special sales promotion of relevant books.

We had started to plan the conference in 1996, wondering how the big changes occurring in the lives of working-class people were being treated by film-makers. We wanted to find out how radical film-makers have managed to work in the double sense of the structure of their industry and the aesthetic forms, the means of representation they have adopted. We also wanted to know why? What personal, cultural and political influences led them to look at the working class, and how have these ways of looking changed? These questions, posed from differing perspectives, run right through the book.

In compiling *Looking at Class* we have followed an approach that has guided much of our own research and writing. We have both been involved in gathering oral evidence since the early 1970s and see personal testimonies as valuable both as sources of individual experience and as indicators of wider social and cultural processes. While the core of the material in the collection comes from the conference, we have supplemented edited versions of the original lectures with interviews and new contributions.

1 Handing on Histories

Sheila Rowbotham and Huw Beynon

Almost every portrayal of working class people in the story-film is either as creatures of fun, Cockney types or rustic half-wits, or as dishonest rogues, tramps and pick pockets. Paul Rotha, 1936[1]

The late 1950s and early 1960s, the period when *Looking at Class* begins, appeared to mark a decisive break in the representation of class. First came the films influenced by realistic novels and kitchen-sink plays and then innovative television drama dealing with social issues. Once again, in the late 1990s, a cluster of comedies have taken working-class themes—obvious examples are Mark Herman's *Brassed Off* (1996) and Peter Cattaneo's *The Full Monty* (1997). Several directors, including Gary Oldman (*Nil By Mouth*, 1997), Shane Meadows (*TwentyFourSeven*, 1997), and Lynne Ramsay (*Ratcatcher*, 1999) have also produced sombre work that has been hailed as renascent 'British grit'.[2] Yet while the work of the late 1950s and '60s pulsated with anger and a sense that change for the better was in the offing, the films of the late 1990s are more pessimistic; they portray a world of disintegration where characters survive against the odds through humour or a desperate tenacity of spirit.

In 'Working in the Field' Tony Garnett asks the question, what nowadays is the 'working class' exactly? It is evident that much has altered in the last forty years, both in terms of work structure and the configuration of daily life. The old manufacturing industries have declined dramatically, and new kinds of production have been radically restructured, along with the public sector. Finance and the service sector have grown in significance; part-time work has increased. The trade unions have been weakened by these structural changes as well as by the legislative assault mounted on them since the 1980s. Assumptions about regular work and secure jobs have been shattered in the process. On the other hand, consumption patterns and the lived environment have been transformed. New housing has replaced the old back-to-backs with their sooty chimneys and outdoor lavatories. Continuing education has become more general. Attitudes to women working, to illegitimacy, to homosexuality and to race have all shifted radically.

These factors have contributed to very different ways of seeing the working class from those that prevailed in the 1950s. It is no longer possible to ignore the entry of women, including those with children, into the workforce, or to

Sheila Rowbotham is a reader in sociology at Manchester University. She has written extensively on women's and labour history and been involved in several films including *Night Cleaners*, *British Sounds* and *Edward and Dorothy Thompson*. Her most recent books are *A Century of Women: The History of Women in Britain and the United States* (1997), *Threads through Time: Writings on History and Autobiography* (1999) and *Promise of a Dream: Remembering the Sixties* (2000).

present an homogenised 'working-class' experience that excludes racial diversity. This sharper awareness of gender and race controverts earlier over simple assumptions about class that took the male Northern working class as the norm and has also led to an interest in regional and ethnic differences in the past.It has also contributed to the recognition of the need to consider communities as well as workplaces.[3]

While we are living through an intense process of transition in which class structure and people's experiences of class are altering rapidly, contemporary Britain remains a profoundly unequal society. Our own view is that far from the working class being abolished, it has been driven into new habitats and acquired new forms and boundaries. This working class in-the-making undeniably possesses very different characteristics from the working class of the 1950s, or indeed of the 1970s. It remains unclear, however, whether this can be characterised as the definitive rupture that some commentators have detected.

Historically it has been the case that the working class has gone through several such makings and remakings—at each turn drawing on symbols, rituals, ideas and belief-systems that were previously established. These have shifted their meanings in the process of being adapted to new circumstances.[4] Living amidst a dramatic period of rapid change makes it difficult to predict how the past will be transplanted into the future and find new roots. It is incontestable that class-based social solidarity has been severely disrupted and that the institutions that once supported collective forms of understanding have been seriously weakened. However, as long as unequal and exploitative conditions persist, there is a strong likelihood of an awareness of class refiguring, even though the manner in which a new consciousness of class will be expressed is not apparent.

These questions have been hard to pose partly because any discussion of working-class experience has become peculiarly unmentionable, politically and theoretically. Indeed words such as 'workers' and 'labour' have assumed an archaic inflection. Several odd disjunctures in perception have emerged as a result. While 'class struggle' has been expunged from mainstream Labour politics, a Gallup Poll in Britain in 1995 recorded that 81 per cent of the population believed there to be a class struggle between the haves and have-nots.[5] Moreover a 1996 poll conducted by the *Sunday Times* revealed that the majority of people in Britain considered themselves to belong to the working class! The *Sunday Times* editorial commented: 'Confused? Either they are or we are.'[6]

Although a growing body of empirical data is demonstrating how the gap between rich and poor has grown over the last two decades, within academia the theoretical discussion of 'class' is enveloped in a fog of confusion.[7] Whereas in the past commentators had privileged class and ignored other categories of resistance, many sociologists and historians in recent years have become wary of class as a category of analysis. From the mid-1980s in both the social sciences and cultural studies, interest in other aspects of identity, gender, race and ethnicity, instead of leading to a more dynamic and inclusive understanding

Huw Beynon is Director of the new School of Social Science at Cardiff University. He was previously professor of Sociology at the University of Manchester. His books include *Masters and Servants: Class and Patronage in the Making of a Labour Organisation* with Terry Austrin (1994) and *Patterns of Social Inequality* co-edited with Pandeli Glavanis (1999).

of class, has increasingly come to replace it. Conversely, gender, race and ethnicity are now frequently viewed in isolation without any consideration of how they, too, are all affected by class.[8]

It is not just that 'class' has fallen into this curious disrepute; the theoretical interconnections between social existence and culture have also been severed. Although 'cultural studies' as an academic discipline derived partly from the work of Richard Hoggart and Raymond Williams, who drew on their own experience of class to think through cultural changes, it was to move very far away from its social and material beginnings. The main thrust has been to dump the restraints of the material along with its lumbering sociological accoutrements. The initial rejection of a crude Marxist reduction of culture to the economic is comprehensible, but the adversarial path then taken proved so extreme that it was to divert attention from the history of material and social practices altogether, bypassing Williams' insight that culture itself is material and that material life includes cultural processes.[9]

When we began to plan the conference on 'Images of Labour' we were aware that our perspective differed from the tendency in recent cultural theory to focus on a specific piece of work and ignore its social surroundings. Our starting point in *Looking at Class* has been the conviction that recognising that the representation of reality is complicated need not lead to the dead end of denying that any reality exists. Reality is both imagined and 'there'.

Conversely, looking at economic and social change is integrally connected to understanding the process by which values, beliefs and ideas are maintained and developed through cultural practices and institutional forms. John Hill observes in his study of British cinema in the late 1950s and early 1960s *Sex, Class and Realism*, that films 'do more than just "reflect" they also actively explain and interpret the way in which the world is to be perceived and understood'.[10] Our own research into the social history of the nineteenth and twentieth centuries has made us aware how this 'symbolic landscape',[11] to use Jessica Evans' phrase in *The Camerawork Essays*, constitutes a crucial means by which transformation becomes manifest. Visual imagery can thus provide some vital clues for thinking about how individuals situate themselves in new circumstances.

At a more hands-on level the 'Images of Labour' conference and *Looking at Class* have also grown out of our own involvement in various forms of radical cultural activity that have sought to democratise thought and creativity. Huw Beynon worked closely with left documentary film-makers, including Amber in Newcastle during the 1970s and '80s, while Sheila Rowbotham was similarly involved with radical documentaries in London, initially through friendship with Marc Karlin from 1969 and subsequently as a consultant on several films. Although there are references to work done elsewhere, these two contrasting places provide the main setting for *Looking at Class*.

A series of groupings, collectives and associations of radical film-makers developed nationally from the 1960s. These in turn have been part of a wider oppositional culture which has included alternative bookshops and publishing

Dream On, 1992
(Steve Conlan: Amber)

groups, fringe theatre, community art and community newspapers. This vigor-
ous radical culture, which flourished in the 1960s and '70s, and managed to
survive through the 1980s and into the '90s, is much less known than the left
theoretical debates that have passed into academia, yet it is a crucial element
in the history of political film-making. Moreover it too has generated a rich seam
of arguments and ideas about art, communication and the media which deserve
greater consideration.[12] *Looking at Class* bears witness to this hidden, subversive
tradition which, despite fierce disagreements, has aimed to return artistry to those
whose labour has always sustained it and to hold on to the hope of imbuing
life with a vision of possibilities that defy the way things are. Our desire to put
on record the contribution of the film-makers and critics in this collection has
been partly prompted by an awareness of the fickleness of historical memory.
Even a relatively recent radical past can be so easily submerged and obliter-
ated.

The personal chronicles record how oppositional approaches have survived
against the odds while charting a series of radical waves in British film. The
theme of how things came to be made also recurs. *Looking at Class* thus documents how the changing conditions of production have affected the circumstances in which people labour—a subject we have both written on in differing
contexts.[13] Instead of separating theory and analysis from the practice of
'making', we wanted to show how they can interact creatively.

We were to find that we were not, in fact, as out on a limb as we had initially
imagined. In recent years there have been distinct indications of unease and

several calls for the study of culture to touch ground. In *The Art of Record*, for example, John Corner stated, 'the development of theoretical work has often increasingly divorced itself from attention to specific practices and artefacts, setting itself up as a relatively autonomous discursive activity "above" the level both of practice and practical criticism.'[14]

Our starting point has been the assumption that seeing how images of the working class are conceived requires understanding the material factors affecting class in the wider society, as well as how these have had an impact on the institutional frameworks in which radicals in film and television have been able to work. From the mid-1990s a new crop of books started to appear that has taken a more social and historical perspective. *Looking at Class* thus appears when there is a growing awareness that the relationship between material existence and culture is dynamic and integrally interconnected. As Greg Philo and David Miller observe in their study of cultural theory and contemporary society, *Market Killing*:[15]

Media representations can crystallise and express the key moments in relationships which define a period or type of society. In this sense media images grow historically and are located in the material world. But they also extend, legitimise or comment on such relationships—they can celebrate or criticise. In this they have a crucial role in the winning of consent for a social system, its values and its dominant interests, or in the rejection of them.

The film-makers in *Looking at Class* have been revealing, defining and illuminating ideas and aspects of life that have been neglected and excluded from the dominant culture since the early 1960s. The individual accounts register how the possibilities of presenting images of class have shifted over time, opening in certain periods in some areas of the visual media, while contracting in others. Both individuals and associations have played a vital role in creating space. For example Tony Garnett describes the importance of Sidney Newman, a left-winger from Canadian drama, in creating the slot of the Wednesday Play in the '60s. His arrival coincided with a moment of radical hope in the possibility of change, which was to be expressed in a series of powerful TV plays protesting against capital punishment, homelessness, prison conditions and the illegality of abortion. To young left-wing film-makers in the 1960s the subjects appeared to be all out there waiting for drama to be made about them. Tony Garnett has described how they were driven by a sense of urgency about politics and a desire to 'make sense of the world'.[16]

This feeling of being able to have an impact upon political and social attitudes was partly based on the particular conditions of TV as a medium in this period. Tony Garnett and Ken Loach were able to reach a mass audience through TV at a time when, as Tony Garnett observes, two channels meant a play would become a talking point the following day.

During the 1980s the arrival of Channel 4 was again to provide an extraordinary exhibition space and source of funding for radical independent film-makers. Combined with Greater London Council funding, Channel 4 made it possible for experimental and radical film-making to develop, as Isaac Julien, Gita Sahgal and James Swinson all testify. However, openings also contain within them certain problems, and James Swinson records a rigidity in the bureaucratic funding categories that sliced people into distinct and fragmented 'identities' of race, ethnicity and gender in the manner of American-style equal opportunities while maintaining a silence on class. Beneath the rhetoric he notes how class attitudes at the new Channel were remarkably similar to the upper-middle-class ethos of the BBC. Alan Fountain played a key role as commissioning editor in the independent Film and Video Unit. His slot *The 11th Hour* was open to innovation and creativity. But he points out that the victory the Channel represented in terms of access was to be undermined by its role in breaking up the regulated working conditions in the television industry.

Looking at Class demonstrates too how the fortunes of different kinds of radical film-makers have varied within the same period. For Ken Loach, working in a naturalistic form and making directly political documentaries, the 1980s were frustrating and restrictive. Loach's documentary *Which Side Are You On?* about the miners' strike in 1984–5, was rejected by London Weekend Television's *South Bank Show*. It was later shown on Channel 4. But a series of films about the Tory onslaught on trade unionism and the effort to devise opposing strategies among trade unionists were never to be transmitted by Channel 4.

By the late 1980s there was a cautious conservatism pervading the media in general. Alan Fountain describes how this process of ideological closure arrived at Channel 4. It was never an overt political contestation, but instead expressed as a sneer—left-wing socialism was simply 'old fashioned'. This political shift in the culture coincided with the battering that the trade unions in general were receiving. Alan Fountain observes that the result of these defeats both inside and outside the industry were to make it harder to treat class issues.

Although the world of feature films is quite separate from TV, the difficulties in operating have led some left film-makers to oscillate between the two. Ken Loach, Tony Garnett and Sally Hibbin have worked in both and comment on the advantages and disadvantages. Sally Hibbin recounts the long, drawn-out process of getting a feature film financed and the need to put together funding from different sources. Channel 4's financing of low-budget work has been crucial since the late 1980s. However, even when a film is made, exhibition and distribution continue to be extremely problematic. Nina Hibbin tells how she ran an alternative cinema in Tyneside from the mid-1970s.

Peter Stead shows how the studio system that prevailed in the 1950s was seen by film-makers in the 'New Wave' as rigid and limiting. When independent companies were established however, they lost the guaranteed distribution outlets that the big organisations that ran the studios secured for their films. Tony Garnett points to the irony of the late 1990s: feature films can be made that are unable to find an audience of any size. Tony Garnett prefers to keep working in television and continues to reach large audiences through series that use popular genres but are scripted by writers with direct experience.

This dilemma of how to reach audiences is a recurring preoccupation. Alan Fountain believes one of the weaknesses of the modernist avant-garde project was the emphasis on creation and a disregard for audience. He argues there has to be a balance between producing a film and reaching an audience. Isaac Julien considers that an audience can be made—something that the experimental black film-makers have in fact managed to a certain extent. He sees a way for himself through the closing down of possiblity on television by doing different kinds of work in various contexts. The outlets he mentions include universities—in the United States especially there is a growing audience. Both he and James Swinson have also worked within the art world, doing video installations. Sally Hibbin mentions the films being made by young people to show at raves, while Alan Fountain with Sylvia Stevens from Faction Films have been exploring using the internet as a global exhibition and distribution network through Mondial.

Though the alternative collectivities of the 1970s and the networks of the 1980s have been largely broken up, new groups and connections were to emerge in the 1990s. Ken Fero from Migrant Media was among the speakers at the 'Images of Labour' conference for example. The group has made several films on civil liberties, state violence and racism—*Tasting Freedom* and *Britain's Black Legacy*. Kerry William Purcell, who writes in *Looking at Class* on *Riff-Raff* (1990) and *Nil by Mouth* (1997), belongs to a new film group, 'Revolutionary Eye Productions', which is working on a film about the White Russian photographer Alexey Brodovitch. Many different kinds of radical work are being covered in film magazines, and on the internet, while the Lux Cinema in Hoxton, east London, has begun to show left films that have been disregarded and marginalised.

Technological developments from smaller cameras to the arrival of video have affected how films can be made. Kim Gordon argues that space for working in the mainstream could be gained once again because the new digital technology is resulting in a myriad of television channels.

As Tony Garnett remarks, radical film-makers are going to continue working in many different ways. It is a fair bet too that disputes will persist between them about *how*, in terms of aesthetic forms. When Alan Fountain was commissioning films at Channel 4 during the 1980s and early '90s, he says he tried to take an eclectic approach. This was a period when there was a powerful theoretical challenge to naturalism and the mixing of documentary and dramatic narrative that had seemed iconoclastic in the previous two decades. From the late 1990s, in contrast, there was to be a certain revival of interest in the differing historical versions of realism and naturalism and in documentary forms. 'Docusoaps' have joined 'dramadoc' and 'docudrama' and are generating a weighty critical literature. Boundaries are notoriously slithery and definitions are much disputed theoretically.[17] Tony Garnett now emphatically rejects the tag 'drama documentary' as a source of confusion, stressing that though he and Ken Loach were interested in documentary techniques in the 1960s, they were creating works of fiction.

The documenting of daily life in naturalistic or realistic ways are not the only aesthetic approaches discussed in *Looking at Class*, and images of class have not been exclusively presented through these forms. However, they have historically been very much associated with the representation of the working class in British films and TV.

While radical film-makers since the late 1950s have been influenced by the world around them, they have also drawn on a long history of ideas, debates and work within radical culture. As Judith Williamson observes, looking at class involves understanding the history of representation, as well as a history of what is happening in society. One of the fascinating and unexpected elements in compiling *Looking at Class* was the way in which cultural traditions intersect and weave through all the accounts. Influences mentioned from within Britain include the British documentary film-makers of the 1930s and '40s, such as John Grierson, Humphrey Jennings and Paul Rotha, and the 'Free Cinema' movement, which made documentary films about the poetry of everyday life during the 1950s.[18] Inspiration has not of course been nationally confined. Italian Neorealism for example is mentioned by Peter Stead and Judith Williamson as an influence on the British New Wave. It emerged after the Second World War and the defeat of the fascists, when left film-makers in Italy sought to renew Italian culture. This moment in Italian cinema has an obvious resonance in the TV work of Tony Garnett and Ken Loach in the 1960s. The Neorealists deliberately focused on 'ordinary' life; they used location shots and a mix of actors and non-actors. Chance affects the characters' lives; endings are left open rather than given happy resolutions.

As Judith Williamson stresses there have been differing historical versions of realism, as well as a much wider range of radical aesthetic approaches. For example, the French students' and workers' rebellion in May 1968 revived interest in the aesthetic debates of the Soviet revolution. Marc Karlin, who from 1969 to 1998 worked with Cinema Action, the Berwick Street Film Collective and Lusia Films, describes not only the influence of the left-wing experimental film-maker Chris Marker upon him but also Marker's infectious enthusiasm for early Soviet film-makers such as Dziga Vertov and Alexander Medvedkin. Dziga Vertov was part of the Montage (mounting) movement that also included the better-known Sergei Eisenstein. Their juxtaposition of contrasting images communicated conflict and suggested meanings, which jumped beyond the conventional sequences of time and space. Vertov insisted on the need to connect form and content in order to create 'a fresh perception of the world',[19] and he experimented endlessly with techniques. For instance A. L. Rees, in *A History of Experimental Film and Video,* notes that for Vertov 'the gaps between shots…are equal in value to the shots themselves.'[20]

Vertov was scornful of fictional feature films as 'cine-nicotine'[21]—a sentiment shared by the iconoclasts of the late 1960s and early '70s. His conception of the 'Kino-Eye'[22] rejected the role of the 'director-enchanter'.[23] Kristin Thompson and David Bordwell say in their Film History that Vertov believed '"life caught unawares" would be the basis for a cinema of fact'.[24] Vertov's conviction that, as a film-maker, he could 'decipher in a new way a world unknown',[25] appealed to radical film-makers imbued with the heady hopes of May '68. So did the mobility of *The Man with the Movie Camera*—the title of Vertov's 1929 film. Mobility and dispensing with elaborate sets were very much the ethos of the late 1960s. Alexander Medvedkin, who travelled around the Soviet Union in the early 1930s making films with peasants and workers rather than with actors, possessed a similar appeal.

French film-makers set up their own alternative groups modelled on the Soviet film-makers. In 1969 the Medvedkin Group included Jean-Luc Godard and Chris Marker. Godard was later to form the Dziga-Vertov Group; while Chris Marker established the Parisian group SLON. These groups inspired similar film collectives in many other countries, including Britain, from the late 1960s.[26] Isaac Julien, from a later generation of radical film-makers, also refers to early Soviet work and specifically the effect Eisenstein had upon him.

The aesthetic influences mentioned in *Looking at Class* extend beyond cinema. For example Tony Garnett describes how he and Ken Loach were initially influenced by Brecht, and both pay tribute to Joan Littlewood's radical theatre. Her Theatre Workshop, as the experimental theatre company Theatre Union, founded in 1935, was known when it reformed in 1945, drew, in turn, on the work of the dramatist and singer Ewan MacColl, with whom she had collaborated in left drama and radio programmes in Manchester during the 1930s. Not only did MacColl and Littlewood seek out authentic voices through oral interviews, they adopted Stanislavski's method of actors identifying with their characters long before the late 1950s when the ideas of both Stanislavski and Brecht were exerting an influence upon British avant-garde theatre.[27]

The technique of mixing stories and fact also preceded the 1960s. *Drama Documentary* was the title of a compilation produced by the left-wing Unity Theatre in London after the Second World War and was used to describe Ted Willis' Unity play about the coal industry, *Black Magic*, in 1946. The basis for both was the 1930s radical dramatisation of the news, *Living Newspaper*, and the Play Unit of the Army Bureau of Current Affairs during World War Two.[28]

Judith Williamson points out that a distinction needs to be made between the representation of 'the working class' by left-wing film-makers and films and TV soaps aimed at a mass audience, which portray working-class characters. She observes how the latter frequently combine realism with melodrama. This has a history. Despite long debates about aesthetics in left circles, in practice this mix of styles was often adopted because it brought working-class audiences to radical theatres. These shows were to influence both musicals and TV; Unity, for instance, nurtured several future key figures in television light entertainment. Instead of presenting the working class as an authentic, or opposing voice, in the manner of the radical tradition of social criticism, the focus is on warmth of feeling and community reminiscent of some of Dickens' novels and music hall.

Jacquetta May notes similar characteristics in *EastEnders*, in which she acted the part of Rachel during the early 1990s. Though working-class soaps,

Night Cleaners, 1975
(Berwick Street Film
Collective)

especially *EastEnders*, often deal with social topics such as unemployment, casual work or race, social criticism is muted by the emphasis on personal fellowhip.[29] Soaps take up issues, they do not portray collective working-class action as Ken Loach has done in films such as *The Big Flame* (1969) and *The Flickering Flame* (1996). The process of interaction between aesthetic forms has continued; for instance the feature film *Brassed Off* (1996) employed some soap-style motifs to convey a story about a miners' brass band facing the closure of their pit, as did *Dockers* (1999), the TV film about the docks dispute, produced by Sally Hibbin for Channel 4.

A dilemma that has been resolved in differing ways at various times by radical film-makers has been whether to work within popular forms of representation or to experiment with existing forms and ways of working as a means of communicating their opposition to conventional assumptions. Whereas Loach and Garnett, as part of the early '60s left in the media, had sought to reach mass audiences through mainstream channels of communication, the impact of the student-worker rebellion, the May Events in France in 1968, was to foster an oppositional approach to radical culture in defiance of the mainstream. Suspicion of the media marked the new student left in many countries and affected journalism, publishing and the visual arts. Working in the mainstream seemed impossible without 'incorporation'; radicals instead set about creating alternatives, in which the emphasis was on producers retaining control over their creative activity and communicating directly without mediation.[30]

This refusal contained a residual ambivalence towards technology, a stance that was to have negative consequences in the long term, as Kim Gordon notes. Historically, however, this distrust of modernity on the revolutionary left can be understood as a prescient protest against incipient changes in the communications industry, which threatened the independence of artistic and intellectual work. It is interesting, for instance, that it was to be the counter culture which pioneered video art and community video.

However, the hippy underground and the left film-makers in the late 1960s and early '70s shared a feeling of impatience with older styles of politics and communication. For those on the left, demonstrating the need for reforms was not enough; the forms of communicating had to break with convention and jolt audiences into a realisation of the need to transform capitalism as a system. Consequently the artistic impulse of the period was not to portray real life but to find forms through which it could be split open and surmounted—evident still in Marc Karlin's desire to freeze and explode images into moments of critical perception and realisation. Moreover Marc Karlin's film *Night Cleaners* (1975) deliberately used blank screens and long close-up shots to give the audience time to consider the implications of the documentary.

While the radical film groups of the late 1960s and early 1970s were wary of co-option, they sought new audiences. *Night Cleaners*, for example, was shown around the country at radical meetings. Marc Karlin's account of Cinema Action,[31] taking Third World films to Merseyside trade unionists, is part of a much wider revolutionary cultural evangelicalism, which began from where Arnold Wesker's 1960s Centre-42 had left off in 1970. Amber,[32] which Murray Martin describes, also played a pioneering role in creating a film workshop in Newcastle in 1968. Amber have kept a co-operative, egalitarian structure, sharing the profits and ploughing them back. Their independent status has been maintained by work for local campaigns which has been locally shown, for television and also feature films.

Groups such as Amber, the Berwick Street Film Collective and, later, Lusia Films were part of a wider 1970s radical film culture. As yet these local histories of cultural and political radicalism have been only sketchily chronicled. Murray Martin's and Nina Hibbin's accounts of Tyneside and Huw Beynon's discussion of the popular TV drama series, *Our Friends in the North*, detail the specific context of the North East. James Swinson recalls community politics in Brixton in the early 1970s, while Isaac Julien takes up another London story, telling how the local radical culture of the East End affected him during the late

1970s. He grew up in a black working-class family amid conflicts with the local fascist groups, and his political awareness evolved partly from his own situation and the conflicting debates about race that he encountered. His interest in visual images was stimulated by radical community-arts activism, such as the photography group Camerawork,[33] and by left film groups, such as Cinema Action and the Newsreel Collective. While studying at art school he was introduced to the experimental structuralist films of Malcolm le Grice[34] and William Raban,[35] which discarded narrative and symbolism. He was also inspired by black cinema, especially the work of Horace Ove[36] and Menelik Shabazz.[37]

Alan Fountain tells how the network of radical film workshops, including the one to which he belonged in Nottingham, contributed to the formation of the Independent Film-makers Association in 1974. Rooted within specific communities, they sustained the impetus to transform the means of communication through the 1970s.

Repeated attempts have been made to create alternative ways of showing both features and documentaries. From the late 1960s, several groups began distributing radical films: the Angry Arts group and Politkino, Liberation, WFA and the Other Cinema. The latter opened its own cinema in 1976 in an attempt to break the hold of the big companies over distribution and exhibition, but this venture failed. The Independent Film-Makers' Association (IFA) envisaged the establishment of an oppositional network nationally for making and distributing films. After the Other Cinema closed, the IFA's efforts were to turn mainly towards the creation of a fourth TV Channel. Ironically Channel 4 was both to stimulate and swallow up many of the small film collectives.

It is sobering to put this recent history in a longer term context. There was a time when radicals in the film industry had sought to develop alternative forms of distribution and exhibition on a much grander scale. One strategy was to demand a greater degree of state involvement, while another approach was simply to set up their own labour movement structures. In 1941, the Association of Cine Technicians (ACT), as the film union was then known, called for municipal state-run cinemas to combat the hold of big business.[38] The idea of alternative cinemas had been around in the labour movement for many years; the Derby Women's Co-operative Guild in 1919, for instance, argued for municipal cinemas 'where children could be shown pictures which would bring the best out of them and give them a love of things beautiful'.[39]

The Co-operative Movement set up its own cinemas in the 1930s and '40s with particular success in the North East and in West Yorkshire. By 1945 the private sector was worried that the co-ops would become the biggest circuit. *Co-op Circuit Menace* announced *Kine Weekly*.[40] The left and the labour movement also created their own distribution networks to communicate their politics. The Communist Party, for instance, used films from the late 1920s as part of their agitation and established two distribution agencies in the 1930s.

From within the Co-operative Movement and the Independent Labour Party, Joseph Reeves formed the Workers' Film Association in 1938. He wanted films to be made by trade unions about their members' working lives, but the

WFA (the National Film Association from 1946) was to act mainly as a distribution network.[41] In 1945 G. D. H. Cole urged the Co-operative Movement to be prepared to make 'a big splash' and take on the cinema distributors: 'We must have control of a great chain of cinemas or producing agencies so that we have a chance of showing a particular kind of film.'[42]

Hope of big splashes for 'a particular kind of film' swiftly died. However, in the early 1950s two Communists, Stanley Forman and Charles Cooper, began importing films from the Soviet Union and Eastern Europe through Plato and Contemporary Films.[43] They, along with Ralph Bond, another Communist veteran from the documentary-film movement of the 1930s and '40s, who was active in the film union, were to help the new radical film-makers' collectives that appeared in the late 1960s, even while denouncing them for being 'ultra left'.

Not only was this oppositional film culture of the radical collectives closely involved with working-class industrial militancy and community politics but it was also critically informed, debating the ideas of Brecht and Walter Benjamin, and aware of new waves in cinema internationally. Its history has been over-shadowed by the theoretical influence of *Screen* magazine, though James Swinson makes the very important point that there was not initially an absolute separation between the new film theory and left film groups. Each grew out of a common radical milieu, though they were later to go differing ways. In the first half of the 1970s some of the practitioners and the theorists were to be found working together. For example the feminist conceptual artist Mary Kelly worked on *Night Cleaners* with the Berwick Street Film Collective. Political awareness on the left about how the modern media was capable of manipu-lating subjective emotions combined with an acute consciousness among femi-nist and gay activists of the communicative power of definitions and visual representation. Both contributed to a rebellion against a crude reduction of visual culture to the economic and social. An exhaustive search for texts that could illuminate culture as an autonomous area requiring its own cryptogra-phy was the issue. Alan Fountain notes how this heady intellectual excitement fed into the contents of *Screen* during the 1970s and how its orientation was to shift during the 1980s as theoretical criticism became more and more divorced from practice. By the 1990s film theory was being academicised through new subject disciplines such as 'cultural studies', while practitioners were being increasingly immersed in the priorities set by the 'cultural indus-try'. As one went off into abstraction, the other vanished into the material.[44] The ironic outcome was that even the more conceptual films, as Alan Fountain and Isaac Julien point out, received relatively little attention.

During the long period of Conservative ascendancy from 1979 to 1997 the left became increasingly disoriented; geared up to tackle social democracy or Keynesian welfarism, socialists found themselves facing an opponent who did not play by the established rules. Work that was politically and socially critical of Thatcherism did continue to appear through the 1980s, even though the work-ing-class movement had been forced on to the defensive: in cinema, for example, Mike Leigh's *High Hopes* and, on television, Sally Hibbin's *A Very British Coup* (both 1988). Several films were to subvert and extend prevailing definitions of the working class with acute and complex portrayals of race, ethnicity and national identity. These include the perceptive *My Beautiful Laundrette*, Stephen Frears' 1985 film based on Hanif Kureishi's script, and *Queen and Country* (Martin Stellman, 1988) about a black ex-serviceman returning to his council estate after serving in the Falklands-Malvinas war to find he has been excluded from British citizenship by the 1981 British Nationality Act. The Thatcher decade also saw Karl Francis' searing *Milwr Bychan/Boy Soldier* (1988), about a Welsh soldier in Northern Ireland—the first Welsh-English bilingual film to be shown outside Wales. The persistence of this critical cinema provoked an outburst in 1988 from the historian Norman Stone who was politically sympathetic to the Thatcherite project. Writing in the *Sunday Times*, he railed against what he called, 'tawdry, ragged, rancidly provincial films'.[45]

However, as Sally Hibbin remarks it was very difficult to express what was happening while actually living under Thatcherism. All the film-makers in *Looking at Class* describe grappling with this question of how to respond to the 1980s, which affected their work in very different ways. It was partly a matter of incomprehension, partly confusion because some aspects of the libertarian left-wing case, such as the suspicion of the state, were incorporated into the new Conservatism. The assumed meanings of 'alternative', 'independent', indeed of 'socialism', were to be gradually emptied, a process accompanied by a peculiar forgetfulness, as if it were too painful to remember what had been hoped for. The political repercussions of defeats and the erosion of memory affected film-makers along with other radical communicators. John Hill makes the point in *British Cinema in the 1980s* that while the working class continued to be represented during the 1980s, it was less likely to be seen as carrying 'any particular set of countervailing values'.[46]

The cultural confusion and uncertainty of the 1980s was accompanied by the challenge of the social movements to received socialist versions of who were the working class and how class was to be represented. Gita Sahgal, who worked on the Bandung File and was in Southall Black Sisters, and Isaac Julien[47] have both played an important part in these 'new social movements' and stress their autonomous significance. On the other hand they do not equate contesting the limitations of a white male image of 'the working class' as the norm with a dismissal of 'class'. Since the mid-1980s social movements have tended to be theorised as distinct or in absolute opposition to those of the working class. Historically this has been a misleading perspective. The local reality was that they developed in interactive tension with the labour movement. These two interviews demonstrate how the impetus to rethink the meaning of class struggle in relation to race and gender was rooted in the turmoil of campaigns against fascism, police violence, immigration laws, racist attacks and murders along with action around domestic violence and gay and lesbian sexuality. All of this was accompanied by the growing militancy of women, including black and Asian women in the trade-union movement during the 1970s.

Isaac Julien tells how he became conscious of an absence during the 1970s. Black people were rarely on TV, and their presence was a noteworthy event regardless of what they were actually doing on screen. Left film-makers from the late '70s were beginning to present 'race', but it was framed as a 'problem', a perspective that filtered out many dimensions of experience. By working in the independent black workshop Sankofa, Isaac Julien was able to challenge both the restrictive expectations of a narrow political agenda and fixed essentialist views of racial identity. Sankofa, along with the Black Audio Film Collective, was set up in a period when funding was available from local authorities, such as the Greater London Council, as well as backing from Alan Fountain at Channel 4.[48]

Both Gita Sahgal and Jacquetta May note the much greater visibility of race on television during the 1990s, remarking how racial difference now tends to be presented without comment. In one sense this avoids the 'burden of representation', to which Judith Williamson refers. On the other hand, while the limitations for Asian and black actors of being expected to represent 'positive images' are evident, there are none the less problems in the denial of the social reality of racial difference—especially as white people are an overwhelming majority in television and possess the power to determine the terms of representation. Gita Sahgal also shows how the lack of explanation means that when race and class coincide the specific implications of the interaction are obscured.

Jacquetta May discusses how the soap, aimed at a female audience, though watched also by men, has been a genre on British TV in which the portrayal of working-class women has developed, albeit within certain limits. Ironically it has been the soaps that have created a space in which several kinds of working-class women's roles can be presented. Despite the boundaries of the stereotypical parts, the women have a crucial importance in the soaps as commentators on behaviour, opinion and feelings. In contrast to other popular genres, such as the action film, the soap foregrounds the personal and the everyday; Jacquetta May shows how working class women have a central position because they serve to reveal the plot, even though the men still tend to drive the action.

The soaps drew on and expanded the stereotypes that had figured in popular British comedies from the 1930s onwards. Hollywood, as Judith Williamson shows, has had a career-open-to-talent tradition of presenting working class women as aspirant and desiring. In contrast female British working-class film characters before the 1960s tended to be stoical wives, blonde and busty or versions of a Widow Twanky send-up. John Hill in *Sex, Class and Realism* remarks on the suffering heroines of early 1960s 'kitchen sink'[49]—though as Robert Murphy says in *Sixties British Cinema*, it is important to see them in the context of the limited roles women had been offered before.[50] TV drama of the 1960s, the work of Loach and Garnett, and David Mercer's unjustly forgotten plays made significant modifications. Working-class and radical middle-class female characters are treated with a new sympathy and complexity in this period. However, as Huw Beynon notes, the real shift in the presentation of working-class women was to be in the 1980s. John Hill argues in *British Cinema in the 1980s* that 'women-led' films, such as *Educating Rita* (1983) and *Rita, Sue and Bob Too* (1987), 'use and subvert the traditions of 1960s working-class realism', while adopting and adapting 'the conventions of the woman's film'.[51]

In *The Art of Interruption*, John Roberts traces how American documentary work in photography has frequently depicted working class women at the point where the customary routines of everyday existence is fractured by intense inner experience.[52] An analogy can be made with film. Despite the obvious differences in the work of Ken Loach and Marc Karlin, both have presented the hidden injuries of class through the mother–child relationship. Marc Karlin's *Night Cleaners* and *The Seven Dreams of Myrtle* (1976) connect the world of low-paid, casual work to mothering and allow space for reverie and desire, which transcends both work and domestic destiny. In his interview he dwells on his meetings with Nicaraguan working-class mothers confronting the tragic loss of their sons in the war. The anguished, wrenching loss of children appears too in *Cathy Come Home* (1966) and later in *Ladybird, Ladybird* (1994); Ken Loach and Tony Garnett's 1967 TV version of David Mercer's play *In Two Minds*, which evolved into the film *Family Life* in 1971, also deals with the psyche explicitly through family relations.

A characteristic that unites the film-makers in *Looking at Class*, despite their divergent approaches to their work, has been the compulsion to reveal areas of experience that are not being considered. Sally Hibbin, for instance, describes her desire to find ways of 'giving a voice'. She sees this as being about the stories you want to tell, rather than an explicit aim to represent the working-class. But Tony Garnett charts how his own observation and experience made him exasperated with the caricatured versions of working-class characters on TV. Angry working class boys of his generation became a sociological phenomena with far-reaching cultural consequences. Their arrival in the media contributed to the impetus to change the terms and forms of class representation.

The testimonies of the film-makers in *Looking at Class* echo a rebellion against the exclusion of 'the people' and the desire to give voice to those outside 'society', which has a long artistic lineage in British culture. While this has adhered to various interpretations of the 'natural' and the 'real', it has also carried the idea, which surfaced among the early nineteenth-century Romantics, of revealing what cannot be expressed. Indeed a concern to represent the working class has frequently been associated with a less definable desire to communicate what is mute and not apparent, to make manifest what can hardly be articulated within the existing culture. This expressive desire appears in many diverse ways in the film-makers' accounts: the potential for freedom in the boy's love for the kestrel in *Kes* (1969) or the reflection upon the fuller life that Gita Sahgal recalls in *Struggle Not Submission*, the interpretation of a text by a

Muslim woman in a refuge for battered women in Southall. An impulsion to look beyond surface appearances is evident in all the interviews.

Equally there is a shared political commitment to challenge the terms of what can be considered. Ken Loach refers to this resolve in relation to left trade union-ism—a subject that has been banished from serious consideration in TV docu-mentaries. As he says in his interview: 'that whole body of experience and ideas has no existence in our political and cultural life; it can only exist as an alter-native.' Alan Fountain, James Swinson and Gita Sahgal make the point that along with the loss of thoughtful TV presentations of the working class, there has been a dearth of documentaries that consider and analyse events and issues in the light of action and movements from below. This clearly excludes the introduction of political debates and ideas, and leaves the working class as part of the given world, embedded in what is and, seemingly, what must always be. The commitment to showing other viewpoints, other ways of seeing, was being throttled on television—which has the mass working-class audi-ence—from the late '80s.

Marc Karlin tackled the silencing head on in, first, *Utopias* (1987) and then *Between Times* (1993). In both films he was impelled by the need to under-stand why socialism had become unmentionable. During the 1990s he wres-tled in fury to release the muffled epic that he believed needed creative expression, retaining from the extraordinary days of May 1968 a feeling for fire-works—what seemed immutable could explode into another consciousness. He still wanted to make the audience stop in their tracks and consider ideas, to break their absorption with the images on screen in order to question.[53]

Despite the marked dissimilarities in their work, the filmmakers in *Looking at Class* demonstrate a common refusal to accept not only explicit censorship, but the implicit culling, which curtails what can be projected outside small left groupings. Tony Garnett, Ken Loach, Sally Hibbin, Marc Karlin, Murray Martin, Isaac Julien, Gita Sahgal and James Swinson all talk, in various ways, about their quest to push beyond what can be comfortably said. Both Ken Loach and Marc Karlin say they want to surprise their audience into recognising other possibilities. In Marc Karlin's films the uncertainty about what these might be is openly debated, and he fought fiercely for the space for this debate from *Utopias* to the film about Milton he was making when he died in 1999.

History and memory are crucial elements in this resistance to the prevail-ing definitions of culture. They were the themes of Ken Loach and Tony Garnett's series about British working-class history, *Days of Hope,* which appeared on television in 1975. Marc Karlin's *For Memory* was being writ-ten in the mid-70s, though it was not shown until the early '80s. In it he showed how socialist memory was excluded from the prevailing culture and filmed the efforts to record and hand on working-class history. Murray Martin insists that nostalgia, remembering the past with affection, should not be equated with sentimentality.

The clue to explaining the intensity of this preoccupation with remembering is there in the Jimmy Nail song about the river that Huw Beynon cites in his account of *Our Friends in the North*. Relationships between generations are 'the bond between our future and our past'. The bond has been severed at several points in contemporary Britain. The shock of economic restructuring and Thatcherism uprooted working-class patterns of life and undermined the cultural bases of the labour movement. It was accompanied by a pervasive questioning of the assumptions, values and theories of socialism—a process that has necessarily affected radical film-makers themselves. It was no longer clear what could be passed on apart from a sense of outrage and stories of defeat. Accordingly, those unable to consent to the society that had come into being were to find it extraordinarily difficult to trace the contours of how it might be changed. This has been a particularly distressing and contradictory experience for radical communicators.

There are obvious ironies. Some aspects of the radical vision of the 1970s were to have an effect, but in circumstances and contexts remote from their political conception. This dislocation has altered their social, political and cultural meaning. Not only is there a greater visibility of black and Asian people on TV but working-class people too are more evident on the media. They are generally presented, however, through the lens of the social assumptions that prevail and are thus confined in contained spaces. For instance Tony Garnett and Ken Loach comment on how the apparently neutral contexts of news and current affairs programmes continue to present loaded images of the working class, while Alan Fountain points out how working-class people are framed on TV game shows. James Swinson also mentions the popular docusoaps, which have prominently featured several working-class women and attracted large audiences. Not only do these take naturalistic styles to extremes but, in a sense, they too probe what cannot be expressed, by crossing the border between public and personal, and reproducing everyday intimacies. By watching a docusoap we are scrutinising normality turn into the bizarre: yet there is no history, no analysing, no explanation.

This is not to say that all documentaries should necessarily analyse or conceptualise, but that the virtual exclusion of opposing radical ideas, proposals, history and alternative possibilities from television has undoubedly diminished and restricted how working-class experience can be seen and understood. In contrast, several of Marc Karlin's films have examined political processes in relation to Britain and to Nicaragua. Ken Loach too has defied the implicit taboo, in both his documentaries and feature films. *Land and Freedom* (1995), for example, included a quarter of an hour on systems of egalitarian land ownership, while in *Carla's Song* (1996) people discuss the Nicaraguan Revolution at length on top of a bus.

Commenting on television, Gita Sahgal states similarly that subjects that were made visible by the women's movement have entered the mainstream media. She instances how domestic violence can be the topic of a documentary but is divested of any reference to feminist political ideas and activism. Any suggestion of alternative strategies is thus sidelined, leaving simply a feeling of helplessness.

Isaac Julien reflects on the time-lag that is evident in the making of feature films, which have been much slower than music in catching what has been happening to the working class. He suggests that very different ways of being working class are co-existing. Diversity of class experience is not entirely new of course. Along with regional and ethnic distinctions, the working class has always had two sexes, even though its historians have not necessarily recorded the incongruences of gender. Not only the types of work women have been paid to do but relationships within families and communities have contributed to different kinds of class experience.

However, the recent period has seen such rapid changes that even a tenuous sense of a common predicament has become fragmented. In Ken Loach's *My Name is Joe* (1998) it is the woman who is employed and the man unemployed. As Huw Beynon notes, given that the heroic images of the working class in struggle have traditionally been mainly male, this kind of gender turnaround, in which masculinity becomes redundant, is a perplexing discord. The old reflexes do not function in the new situation. British films in the 1990s returned again and again to the theme of masculinity—bemused, stranded, self-destructive—and usually this was to be working-class masculinity.

Isaac Julien points to another significant change in the relation between work, class and masculinity. The market has reached the male body, which is now commodified in ways that were formerly restricted to femininity or to exceptional groups of men, such as the film star, male model, or dancer. One reason why *The Full Monty* struck such a chord among audiences is that it not only defies the destiny of global restructuring but also jokes about the display of the male body, making explicit what is implicitly disturbing in the culture. It takes working-class experience and transcends the actual limits of real life through fantasy and fun.

Kerry William Purcell argues that visual expression of the new circumstances of class, which are still relatively little documented and understood in terms of their implications for consciousness, requires a new aesthetic form. He cites Gary Oldman's film *Nil by Mouth* as a cultural perception of class from within, in contrast to Ken Loach's *Riff-Raff*, which looks at the impact of casual work in the building industry from without.

Sally Hibbin, who produced *Riff-Raff*, brings another interpretation to the film, arguing that though the character of Larry, played by Ricky Tomlinson, is handled lightly, he stands for the older tradition of trade unionism. Larry's struggle for better conditions on the building site can be seen as an attempt to communicate the past to the future the younger men might still make. He is proved tragically right about the fatal consequences of neglecting health and safety but is sacked himself. The humourous shot of him caught naked in the bath of a new apartment suggests the vulnerability that many trade-union men of his generation have been forced reluctantly to accept.

Coming from the left, Loach obviously has the problem of trying to present the possibility of an opposing socialist view, which has become hardly credible because the labour movement has been defeated many times during the last

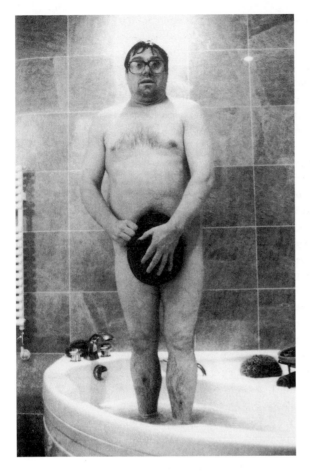

Riff-Raff, 1990 (BFI/
Parallax/Channel 4)

two decades. Interestingly Douglas Urbanski, who produced *Nil by Mouth* with Gary Oldman and Luc Besson, says that they approached the problem of life and work in the inner city from a diametrically opposing perspective. They aimed to show how Thatcherism needed to be taken further, believing the removal of state provision would end dependency and enable people themselves to surmount class divisions.[54]

Judith Williamson argues for changing images of class by using a much broader history of film conventions than the naturalism that has predominated in left film-making in Britain. While Isaac Julien says that in his own work, in which speculation about race, class and sexuality interweaves, a complication in representing new apprehensions is that the recognised experimental films tend to be conceived within the fabric of a middle-class imagination. This makes the presentation of images that push against the existing forms problematic.

Historically it has been the case that new forms of working-class resistance have drawn partly on the past. New kinds of organising, new ways of understanding and seeing have arisen out of a combination of what has been and what is coming into being. It may be that a similar process will occur in the aesthetic forms and cultural idioms in which working-class experience is communicated. Meanwhile what surfaces in a period of rapid change can be apprehended in ways that are unexpected— like the random collectivity of the inner city James Swinson caught by accident in *Street*, his video installation of the city street.

James Swinson is troubled by how to convince his students, who are in rebellion against 'theory', of the need to balance analysis and imagination. The dilemma he faces has wider ramifications. As Alan Fountain argues, a chasm has opened between making films and theorising their making. It has swallowed much of the work that endeavoured to connect doing and reflection.

Looking at Class crosses several abysses: the divorce between makers and thinkers; the split between those who examine the material and social world and those who study culture; the gulf between the experimental and the popular. It also addresses several silences and silencings, not simply the difficulty in expressing and comprehending the metamorphosis that has affected the working class but also the lack of space for politics, history and analysis in representing everyday life within contemporary communications.

While we have tried to be as inclusive as possible and to cross over 'genres', inevitably there are gaps—horror and science fiction for example.[55] Thrillers are mentioned by Huw Beynon and cop series by Tony Garnett, but neither is examined in any great detail. Agitational films about actual labour struggles are touched upon but not given comprehensive coverage.[56] Indeed *Looking at Class* reveals how much more needs to be said on the subject of the images of class in film. There are clearly many more fascinating individual accounts to be collected—from many places besides London and Newcastle—and much unwritten history to be explored about the structures of the radical visual media of the last few decades.

Although we are aware that we are only scratching the surface of a much bigger story, none the less these recollections and reflections hand on histories and intimate histories within histories. Many of the films discussed in this collection have provided visual markers for us both, crystallising shifts and presenting dilemmas that have preoccupied our own research and memories. We have also experienced the disturbing manner in which a social critique from the left has been marginalised and eclipsed. By gathering together the speeches, interviews and essays we hope that *Looking at Class* might re-open a dialogue among radicals who participate in and reflect upon films and television, regardless of their divergent views and ways of working—just as Marc Karlin, in *Utopias* hoped to seat socialists of different persuasions around one table.

Notes

1. Paul Rotha, 'Films and the Labour Party' (1936) in Aitken, *The Documentary Film Movement*, p.174.
2. V. Thorpe, 'Reality Bites Again', *Observer*, 23 May 1999.
3. For an elaboration of these points and further references, see Beynon and Glavanis (eds), *Patterns of Social Inequality*; Beynon, Hudson and Sadler, *A Place Called Teeside*; Hudson and Williams, *Divided Britain*; K. O'Morgan, *The People's Peace*, chs 12 and 13; Rowbotham, *A Century of Women*, pp.488–505, 548–91.
4. On 'remakings' in the past see Savage and Miles, *The Remaking of the British Working Class*.
5. Gallup Poll 1995, cited in H. Beynon, 'A Classless Society?' in Beynon and Glavanis (eds), *Patterns of Social Inequality*, p.36.
6. *Sunday Times*, 22 September 1996; quoted in Beynon and Glavanis (eds), *Patterns of Social Inequality*, p.49.
7. W. M. Reddy, 'The Concept of Class' in M. L. Bush (ed.), *Social Orders and Social Classes in Europe since 1500*, Longman, London, 1992.
8. For critiques of these trends see L. Segal, *Why Feminism?*, pp.200–209; H. S. Mirza, *Black British Feminism: A Reader*, Routledge, London, 1997, pp.3–21.
9. See Williams, Marxism and Literature. On Williams see P. Edwards, 'Culture is a

Way of Life', *Red Pepper*, August 1999. See also Thompson, *The Poverty of Theory*, pp.352 and 356.

10. Hill, *Sex, Class and Realism*, p.2.

11. J. Evans, Introduction to Evans (ed.), *The Camerawork Essays*, p.17.

12. On the background in radical culture see Fountain, *Underground*; Griffiths and Llewellyn-Jones, *British Women Dramatists*. On film see Dickinson, *Rogue Reels*; Mitchell, 'How not to Disappear from That Choice' and Raban, 'Lifting Traces'.

13. See, for example, Beynon and Austrin, *Masters and Servants*; Rowbotham and Mitter, *Dignity and Daily Bread*.

14. Corner, *The Art of Record*, p.9; Higson, *Waving the Flag*, pp.17–18. See also McRobbie, *Back to Reality?*, and Hill, *British Cinema in the 1980s*.

15. See Philo and Miller (eds), *Market Killing*, p.13.

16. Tony Garnett, 'Television in Britain: Description and Dissent', *Theatre Quarterly*, 2, April-June 1992, pp.19–20, quoted in J. Petley, 'Factual Fictions and Fictional Fallacies; Ken Loach's Documentary Dramas' in McKnight, *Agent of Challenge and Defiance*, pp.104–11. On Ken Loach's work see also Fuller, *Loach on Loach*.

17. Corner, *The Art of Record*, pp.1–55, and Cook, *Dennis Potter*, pp.27–30; see also Paget, *No Other Way to Tell It*.

18. On the documentaries see Aitken, *The Documentary Film Movement*; on Free Cinema see Stead, *Film and the Working Class*, p.179, and Caughie and Rockett, *The Companion to British and Irish Cinema*, pp.27–30.

19. Dziga Vertov in Macdonald and Cousins (eds), *Imagining Reality*, p.56.

20. Rees, *A History of Experimental Film and Video*, p.50.

21. Vertov in Schnitzer and Martin (eds), *Cinema in Revolution*, p.81.

22. *Ibid.*

23. *Ibid.*, p.83.

24. Thompson and Bordwell, *Film History*, p.140.

25. Vertov, quoted in Macdonald and Cousins (eds), *Imagining Reality*, p.56.

26. Thompson and Bordwell, *Film History*, p.649; Dickinson, *Rogue Reels*, pp.41–5.

27. R. Samuel, Ewan MacColl, Obituary, *Independent*, 30 October 1989.

28. See Chambers, *The Story of Unity Theatre*, pp.201–3, 240–42, 331–3.

29. See Geraghty, *Women and Soap Opera*, pp.51–9, 84–106; on the 'drama of everyday life' in British films see Higson, *Waving the Flag*, pp.212–71, and on Dickens and Englishness see Richards, *Films and British Identity*, pp.326–50.

30. See Dickinson, *Rogue Reels*, pp.35–45.

31. On Cinema Action, *ibid.*, pp.263–88.

32. On Amber, *ibid.*, pp.247–63; Dickinson, Cottringer and Petley, 'Workshops: A Dossier', pp.16–17.

33. On Camerawork see Evans (ed.), *The Camerawork Essays*.

34. On Malcolm Le Grice, see Rees, *A History of Experimental Film and Video*, pp.77, 84–5, 90, 94, 108, 112.

35. On William Raban, *ibid.*, pp.116–17.

36. Pines, *Black and White in Colour*, pp.120–31.

37. Hill, *British Cinema in the 1980s*, p.58. P. Cook, 'Border Crossings: Women and Film in Context' in Cook and Dodd (eds), *Women and Film*.

38. Dickinson, *Rogue Reels*, p.20.

39. Derby Co-operative Society, *Monthly Reports,* Women's Guild, October 1919.

40. *Kine Weekly*, quoted in Burton, *The People's Cinema*, p.80. There were also trade-union and village cinemas (information from Nina Hibbin, November 1999). On film and the labour movement see Stephen G. Jones, *The British Labour Movement and Film, 1918–1939,* Routledge, London, 1987.

41. See Burton, *The People's Cinema*, pp.40–51.

42. G. D. H. Cole, quoted *ibid.*, p.80.

43. Dickinson, R*ogue Reels*, pp.31–2, 210–23. On the Communist Party see B. Hogenkamp, 'The Sunshine of Socialism', pp.192–206.

44. See Forsyth, 'Marxism, Film and Theory', and Philo and Miller (eds), *Market Killing*; in relation to photography see Roberts, *The Art of Interruption*, pp.144–71, and, more generally, Roberts, 'Philosophising the Everyday', pp.16–30.

45. Norman Stone, quoted in Hill, *British Cinema in the 1980s*, p.134.

46. Hill, *ibid.*, p.144.

47. On Isaac Julien see Hill, *ibid.*, pp.219–40; Thompson and Bordwell, *Film History*, p.691; Roberts, *The Art of Interruption*, p.156.

48. On Sankofa see Dickinson, *Rogue Reels*, pp.55, 70; on the Black Audio Collective see *Rogue Reels*, pp.304–18.

49. Hill, *Sex, Class and Realism*, pp.160–75.

50. Murphy, *Sixties British Cinema*, pp.28–33.

51. Hill, *British Cinema in the 1980s*, p.174.

52. Roberts, *The Art of Interruption*, p.86.

53. On Marc Karlin see articles in 'Remembering Marc Karlin', *Vertigo*, 9, summer 1999; A. Fountain, 'A Visionary Life', *Red Pepper*, March 1999; J. Wyver, 'Marc Karlin', Obituary, *Independent*, 28 January 1999; J. Ellis, 'The Conscience of Radicals', Obituary, *Guardian*, 25 January 1999; S. Rowbotham, 'Marc Karlin: Reel Dreams and Real Lives', Obituary, *Guardian*, 25 January 1999; S. Rowbotham, 'Marc Karlin, 1943–1999', *History Workshop*, 48, 1999, pp.267–9.

54. Interview with Douglas Urbanski by Sheila Rowbotham, September 1999.

55. See for example D. Kellner, 'Poltergeists, Gender and Class in the Age of Reagan and Bush' in James and Berg (eds), *The Hidden Foundation*, pp.217–39.

56 See D. E. James, 'For a Working-class Television: The Miners' Campaign Tape Project', James and Berg, *ibid.*, pp.193–216. On the left and film see Hogenkamp, *Deadly Parallels*.

2 Images of Labour/Images of Class

Huw Beynon

The image of the industrial worker has been a powerful one that has sustained many popular and political ideologies. This was particularly the case in the third and fourth decades of the twentieth century when an heroic imagery of manual work was developed by intellectuals and labour institutions who drew upon aspects of earlier nineteenth-century iconography. This heroic image was most commonly linked with particular kinds of work and occupations in heavy industry. In the latter half of the century, the ascendance of the assembly line and a mass consumption society encouraged the construction of images that drew upon themes of alienation and dehumanisation. As the century drew to a close with many trade unions defeated or in retreat and with labour markets deeply fragmented no single coherent 'image of labour' seems to be available. Instead intellectual and visual themes have alluded to the multi-faceted nature of experience and more complex sets of identities and representation open to 'labour'.

Heroic labour

Nostrums about hard work not hurting anybody, and about not being afraid to get your hands dirty were fashioned into a central part of a code of ethics for the industrial working class in the first half of this century. It was both a method of judging your fellows, and an acerbic assessment of those who considered themselves to be your superiors. This image of labour was taken up by the institutions that represented industrial workers. A large statue of a manual worker, which conveys an image of power and strength, fronts the impressive headquarters of the Trade Union Congress in London. In Washington, DC, the offices of the AFL-CIO—the US equivalent of the TUC—greet visitors with two striking murals of marble and glass. Each measures seventeen by fifty-one feet; the one in the south lobby takes its title from Thomas Carlyle—'Labor is Life'— and 'depicts the role of workers and their families in America's development'. In the north lobby this is extended to contemporary America as *Labor Omnia Vincit* and locates human labour in the context of the space age and advanced technology. The emphasis in these and other images is upon the central importance of industry and technology to society, and of the critical role of the worker (of labour), who through physical strength, skill and endurance provides the basis for society's existence.

In many accounts this condition of labour rendered heroic images within which the worker was seen to be both powerful and exploited; the antithesis of middle-class comfort and respectability yet the lynch pin for it. Orwell's writings were of this kind. Lacking sympathy with the superficiality and condescension of middle-class life, he identified emotionally with manual workers. In the 1930s he went down a coal mine, and he marvelled at the ability of his guide to work strenuously under conditions which, in themselves, were exhausting to the visitor. Mark Benney made a similar observation on his journey underground in Durham. There he watched the miners work:[1]

Norman, his black muscular body glistening in the olive coloured light of his lamp, worked easily and quickly, crawling around with the agility of a mole. There was, too, an urgency behind his work that seemed almost unnatural. His shovel drove forward and cast back not only in a steady rhythm, but a fast rhythm…It was full-blooded, unrelenting and unflagging effort, that would have seemed wholly admirable in a man working in the full light of day; down here, in the darkness of a two foot seam, it was almost unbelievable.

Yet, as Orwell observed:[2]

You could quite easily drive a car right across the North of England and never once remember that hundreds of feet below the road you are on, the miners are hewing out coal. Yet in a sense it is the miners who are driving your car forward. Their lamp-lit world down there is necessary to the day-light world above, as the root is to the flower.

This sense of manual work being indispensable yet unnoticed framed the politics of trade-union leaders in the early part of this century and their attraction to the Labour Party. It came to have a strong impact upon writers, photographers and film-makers. In the 1930s the work of the Mass Observation project under Charles Madge and other communist intellectuals was dedicated to uncovering the detail of the daily lives of manual workers and their families. Documentary film-makers began to do the same and during the war many of these were used by the government in an attempt to retain the morale and support of the work forces necessary for the war effort. Jack Common, the Tyneside essayist and associate of Orwell, agreed to script a film about the ship yards on the Tyne. Dylan Thomas was similarly employed in South Wales. Common's film was a startling one. He had lived on Tyneside through the depression and knew how the shipyard workers felt about the way they had been treated. The film is a call to arms—encouraging the shipyard workers to return and take on the task of building ships for war. It ends with a worker turning to face the camera and saying in strident terms what many of them felt: 'Now you know you need us—don't forget this when the war is over.'

Sentiments such as these saw the miners push for the nationalisation of the industry and for the implementation of a 'Miners' Charter' which would address the general conditions of life in the coalfields. Against such a background, the miners of the North thronged into Durham City with their families for their annual gala in 1947. By all accounts there were a quarter of a million people there on that day. Michael Foot was one of the speakers, and he remembers it in this way:[3]

I started there in 1947. That's when I shared the platform with Arthur Horner...The Durham Miners' Gala...in those days it was absolutely sensational...the music, the banners and all in that beautiful city. It overwhelmed you really. In those days it was, far and away, the best working class festival that there was in this country. Far and away the best. It was just marvellous.

The impact of the Gala, and events like them, was powerfully visual and emotional. Each village carried a large colourful banner with its own motif. This was well understood by the National Coal Board. At the time of Nationalisation, the NCB employed four film crews. These produced newsreels Coal News—to be shown in the local cinemas on the coalfields. They also produced feature-length documentary films and several of these featured the coal miners' galas. The power of the images involved here was still evident in 1983 when the Durham miners' union celebrated their one-hundredth gala. On this day as many of the old lodge banners as could be found were paraded through the city. The community film group Chapter from Cardiff was at that time one of the work-shops supported by Channel 4. It was commissioned by the Durham NUM to make a video tape of this event. Lawrence Daly, the retired General Secretary of the National Union of Mineworkers, sent messages to say that he had to have a copy of this video tape: 'I just want to see those banners going over the bridge at Durham.'

In 1983, of course, the coal-mining industry was severely depleted. In 1947 there were 740,000 miners working in British coal mines. By 1983 their number had declined to 230,000. Today, and after a year-long strike to 'save jobs and communities', just 12,000 remain. This represents an enormous change that relates to other complicated sets of changes that have taken place in Britain over decades, at different paces and with different consequences.

Alienated labour
In the 1960s, the coal mines closed down and miners and their families moved into different kinds of work. Public attention focused upon the car industry and the related factories that poured out the vast numbers of mechanical parts to be assembled in Dagenham, Longbridge, Ryton, Halewood and the other assembly plants that had come to dominate our large cities. Here was quite a different kind of manual work and one that was less easily converted into romantic and heroic imagery. Mass production work was inherently monoto-nous, requiring patience and endurance and that restless alertness that Sartre identified as endemic to the condition of manual work in the second half of the twentieth century. Here too the changes were often represented though visual imagery or allusion. In 1959, for example, the business magazine *The Economist* remarked upon changes that were taking place in the lives of the

working class. In expressing these changes it cited the television aerials on roof tops and the 'housewives' tight slacks on the back of motor cycle and family sidecars on the summer road to Brighton'. Orwell had earlier commented on the significance of changes in dress and the ways in which these had begun to blur differences between the classes. Others have paid attention to the ways in which work and the modern factory were changing attitudes and perceptions.

In his classic novel *Saturday Night and Sunday Morning*, Alan Sillitoe pays attention to the changing realities of working life and the impact of these upon personal relationships. It revolves around a man in his early twenties—Arthur Seaton—whose world is described as involving:[4]

a brief glimpse of the sky at mid-day and evening, a prison-like system, pleasant enough because he could be happy in knowing that by this work he never had to worry where the next meal, pint, smoke or suit of clothes was coming from.

He endures the monotony. Freed from the threat of the dole he lives in the present and concludes: 'It's a hard life if you don't weaken.' Sillitoe's novel was path-breaking. Working within a realist tradition it managed to establish a sympathetic account of manual labour that eschewed romantic and heroic images. This facilitated the production of one of the very best examples of British film-making in 1960, with Albert Finney in the leading role.

This image of manual work involving men in a perpetual and tedious set of exertions came to dominate. It was developed effectively by Godard in *British Sounds* (1969), a film that began, quite exceptionally, with a long tracking shot of an assembly line. In this way the French director captures directly the monotony and noise of modern assembly-line work and the pace of the manual worker as an appendage to the assembly line. As a statement on the contemporary condition it mirrors the traffic jam in *Weekend*, but here there is no humour. Shot in colour, the emotions are grey ones; endless lines of cars but with workers attached. And in the sound-over, readings on alienation from *The Communist Manifesto*, and the voice of a young girl remembering events from the history of the British working class.

This theme of alienation was developed in different ways in a number of different films in the 1970s. Importantly it came to be seen as a theme that was not simply a feature of work-places. Alienation involved the commodification of human labour and this process affected the whole of life. This was the dominant feature of Elio Petri's phenomenal *La Classe Operaia Va in Paradiso—The Working Class Goes to Heaven* (1971). Here too the theme is one of relentless degradation. This unremitting account of factory life is, however, tinged with humour and irony. No more so than when an old militant worker is visited in a mental hospital. He had been sacked for attacking a foreman who had refused to answer his question: 'What are we making in this factory?' This sense of irony reflected the times. In Liverpool in the 1970s Ford workers told jokes about men who had decided to leave the factory to get jobs elsewhere. One is supposed to have obtained a job in a sweet manufacturing plant. His job involved separating the blue sweets from the reds. He left because he couldn't stand the decision-making.[5]

Petri's film is built around the life of Massa, an assembly-line worker, in whose view 'the factory is a prison'. Like Arthur Seaton he is a highly productive worker; he tends the machine making piece after piece after piece. He explains how he manages to achieve this: 'You gotta pick out something that'll hold your concentration. Me I concentrate on Adelgisa's ass over there.'

In this deeply sexist way he links his productivity as a worker with mechanical sex: 'a piece…an ass…a piece…an ass'. This link between repetitive standardised alienated labour and a repressed sexuality is both profound and persistent. It is drawn not only by Petri and Godard but also in a number of Hollywood productions. Here the relationship between the psycho-sexual depths of working-class life and their relationship to the capitalist ethos are less well developed but present nevertheless. In the under-rated Joe (1970), for example, the working world of the lead character is alluded to as he sweats in front of a furnace. In the bar he rails against people with a more privileged life than his and the way in which they show disrespect for his world—his America. In front of a radical poster of Nixon ('Would you buy a used car from this man?') he exclaims—'If you can't buy a car from the President of the United States who can you buy a car from?' His hatred is directed most firmly toward the hippies and in this a company executive, whose daughter has dropped out to live in a commune, shares his sentiments. They join forces and it becomes clear that Joe's hatred is both more intense and violent. The business man has lost a daughter and wants her back; the worker finds the value of his whole life threatened, and he wants to kill. A later film Blue Collar (1978) was situated more centrally in the work-place—a car-assembly plant in Detroit. Directed by Paul Schrader it provides a graphic and perceptive account of the ways in which in the tortured world of the assembly line, human values become distorted and people become divided from each other. As in Petri's film, the workers have humorous and perceptive understandings of the modern factory condition. A black worker, Zeke (played by Richard Pryor), argues that the assembly plant is 'just short for plantation'. And a strong bond develops between him and his friends Jerry (Harvey Keitel) and Smokey (Yaphet Kotto) Their attitude to sex and women is captured in a vicarious orgy scene. More generally, in the plant they become split apart. The factory produces divisions, dissension and distrust. However, unlike The Working Class Goes to Heaven (where such divisions are understood in the context of capitalism and alienation), in this film, the source of division is seen to be the trade union. Hollywood's view of industrial life was established with On the Waterfront, where union corruption was seen to be rife. Blue Collar extends this view, unrealistically, to the car plant and the UAW, in a way that weakens its overall impact.

This relationship between work, friendship and sexuality is dealt with in an interestingly different way, from the perspective of women workers, in Letter to Brezhnev (1985). Here two young Liverpool women prepare for a night out after a week working in a food-processing factory. In Sandra's view you simply have to go crazy at the weekend if all week 'you've been sticking giblets up chickens' arses'. Here too vicarious sex is on the agenda, and Russian seamen fit the bill. For Sandra this involves a laugh and a good time. For her friend it involves looking at the moon, love and a letter to Brezhnev.

'Labour' then, is not just work; these films tell us that work affects the whole of life. Massa's life is dominated by his work and only an accident to his finger breaks him from the routine. At home he is as he was at work. The cutlery must be in the right place on the table; everything must be ordered and in place. This theme was also picked up in *Shirley Valentine*—one of a number of feminist-influenced films that began to look at these issues in different ways. Shirley gives the steak, bought for Thursday's dinner, to the neighbour's dog. The dog had been restricted to a vegetarian diet and she takes pity on him. Her husband—played by Bernard Hill—has to settle for egg and chips: 'What's this. It's Thursday. It's steak on Thursday. This isn't steak.' By this time though the world was beginning to change. Here the changes are worked though in their relationship and the film ends with them having a new kind of understanding of life and of each other. This optimism was short lived however.

The destruction of labour

In the 1980s in Britain industrial workers of all kinds experienced massive changes in their working lives. In three years more than three million manufacturing jobs were lost as factories closed down or were moved overseas. The car industry was especially badly hit with the British car makers being buffeted by rounds of take-overs and mergers. The car workers, it seemed were going the way of the miners; as were the shipyard workers, the steel workers and those, like Arthur Seaton, who in mechanical-engineering factories supplied components for the consumer industries. The scale of the transformation involved here is perhaps best captured by the fact that employment in all of these industries (coal, steel, shipyard, cars, mechanical engineering) is today exceeded in the hotel and catering industries. At the turn of the century there were five times as many 'personal financial advisers' as there were coal miners in the UK.

The new industrial jobs were increasingly concentrated away from the cities and the coalfields. The new electronic industries grew up in East Anglia, along the M4 corridor, in Silicon Glen in Scotland and along the coastal plain in South Wales. More and more people, however, were being employed in the 'service sector' and were self employed. These changes became the subject of considerable comment and speculation. Writing in the *Spectator*, Sandra Barwick commented on how:[6]

What would once have been defined as the working class has shrunk and is still shrinking…The 'working class' label has an old quaint, Hovis advertisement clogs and cobbles ring to it. This has led, especially on the left to a discernible and typically British sense of loss. A few sociologists, in an atmosphere of nostalgia, have even suggested that television is partly responsible for the breakdown by providing in-house distraction, isolating workers from activities which reinforced solidarity, a sense of community, the Working Men's Club, the party, the Gala, the march.

These changes began to be widely celebrated in the broadsheet newspapers. Ann Barr and Peter York, for example, introduced *Observer* readers to the 'New Babylon' in which people will be presented with careers of an astonishingly exotic—almost whimsical—variety…and these in turn:[7]

influenced the idea of what work could be in more everyday situations. The 'explosions' in media, financial services, property values and leisure of all kinds have opened up extraordinary opportunities for people who were lucky, (mostly) well educated, and well placed (Southern etc.). There were openings not only in investment banking and the television industry but interior decoration and specialist retailing.

In the 1980s these themes came together to provide a powerful and pervasive account of social change. In this, unfortunately, critical traditions, which once emphasised the damaging effect of work upon workers, gave way to those that celebrated the enriching aspects of employment. These were regularly contrasted with the debilitating experience of unemployment. In this way, the major division within society became understood as that between those with and those without work. Moreover work became invested with internal moral meaning and righteous virtue, regardless of its content or the social value of the activity of which it was a part.

Ironically, in this new context, many of the 'new workers' began speaking in the language of the old. Teachers and university lecturers talked of working at 'the chalk face' and their trade unions developed this metaphor in their negotiations with the employers, when they threatened 'industrial action'. More than this; in offices, people began to refer to the computers as their 'machines', and 'workerholism' became an acceptable illness among the new middle classes. While in Orwell's days these people looked down upon industrial workers and their work, in the 1980s and 1990s they publicly embraced the ethic of work and endeavour. *The Times* commented on how:[8]

In the 1980s a new type of working—'macho' working became increasingly prevalent. An urge to perform seemed to overtake people, perhaps most notably in the City…It became de rigueur to arrive at the office before everyone else and to be the last to leave. The 'power breakfast' was born, the better to get meetings out of the way before the rest of the day started. At the office, meetings were scheduled at 8 am then, ludicrously, 7 am, when the people around the table might have said goodbye to each other only a few hours earlier. British Rail was asked to provide more early morning trains.

This new context—the pressurised corporate office—has been fruitfully explored in several Hollywood productions. Jack Lemmon's performance in *Glengarry*

Glen Ross (1992) draws out the pathos of life as a salesman. With the intensity of Arthur Miller's *Death of a Salesman*, this film explores the painful emotional labour that underpins much service-sector employment. Repeatedly the pressure comes from money—the need to clinch an insurance deal. This theme is explored with gusto by Oliver Stone in *Wall Street*—'lunch is for wimps'; 'greed is good' (1987). Here a young careerist played by Charlie Sheen looks for fortune in the large Manhattan brokerage firm run by Gordon Gekko. Gekko, played by Michael Douglas, is iconographic of the Thatcher/Reagan years. The film whilst exploring the world of the corporate raider becomes a morality tale. Sheen trades on information gained through his father (played by his real dad, Martin, to give added poignancy to the generational shift) to trigger insider share trading that threatens his father's future. Here, good triumphed over evil and the values of manual work and commitment to a trade won out over the power of money. That this has not always been the case is pretty obvious. What these films and others like them (*Jerry Maguire*, 1996, *The Bonfire of the Vanities*, 1990, *Boiler Room*, 2000) achieve is a critical portrayal of the new money economy.[9]

Interestingly the British cinema has produced no films of this kind. However, the world of accountancy and money was examined critically in *Brassed Off* (1996). Set in Grimethorpe on the Yorkshire coalfield this film contrasts the logic of money and the world of consultants and auditors with the daily life of the local community that relied upon the coal mine for its security. The life of the community is explored (somewhat romantically) through the world of the colliery brass band and its conductor (Peter Poselthwaite). In a final evocative scene he (having escaped from his hospital bed) celebrates the band's victory in the national competition and extols the virtues of a life where endeavour and solidarism count for more than money—'brass'. This film filled cinemas in the North of England and South Wales for months on end; many local people seeing it time and again. It tells of a world we have lost.

A Lost World
In the UK and the USA we have witnessed a major change in the pattern of employment and the organisation and experience of labour. Employment in manufacture began to decline relatively in relation to services in the 1950s; it went into absolute decline in 1968, and this became cataclysmic in 1979. In 1966, 8.6 million people were employed in manufacturing, in 1981 there were just 5.4 million and this remained stable. By the 1990s, employment in those three great industrial sectors (construction, mining and manufacture) made up no more than a quarter of the country's jobs. In contrast employment in the service sector increased as new kinds of 'services' were offered for sale. By the 1990s services provided over 15 million jobs and 70 per cent of total employment.

These changes have been hastened by the neo-liberal policies of Thatcher and Reagan, continued under a different guise by Blair and Clinton. They have been associated with the increasing internationalisation of product and money markets, the growing ascendancy of multi-national corporations and the implementation of a major technological revolution around the silicon chip, the micro-processor and the computer. The combined effects of changes like these have been almost revolutionary. In the UK the size of the labour force increased - from just over 20 million to almost 23 million. At the same time the number of unemployed and 'economically inactive' people also increased—quite dramat-ically so in the 1980s. Young people found it increasingly difficult to get employ-ment, as did older people. In this way the core labour force became one in which people between the ages of 25 and 50 dominated. It became harder to get into employment in the first place. In later life, people forced out through redundancy schemes, take-overs and closures began to find that it was more and more difficult to get back in. In these years it became common for people to talk of being 'on the scrap heap'—an allusion to the machine world that repre-sents the final insult to human labour.

This was the context of another successful British film—*The Full Monty*. Like *Brassed Off* it was set in Yorkshire, this time in the steel town of Sheffield. The first scene finds the central character (played by Robert Carlyle) attempting to steal a girder from one of the closed steel factories. He is helped by his son, who complains that this isn't what other boys and other fathers do when they are together. We learn that he is divorced and that his wife has remarried and lives in a middle-class housing estate. The closure of the steel industry, redun-dancy and his own growing sense of hopelessness, we surmise, hastened their divorce. Tragi-comic scenes dominate the film as the pain of divorce, unem-ployment and attempted suicides are explored though humour. Eventually the group of redundant workers endure but only through inverting one of the domi-nant structures of their previous lives. They become strippers and appear naked—the full monty—before a female audience in a local club.

The Full Monty was a popular film that, like *Brassed Off*, entertained audi-ences in the old industrial regions for months. Unlike *Brassed Off* it also had a much wider appeal. It was phenomenally successful in the USA where book-lets were produced, translating many of the working-class phrases and Yorkshire dialect. Perhaps this success isn't too difficult to explain. The film is entertaining and the narrative is one that emphasises working-class endurance, imagination and survival. This, of course, is the way Hollywood has best dealt with the world of labour. In *Saturday Night Fever*, John Travolta plays a work-ing class boy for whom dance and style allow him to escape the mundane nature of his work and the drabness of his home life. This theme of redemp-tion and success was also to be found in *Rocky*, as Stallone trains hard to take full advantage of the big chance that allows him to escape drudgery and despair. *The Full Monty* then was appropriated to the American dream. That this is not the only way to represent working-class life—in the UK or USA—is demonstrated in the films of Martin Scorsese. In movies like *Mean Streets* and *Taxi Driver* we enter the worlds of people who have become deeply disturbed in their attempt to construct a life in urban USA. Even in success (as in *Raging Bull* or *Casino*) there is no contentment; only the fear of betrayal and of vulner-ability in a hostile world.

Nevertheless, the theme that underpins *The Full Monty* became a pervasive one in societies where the deregulation of labour markets produced increasing levels of insecurity and uncertainty among workers of all grades. This was revealed most poignantly on the Liverpool shore line where dockers went on strike in an attempt to prevent the dismissal of a group of workers. In response the company also sacked the strikers whilst offering them the possibility of being re-hired on new contracts. The strike lasted over a year and had many echoes of the struggles of the miners a decade earlier. These events were dramatically portrayed in the Channel 4 film *Dockers* (1999). The film was scripted through collaboration with the redundant dock workers and takes the form of a morality tale with honourable men and women holding out against the encroaching disci-pline of the company and the bureaucratic inertia of the trade union. Unlike *Wall Street* there are no happy endings. The workers do not find paradise, they end up unemployed, and we are left to contemplate the friable nature of solidarity and the ending of a once-powerful working-class culture.

The sense of ending, of a finality, is exceptionally strong in *Dockers*. Read against other films of this kind made by Ken Loach in the 1990s (*Riff-Raff*, *Raining Stones*, *Ladybird, Ladybird*) it is a chilling experience. What would be the future for these people made redundant in Liverpool? Did they too face unemployment and indebtedness, terrorised by social workers? In *Dockers* these workers were complaining about the casualisation of their work contracts. Given the history of dock work (where dockers once stood in 'the pen' to be called for work by the foreman) their sensitivity to this change is understandable. The more so when we understand that the introduction of casual contracts has become an increasingly general feature of employment in the UK and the USA. The dock workers had struggled to establish job security and continuity of insured employment. This, in a way, was the nearest to paradise that they could hope for. The deregulated labour markets of the 1990s cut across hopes such as these.

Fragmented labour/complex society

Generally in our society the stable superannuated labour force which charac-terised the 1950s has been severely eroded. The labour force of the 1990s is made up of a number of different kinds of employees: part-time workers, temporary workers, casual, even self-employed workers. As we enter the twenty-first century these hyphenated workers are becoming a more and more significant part of the economy. This has been particularly evident in the film and television industries where production is increasingly organised on a sub-contracting basis. In this maelstrom of change people who once worked for an employer now work for themselves. This is particularly the case in the growing service sector. Most commonly self-employment has come about from necessity rather than choice. This has been the case with many of the fami-lies that came to the UK from the Indian sub-continent; a phenomenon that is explored in interesting ways in *My Beautiful Laundrette*. This film was the first of several that focused on the emerging multi-ethnic content of labour, explor-ing the problems and possibilities of different cultures coexisting within a rapidly

Dockers, 1999
(Parallax/ Initiative
Factory/ Channel 4)

changing capitalist world. In both *Bhaji on the Beach* (1993) and *East is East* (1999) gender relations and the position of women within this new reality are seen as critical aspects of change.

Alongside the self-employed worker has come the temporary worker and the agency worker moving from one place of work to another. However, it is part-time work that has provided the main source of employment growth in the 1980s and 1990s. In 1995 for example there were three and a half million fewer full-time jobs than there were fifteen years earlier. The dynamic in the jobs market has been in part-time employment, usually for women. This 'gender bias' in part-time work is being modified slightly as increasing proportions of men find employment on this basis. In the hotel industry, for example, part-time employment made up 26 per cent of all jobs in 1971 (21 per cent for women and 5 per cent for men). By 1991, the proportions had almost doubled with the part-time jobs of women (33 per cent) and men (11 per cent) providing almost half of the jobs in the industry. This practice has been encouraged by government initiatives which emphasise the attractiveness of this type of employment, seeing it as indicative of an increasingly flexible labour market.

These changes have been profound ones and have contributed to the transformation of the Labour Party into New Labour, a new style of politics that has embraced these changes, pointing to the advantage of flexibility in a globalising world. These new arrangements have often been presented as positive, offering greater opportunities for women re-entering the labour market. The fact that many women have historically developed their employment careers through a complex process of juggling time and commitments was seen to make them more able to deal with the new reality. In all of this talk, however, the pressures and constraints experienced by these women have often been overlooked. In the late 1980s a waitress at a Yorkshire hotel explains how:[10]

Craig my eldest son was five when I started work here. It was just evenings then. I started off as casual at night when the children were little and my husband looked after them. I just did banquets…Then I gradually started doing weekend breakfast and the odd lunchtime. Then I did the week breakfasts and it fitted in quite well as my husband was working local and he could see them off in the morning for me. Then they grew up and they got to an age when they could be left on their own.

Combining paid employment with the demands of child-care and a family is becoming more and more common; requiring more and more gymnastics with the clock, the childminder, the oven and the take-away food store. The stresses and tensions involved here are obvious. Their lighter side formed the theme for George Clooney's move on to the big screen in *One Fine Day* (1996).

The old industrial economy of Britain was highly regulated; it employed large numbers of highly unionised workers employed on full-time contracts. As we have seen, most of these were men, and they were paid what was recognised as 'a family wage', a form of payment that sustained the idea of the man as the bread-winner. This 'family wage', like coal and steel production, is a thing of the past. Most generally the standard of living for families in the UK is sustained by more than one income. Women's wages (once slandered as 'pin money') have become an essential part of household income. Oddly, at a time when work is becoming scarce, more and more people are working longer hours. In Britain we work longer hours than anywhere in Europe. Twenty per cent of us work on Sundays and 15 per cent of us are routinely paid to work over 46 hours a week.

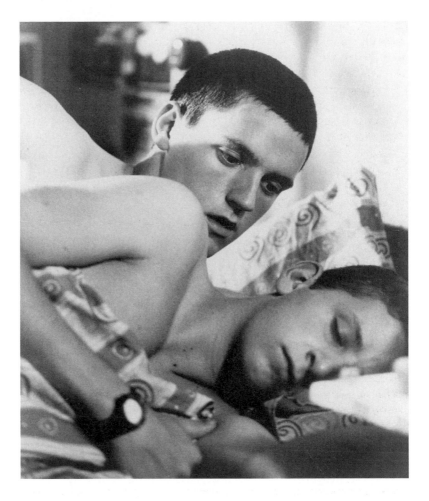

Beautiful Thing, 1995
(Film Four: World
Productions)

Equally, it is clear that many of the jobs created in service industries are manual jobs, many requiring few skills, most of them done by women. This has contributed greatly to a general and profound increase in the proportion of women in the labour force, a change which, perhaps more than any other, provides a clue to the detailed ways in which work and employment have altered since the war. In the recent past manual industrial labour has been a man's affair. Film and documentary photography have reflected this. It was this experience that produced that powerful, heroic, and masculine symbol of labour outside the TUC. This reality changed in the 1970s and 1980s. Women now dominate in many parts of the labour force. This is especially the case in the sectors associated with the rise of industries based upon information technology. Here, women play a central part: they manufacture the micro-chip in factories in the Far East and they assemble the computer boards in the lowlands of Scotland. It is also women who, for the most part, look at computer screens and 'hammer away' at key-boards. Studies of audio-typists have noted how:[11]

Consequent upon their isolation, the typists' work appears doubly monotonous. Like manual workers in mechanised jobs, they are prevented from making conversation with their workmates by the noise of the machinery...In the building society, the audio-typists turned the machinery to their own advantage by listening to music cassettes on playback machines while copy-typing! While this might be seen as an attempt by the typist to gain control over the work environment, it might more accurately be seen as one of the ameliorating aspects of routine, alienating work long established in factories.

Ratcatcher, 1999
(© Pathé)

The parallels with factory work are not overdrawn. Manual labour in the twenty-first century will be emerging in new and different ways. This growing complex of jobs and labour contracts combine with gender and ethnic difference to produce a mosaic that is not easily represented in simple images. This is particularly difficult for those intellectuals and film-makers whose concern has been to understand and portray the ways in which labour contributes to and is constrained by capitalist society.

In the 1980s and 1990s there has been a systematic and systemic weakening of previous sets of images and understandings. The collapse of the Soviet Union accelerated a view of an ascendant capitalist ethic. Indeed many of the former symbols of working-class power have been appropriated. In Britain, what remains of the coal industry used images of coal miners as propaganda for the advantages of enterprise and entrepreneurship. Cardiff Bay Development Corporation (and many others) use images of Marx to advertise their activities. 'Capitalism', once a taboo word, has become common currency and Marx has been hailed by the World Bank as the prophet of globalisation. New Labour views images of labour as being of the past, redolent of 'Old Labour'. These profound political changes arch over those in the economy, accentuating the sense of fragmentation and detachment.

What all this has done is to raise problematic and unfamiliar questions of how working-class lives can be adequately represented and discussed. It also raises critical questions for British cinema. After each round of Oscar cere-monies it has become common to hear that 'the Brits' have dominated and that British cinema is in the ascendancy. This is rarely the case. Most successes are at the margins and major ones almost always involve US money. 'Successful' British films have either been whimsical romps through English eccentricities (as in *Four Weddings and a Funeral*) or the costume drama, of which there are endless examples. This is a reconstruction of British life as seen from California.

More interesting have been attempts to explore the under-side of British soci-ety through the use of 'black humour'. This was most clear in *Trainspotting* (1998) and in the burgeoning collection of gangster films, best demonstrated in *Lock, Stock and Two Smoking Barrels* (1999). Other serious attempts are being made to deal with labour and class in contemporary British society in new and imaginative ways. On television Tony Garnett faithfully explored the world of hospital work in *Cardiac Arrest*. More generally the world of work and labour is dealt with tangentially. In Mike Leigh's *Secrets and Lies* we touch upon the world of a self-employed photographer, an optometrist and a street cleaner, each dealing with each other and their own pasts. It is an optimistic film that deals with issues of ethnicity, racism, success and failure. Another film, Lynne Ramsay's *Ratcatcher* (1999), humanely explores the impact of the bin-men's strike on a Scottish housing estate in the late 1970s. This retrospective account was partly inspired by observation of the life of her elder brother. It focuses with great sensitivity upon the harsh pressures that economic change have inflicted upon working-class masculinity, and how sensitivity and love can be overwhelmed and crushed. These, and others like them, sustain the hope that space still remains for cinema to explore this new fractured reality and provide images and forms that will enlighten and develop our understanding of labour and class in the twenty-first century.

Notes

1. M. Benney, *Charity Main: A Coalfield Chronicle*, EP Publishing, Wakefield, 1978, p.40.
2. G. Orwell, 'Down the Mine', in *Inside the Whale and Other Essays*, Penguin, London, 1957, p.63.
3. Interview with the author, April 1981.
4. A. Sillitoe, *Saturday Night and Sunday Morning*, W. H. Allen, London, 1958. For a full discussion see Laing, *Representations of Working Class Life*.
5. See Huw Beynon, *Working for Ford*, Penguin, Harmondsworth, 1973.

6. Sandra Barwick, 'Goodbye to the Class Struggle', *Spectator*, 8 September 1990, p.9.
7. Ann Marr and Peter York, 'Work—Just the Job', *Observer*, 8 November 1987, p.14.
8. *The Times*, 7 June 1990.
9. Nigel Andrews, 'The Enduring Filthiness of Lucre', *Financial Times*, 31 March 2000.
10. Juliet Webster, 'Word Processing and the Secretarial Division of Labour', in K. Purcell (ed.), *The Changing Experience of Employment*, Macmillan, London, p.128.
11. *Ibid.*

Section II

CHALLENGING THE CLASS DIVIDE

Sheila Rowbotham

In 1937 a group of intellectuals arrived in Bolton, Lancashire, to study daily life in the town. They were from Mass-Observation, the group that pioneered the investigation of popular culture, combining material detail with notes on attitudes and dreams. The Bolton investigators were to discover the two most popular films showing in 1937 were *Victoria the Great*, starring Anna Neagle, and *Stella Dallas*, an American film about a radio-soap heroine—ordinary woman *par excellence*.[1]

In the 1930s Hollywood was already providing an alternative to stuffy class-bound Britain, especially for young working-class women. British intellectuals, on the left and on the right, were aware of this American influence on British culture and tended to regarded it with suspicion. They feared that 'mass' popular entertainment would undermine the authentic expression of older ways of life in working-class communities and destroy aesthetic standards. Peter Stead shows how these suspicions lingered in the early 1960s and points out how Karel Reisz's *Saturday Night and Sunday Morning* (1960) was to mark a breakthrough. Not only was it a film that portrayed a working-class rebel with sympathy, but it crossed cultural boundaries in terms of audiences as well.

In the early 1960s Nina Hibbin, then working as the cinema critic on the Communist Party's *Daily Worker*, hailed the British New Wave with enthusiasm. There was a close connection with developments in the theatre. For example, Tony Richardson, who had directed John Osborne's influential play *Look Back in Anger* in 1956, formed a film-production company, Woodfall, in 1959, which adapted John Braine's novel, *Room at the Top*, into a film. Woodfall were also to have a great success with *Tom Jones* in 1963.

Nina Hibbin's broad interpretation of culture went back to her own participation in Mass-Observation. Mass-Observation's collection of data on opinion was to become a means of testing out morale in wartime, later, in the commercially minded 1950s, turning into 'market research'. During the 1930s, however, the project was part of a much wider fascination with documenting every-day life in both Britain and the USA. Along with sociological investigation went interest in folk music and folk art, radio programmes recording working-class lives, photography and, of course, documentary films.

The British documentary film-makers of the 1930s and '40s varied greatly in their cinematic styles and political outlook, ranging from the social idealism of John Grierson to the lesser-known Communist Ralph Bond. However, they shared a moral commitment to a cinema that engaged in the inter-relationship of social existence and also set out to provoke thought. This sense of purpose and distrust of showmanship along with their practice of presenting 'real life' by breaking with Hollywood conventions of location and subject matter were to influence succeeding waves of radical British films.

The pioneer documentary film-makers confronted several dilemmas that were to recur. First, their films took working-class subjects but were less appealing to working-class audiences than cinema that entertained with stories—either from Hollywood or the popular British cinema. Second, their resulting dependence on the state or private firms for funding restricted the critical content. Third, they encountered a problematic tension between presenting sociological evidence through working-class testimony and their own creative artistry as film-makers. Ironically their aesthetic eye tended to present poverty, exploitative work and industrial devastation as cinematically beautiful.[2]

This aestheticisation of the Northern industrial landscape and of the male working-class body reappeared in the kitchen-sink films of the late 1950s and early '60s that Peter Stead describes. However, this 'new wave' in film developed from the differing circumstances of the post-war society and was connected with wider philosophical and cultural currents, which emphasised 'the real', authenticity and spontaneous free expression. During the 1950s these preoccupations were to have an explosive impact on British drama and fiction, which began to express the class resentments of a strata of educated, young working-class men (and to a lesser degree women), who found themselves implicitly excluded from the public-school 'establishment'. Alan Sillitoe's novel Saturday Night and Sunday Morning was one example among many.

Although the film of the book, starring Albert Finney, heralded a new crop of realistic grainy films, it was actually rooted in the working-class experience of the 1950s. Peter Stead points out how it was also influenced by the 1950s 'Free Cinema' movement. This grouping, which included Reisz, produced several documentaries that took a poetic look at everyday life. Instead of focusing on 'labour', they were interested in jazz clubs, pubs and fairgrounds—the working class at play rather than 'proletariat'. Free Cinema prefigured the early '60s sensibility, which foregrounded personal rebellion rather than the collective experience of labour that had inspired the 1930s documentary movement.

Although it was the Angry Young Men who became most celebrated, playwrights Shelagh Delaney and Ann Jellicoe were both raising questions of sex and gender several years before a women's liberation movement occurred. Shelagh Delaney's A Taste of Honey appeared as a film in 1961, and Ann Jellicoe's 1961 play The Knack was to be filmed by Richard Lester in 1965, by which time kitchen-sink realism was on the wane, and the bright new world of David Bailey's Swinging London was in the ascendency. Lester had also directed A Hard Day's Night about the Beatles in 1964. The Beatles presented a very different form of working-class floppy, jokey masculinity from the tough working-class hero in Saturday Night and Sunday Morning. But the theme of the individual cocking a snook at the middle-class establishment persisted. In the first half of the 1960s this individualism had a radical meaning; it presented a challenge to the conformity of the Conservative 1950s and implicitly rejected the denial of the individual that had been part of the Stalinist version of Marxism.[3]

Peter Stead refers to the desire of British film-makers in the early 1960s to emulate Elia Kazan's On the Waterfront (1954). The film sided with the individual who stood out against the group—in this case the corrupt trade union. It was perceived as a rebel production but, as Peter Stead relates, it was actually Kazan's justification for testifying against his friends on the Hollywood left who were prevented from working by the McCarthyite purge of Communists and Communist 'sympathisers'.[4] The young rebels who donned donkey jackets in imitation of Brando's Terry, and marched against the nuclear bomb were only dimly aware of McCarthy, however, for Nina Hibbin and many others in an older generation of the left, On the Waterfront was a 'treacherous' film. The fear and bitterness of those McCarthyite years contributed to that break in what could be visibly remembered, which Peter Stead recounts, and was especially marked in the US.

Ironically several Hollywood leftists were to become exiles in Britain and make an impact on British television. The children who sat innocently watching British TV in the 1950s humming along to 'Robin Hood, Robin Hood, Riding through the Glen', were unaware that American radicals fleeing McCarthy had contributed to the popular series. A few years later some of the same children, grown older and radicalised, were to discover the work of the blacklisted Hollywood film-makers, including Salt of the Earth (1953),[5] a film about a desperate strike of Mexican Americans, made by the Communist Herbert Biberman. In 1969 it found new life in meetings organised by the 'Angry Arts' group, which included several American activist exiles. In the early 1970s it was screened on the night cleaners' picket line outside the Ministry of Defence in Fulham, London, while the Berwick Street Film Collective made their documentary Night Cleaners. In these barely perceptible ways, links survived between the 'old' left and the new, in defiance of that erosion of memory that Peter Stead describes. Nina Hibbin's story reveals the tenacity of this subversive radical culture.

Notes

1. See D. A. Mellor, 'Mass Observation: The Intellectual Climate', Camerawork, 11, September 1978 (repr. in Evans (ed.), The Camerawork Essays, pp.133–44); K. Worpole, 'Oppositional Culture: Yesterday, Today and Tomorrow', Camerawork, 11, September 1978; Richards and Sheridan, Mass Observation at the Movies; Spender, Worktown People.

2. Corner, The Art of Record, pp.22–4, 56–71; Aitken, The Documentary Film Movement, pp.1–35; Macdonald and Cousins, Imagining Reality, pp.93–125.

3. On early 60s films see Stead, Film and the Working Class, pp.178–210; Murphy, Sixties British Cinema, pp.10, 63–4; Hill, Sex, Class and Politics, pp.145–76.

4. On the American background see Stead, Films and the Working Class, pp.147–77, and Neve, Film and Politics in America, pp.171–210.

5. On Salt of the Earth see L. S. Robinson, 'Out of the Mine and Into the Canyon: Working-class Feminism, Yesterday and Today' in James and Berg (eds), The Hidden Foundation, pp.172–92.

3 A Paradoxical Turning Point: 1959 to 1960

Peter Stead

Clancy Sigal, the American writer who came to live in England during the 1950s, wrote a magnificent autobiographical novel, *Going Away*, which was published in 1960. It tells the story of an American working in Hollywood as a scriptwriter. Becoming disillusioned with Hollywood, he decides he wants to leave America. The book describes him crossing the United States to take the boat from New York to Great Britain. As he goes through the country, he looks up old friends of his parents, people from the 1930s labour movement in Chicago. He seeks out the veterans of labour struggles in America, and he visits some of the shrines, as it were, the famous landmarks of American labour history. His book is a wonderful counter-history of America and one of the best books written about the American left.

Clancy Sigal was saying that the big events in American history were usually assumed to be the great battles of the American Revolution and the Civil War, such as Yorktown or Gettysburg, but in his family they remembered other battles—the great strikes, Haymarket, Lawrence, Paterson and the people who died in them. An enormous labour struggle occurred in America at the end of the nineteenth and beginning of the twentieth century. Few Americans know this history, and very few students of American history, in this country, know about it. But Clancy Sigal was remembering and celebrating different kinds of memory, different kinds of consciousness.

Even as *Going Away* was being published, Clancy Sigal himself had left his base in London and was going north to the Yorkshire coalfield, talking to the miners, becoming friendly with their leaders and writing another novel, which became, of course, *Weekend in Dinlock*. He was particularly impressed as an American writer by the fact that the mining community had a miners' lodge, delighted to find a political organisation like that. In American society and indeed in much of Britain, he felt that small local communities had lost their autonomy, and that authoritarian directives from capital cities were closing in and crushing local democracy. In this Yorkshire mining village in contrast there was still a forum for a public debate, things were challenged by the community and action was possible. Having celebrated American labour history, Clancy Sigal goes to the heart of what he conceives as working-class community and democracy in Britain and makes this the subject of his fiction.

Clancy Sigal's journey was indicative of a wider mood among novelists, dramatists and academics on the left. Richard Hoggart's *The Uses of Literacy*,

Peter Stead has written widely on issues relating to the history of the culture of the British working class. He lives in South Wales where he is well known as a cultural commentator and broadcaster. His books include *Film and the Working Class: The Feature Film in British and American Society* (1989).

published in 1957, had stimulated a debate about the working class and culture. Raymond Williams was to take up the same theme in the early '60s. There was a strong feeling among many socialist intellectuals that a working-class culture was under threat from the mass media. At the same time there was a renewed interest in labour history. In the early 1960s, the social historian E.P. Thompson was working on his book *The Making of the Working Class*. When it came out in 1963, it was to inspire a labour history that looked at class in new ways. Intellectuals on the left were beginning to rediscover a labour past that stressed the importance of communities and democratic politics.

The late 1950s and early '60s were also a moment in which radical film-makers were beginning to think shouldn't we, as film-makers, go in search of something different? Shouldn't we go in search of working-class communities, of a different kind of consciousness? Some, like Lindsay Anderson and Karel Reisz, were coming from the 1950s 'Free Cinema' movement, which had tried to create a cinema based on free expression and poetic realism. These film-makers were increasingly inclined to reject the 'in-house' nature of the British studios, a hermetically sealed world that created artificial products. There was a conviction that one of the reasons British cinema lost out to America was that it was not sufficiently realistic and excluded large sections of the population.

This debate about the nature of the British cinema, or to be precise the English cinema, which was coming to the boil once again in this period, had been going on, really, from the 1920s. Since then people had been asking why isn't there a cinema in England that captures and feeds off realities in English life in the same way that, for all its faults, American cinema clearly did? In 1927, writing in the *Daily Express*, a critic called G. A. Atkinson declared: 'The American film stands in the main for the American spirit, a certain joyousness, optimism, youthfulness and determination.' In contrast 'the British spirit has not yet found national expression on the screen.'[1]

That phrase 'national expression' was to occur over and over again. To commentators on the left this meant that real issues were not being tackled in realistic ways. In particular, of course, they were concerned at the absence of any cinema faithfully dealing with working-class communities and politics. For example, in 1939 the writer and broadcaster J. B. Priestley had called on the studios to combine with the documentary film-makers:[2]

Nearly all our films are much thinner in their social texture than the French films and the better Hollywood products. When they show us an England, it seems to have been taken from a few issues of the *Sketch* or *Tatler* and a collection of Xmas cards. Only the faintest dribble of English life is allowed to trickle into most of our films, from which everything not of immediate entertainment value has been so carefully removed that most of the entertainment has vanished too.

Priestley was initially sceptical about the cinema; his love was the theatre, and he had a Dickensian appreciation of English popular culture. He came to film via American cinema and was one of the first British intellectuals to understand what was going on. He was aware not only of Hollywood's power to entertain but also its capacity to feed off things that are real in American life. He recognised it was 'only a thin overworked seam of real life',[3] none the less, in contrast to the British cinema, it was there. Interestingly, Priestley also raised an issue which was not taken up for some time. Perhaps this dissimilarity was a result not only of a failure of British cinema in relation to the energy and vitality of American films, but also of something inherent in American society that made it more cinematic than British society. This would suggest that the problem was a deeply rooted one in British society, and that the obstacles to be overcome were not just about how you filmed. I think Priestley's observation was extremely perceptive not only for the 1930s but in a contemporary sense as well.

During the Second World War this debate about cinema and national expression assumed quite an optimistic note, especially in terms of documentary films, and, at the end of the war, the documentary movement was still calling for 'national expression' in the cinema. The idea was to resurface in a more heated way at the end of the 1950s. In 1957 Tom Maschler edited *Declaration*, an influential book about commitment in the arts, and Lindsay Anderson's famous essay 'Get Out and Push' appeared in the collection. Anderson complained that English cinema, was 'snobbish, anti-intelligent, emotionally inhibited, wilfully blind to the conditions and problems of the present, dedicated to an out-of-date, exhausted national ideal'.[4]

Despite his criticisms of Hollywood films, Anderson admired their realism. Even though he condemned the politics of films such as *On the Waterfront*, he knew that they possessed an energy that British cinema had never come anywhere near. However, what he and other left film-makers were up against was a society where class was such a major barrier that it could not be avoided.

As the 1950s came to a close there was a widespread recognition, which went well beyond the left, that English cinema, like English drama, was stilted and phoney, and that it needed to relate to contemporary reality. The years 1959 to 1960 constituted a turning point, however, the move towards greater realism did not come about in the way Anderson had envisaged. The thunder of the left-wing intellectuals who had been calling for a full-bloodied cinema was stolen by more traditional film-makers. They moved into the sphere of social relevance on their own terms, and the result was an interesting false start. Two significant examples of films that responded to the demand for a contemporary realism by taking industrial relations as their theme were *I'm All Right, Jack*, a comedy produced and directed by John and Roy Boulting, which appeared in 1959, followed by *The Angry Silence* in 1960, directed by Guy Green. The latter was a film about sending a worker who refused to join an unofficial strike to Coventry.

The political context added to the controversial impact of both films. The last year of the decade was the one in which the Conservatives won their unprecedented third election victory. Their success was influenced in part by anti-union feeling. Wild-cat strikes were in the news, and there was a strong

I'm All Right, Jack,
1959 (British
Lion/Charter)

message in the media that unions were both powerful and irresponsible. *I'm All Right, Jack* was released in London seven weeks before the election and went on general release just after it. The title itself was to become a satirical catch phrase about British trade unionists.

The reaction from left critics in papers such as the *New Statesman* or *Tribune* was predictably indignant. Penelope Houston, for instance, declared that *I'm All Right, Jack* had obviously been made by 'sour liberals'.[5] To Pauline Kael in the US this passionate rejection of the film seemed excessive. She regarded the criticism of the unions as 'affectionate' and remarked that Penelope Houston's 'jargon' was 'not far removed from the shop stewards'.[6] There was a tendency for left-wing critics to fall into the trap of sounding just like the defenders of sacred cows that the film was making jokes about.

Of course the shop steward in question, Fred Kite, happened to be played by Peter Sellers, who turned an otherwise unremarkable film into a box-office hit. This popularity, along with the apparent invincibility of Conservatism, explains the anger directed towards the humour in *I'm All Right, Jack*. Moreover the Boulting brothers in the past had been thought of as being pro-labour and on the left. In the late 1940s they had created *Fame is the Spur*, about the Labour Party, and *Brighton Rock* based on Graham Greene's novel about youth violence, so there was surprise when they made *I'm All Right, Jack*. They responded by saying that they were making a series of films, satirising all aspects of British society. They also claimed that in this particular film they were making fun of everybody and ridiculing both sides in industry. Management and the ruling classes were satirised in the characters of Major Hargreaves played by Terry-Thomas and the silly idiot from an aristocratic family who has wandered into a factory, acted by Ian Carmichael. They also insisted that the humour was aimed at abuses in the unions rather than the unions themselves. It is true that the Kite character's pomposity, preten-tiousness and his authoritarian unthinking pro-Soviet sentiments could have made him a target of the anti-Stalinist new left. He could be interpreted as a certain type of trade unionist not as a representative of all trade unionists.

The problem was really that the jokes in the script about the workers were much better than those about management. The presentation of management politics is just silly. The Boultings try to load everything into the plot. In fact, the second half of the film is mostly a satire on television, and in particular the way in which television news was put together. Because it was such an over-loaded film, the audience tended to lose sight of any general purpose and just remembered the funny jokes about the union at the start of the film.

Also, of course, the Boultings could not have legislated for Peter Sellers' absolutely magnificent performance as Kite. They had had a particular shop steward at the film studios in mind when they created the character and were getting their revenge on somebody who had been a bit obstructive. Major Hargreaves denounces Kite as 'the kind of chap who sleeps in his Vest—a real shocker'. But it was Sellers himself who deepened the part of Kite and gave the film a biting edge. It was he who suggested the haircut, the Hitler moustache and added the gestures. This is a great comic actor in the process of perfecting his art.

I'm All Right, Jack is an interesting film in social terms because it was so popular. It was to be by far the most successful film of 1959. There was noth-ing in particular about its promotion that suggested it was going to be a great hit. Indeed David Kingsley, chairman of British Lion, the distributors, claimed it had succeeded really because of 'word of mouth'.[7] People said there was a very funny film on locally with lots of jokes about the unions. People started going to it, and it just took off.

In general the press did not play on the anti-union side of the film. They treated it as a normal, run-of-the-mill comedy. The general attitude was 'the shower are back!'—meaning the team who had done *Private's Progress* (1956) and other farces about aspects of British society. The Boulting brothers' publicity also simply promoted the film as a comedy.

However, in 1959 the newspaper columns were actually full of reports of industrial action. For instance there were bus strikes in Swansea and major disputes locally with an American company that was refusing to recognise the union. In interpreting the impact of *I'm All Right Jack* we need to recognise the Boultings' commercial sense. They perceived there was a debate about trade unionism, and they gambled on there being a comedy in industrial relations. They threw in the stuff on television for good measure. As it happened, partly through artistic confusion, partly through the genius of one actor, it became more memorably an anti-union film than was perhaps intended initially. But the anti-unionism in the film did not occasion any great cultural debate.

The following year, however, when *The Angry Silence* appeared quite suddenly the debate started. The Trades Council in Ipswich, where parts of the film had been shot on location, passed a resolution calling for a boycott of the film. The South Wales miners asked cinemas run by the labour movement and miners' welfare institutes not to show the film. Richard Attenborough, who starred in *The Angry Silence* responded by saying: 'This sort of Fascist behaviour is just what the film is about.'[8] The Swansea evening paper tried to keep the conflict going by interviewing David Kingsley from British Lion, who of course insisted the film was merely attacking apathy and abuses in the trade unions. British Lion promoted the film as the frankest and most daring film ever made about British society. The fact that they were prepared to back *The Angry Silence* is indicative of the significant cultural shift that was occurring at this time.

The story behind the making of *The Angry Silence* is very interesting. The film was produced by Beaver Films, a company set up by Richard Attenborough and Bryan Forbes. Forbes had been working as an actor, writer, producer and director since the late 1940s and he was married to actress Nanette Newman. It was she who had spotted the original story about a worker who had been sent to Coventry and then actor Michael Craig who worked on the script. Richard Attenborough was, however, the driving force. He saw the gritty beauty of the story and, of course, a part for himself. To make sure that British Lion accepted this film, Attenborough invested a great deal of his own money in it, and he negotiated a deal that was highly disadvantageous to him personally. He wanted to make this particular film, because he had made his name as a juvenile delinquent in films such as *Brighton Rock* and was keen to graduate to more challenging and more adult parts.

The Angry Silence tells the story of a strike in which we see a Communist agent arriving to ferment conflict and working with shop stewards to that end. There is no explanation of why the strike takes place or what is at stake. We see no discussion between the men at all. The strike simply leads us to the dramatic sequence, in which one man (Richard Attenborough) with a beautiful Italian wife (Pier Angeli) and two children takes a stand against an industrial dispute. It is the fortitude, the bravery of this one man that forms the basis for the whole film. He is injured and loses his eye, his child is tarred and his wife goes through a great deal of emotional stress. Not only is he persecuted by the men, but by hooligans as well—the juvenile delinquents who had figured so prominently in British social-problem films inevitably have to be brought in.

While *The Angry Silence* continues a tradition of British Social-problem films, it was rare to have a film dealing with industrial relations, showing the workings of a trade union with shots inside the factory and on location in Ipswich. Indeed how many British films have been shot on location in Ipswich or even on location in industrial cities? The irony is that this realistic break-through occurs in an anti-union film. We are inside a factory for one reason only, in order that Richard Attenborough can do his thing and be praised for a great realistic performance, hopefully one that will be compared favourably with those in the American cinema.

Though left-wing critics pointed out how the film was absolutely unrepre-sentative of ordinary working people, many critics did praise the film for its drama, topicality, honesty and realism. *The Angry Silence* also earned praise in America for being about 'real people' and was paradoxically contrasted to American films in its depiction of the 'little man'. This was an ironic reversal of what many British intellectuals interested in cinema had been saying about the two countries' film cultures. The praise the film received served as a justifica-tion for Attenborough's opportunism as far as his own career was concerned.

While Attenborough's personal motives give us an immediate reason for the film being made, this is not the whole explanation. To understand why British Lion were prepared to take on a film about industrial relations it is important to remember how the British film industry desired to emulate Hollywood's successes. *The Angry Silence* was, of course, inspired by *On the Waterfront*, which had come out in 1954. Acclaimed as one of the greatest films of its era, it contains superb location shooting, in the New Jersey dockyards and, of course, tremendous, revolutionary acting from Marlon Brando. Elia Kazan was a director of genius and Brando a terrific new force in cinema. There were many things going for *On the Waterfront*, though, politically of course it is a strangely confused film and was meant to be Kazan's defence of co-operating with the McCarthyite investigations: in it Kazan was deliberately defending the role of the informer. Whatever your views about the stance taken, it is undeniable that a great deal of the power of the film comes from its roots in an actual political position. Its edge owed a lot to the fact that it was produced in a particular era.

Then along comes *The Angry Silence*, supposedly the British answer to *On the Waterfront*. However, the position is very different. What you have here is Attenborough and Craig simply wanting to make money and further their own ambitions, without any real political edge and, of course, without any revolu-tionary acting or directing. It is perfectly clear that you are seeing two Chelsea men slumming it in Ipswich.

Attenborough just about gets away with it, because of what one critic, Norman Cecil, called his 'bantam fortitude'.[9] He has that irritated, agitated air that enables him to carry the part off. But Michael Craig, who co-wrote the story, is appalling in the film, and the sexism in his part is atrocious. When he says the line 'I feel so dirty', it is as if he were almost apologising for the entire plot: there is a kind of dirtiness about the film as a whole.

The background then to the production of both *I'm All Right, Jack* and *The Angry Silence* was actually an impulse, evident in both British and American oppositional culture, to return to roots. In both countries this involved a turn to community and a desire for greater realism. But in Britain this campaign for a more realistic cinema, one that dealt with serious issues, to which so many people had been looking forward, was pre-empted by the commercial opportunism of the studios who moved in quickly and made these two amazing films in 1959—although *The Angry Silence* did not appear until the following year.

There were many complicated reasons why the British film industry had failed for so long to respond to British society, even in the limited way that Hollywood had done to American society. A basic factor was lack of money. Production values were always very much higher in Hollywood. Wall Street invested in Hollywood in a way in which the City never did for the British film industry, which, as a result, never rested on a secure financial foundation.

British culture was also more overtly class bound, and this had implications for film. Until the 1950s cinema was not highly regarded in Britain by many middle-class intellectuals. Few writers bothered with cinema, and the British studios made very little effort to attract writers. While intellectuals thought they were too good for the movies, as far as the British studios were concerned, the movies were too good for them.

There is a persistent mythology about how Hollywood treated writers badly. We have all heard about the great Nobel prize-winning writers stranded in the bungalow in Hollywood, writing something for the studios that was sent in and then scrapped. We can see them sitting there, feeling totally confused, alienated, wondering why they ever left New York. But take Scott Fitzgerald for instance. First off he was paid an enormous amount of money for all his writings before he went to Hollywood. Then after he had squandered it all on champagne and was actually forced to go and earn a living in Hollywood, the studios paid him all over again. It is true of course that the writing was ignored for the most part. Perhaps one line of Scott Fitzgerald's might get into a film, because the studios had their own story writers and editors to doctor the scripts: the Hollywood studio bosses knew exactly what they wanted. But they still respected quality, and so they paid people such as Scott Fitzgerald, William Faulkner and the left-wing playwright Clifford Odets, along with many Europeans to work for them. They tried to get everybody, even the Soviet director Sergei Eisenstein, so they could get his name on the credits.

The British studios in contrast were a world apart. They operated a form of restrictive practice, in which entrepreneurs, tycoons and technicians did everything in-house. The studio system in America combined its high degree of professionalism with a desire to buy whatever talent was going. Whereas the British studios did not even try to attract the minor British writers. The result was that British writers had not come to terms with cinema, and cinema had not come to terms with them.

Christopher Isherwood saw something of the British studios before he went to Hollywood in 1939 to work as a script writer for Metro-Goldwyn-Mayer. His

1945 novel, *Prater Violet*, is the best description we have of the British film studios in the 1930s. It was impressed upon Isherwood that there was no real room for him and his kind in the studios. They did not want dramatists or novelists or indeed 'literature' at all; they wanted mere technicians. He also notes that there was a basic problem about working-class dialogue. If you wanted a sausage salesman, you could not get anybody to write such a part. Shakespeare or Tolstoy could have done it; but nobody in the British studios could. He was told he had to do working-class dialogue, but the only people he had really ever heard speaking were public-school boys and bohemians in London's West End. So he did what other middle-class people did, he borrowed it from other films or just made it up. It is not surprising that working-class characters in British films tended to be stereotypes.

The artificiality was compounded by the West End theatrical training that taught everyone posh accents, so you got 'the coalminer's daughter syndrome'. Cinema managers pointed out that in films depicting British working-class life, the daughter would appear and start speaking with a cut-glass accent and the whole cinema would roar with laughter. In contrast audiences accepted American accents as realistic, partly through ignorance. It was not just that class was more visible in British society. There were other differences. British public life was much more formal than in the USA. Deference was more engrained. There was less space for personal self-expression. The individualism that was so central a theme in the American film was quite alien to British culture, where people were trained to behave in accepted ways. Also, as Priestley noted, the pace and vitality in American society and the sense of movement in its cinema was not there in Britain.

In looking at the failure of cinema to depict the British working class in the 1950s, we are going to the very heart of a class culture that had never come to terms with cinema as an art form, because of its own social and intellectual prejudices. From the 1930s left-wing film-makers and critics had been saying that the result was a form of censorship, which excluded the majority and restricted the expression of a whole range of experience.

It is interesting to ask why, despite the institutional achievements of the labour movement, the organised working class had never been able to mount an effective challenge to this class bias in the culture. Here we have to acknowledge that there was a problem within the working class itself as well. Trade unions continued to be a central force in its life in the 1950s. They occupied, however, a particular position in British society as a whole.

The fact that union power had been recognised from the 1890s onwards and had been accommodated within the system meant that the unions never had to consider fighting the battle outside their own terms of reference. There was no need for them to wage a cultural struggle because they were supported so decisively from within. From the mid-1890s onwards, as the British corporate state developed, it was prepared to work with the trade unions. And during the twentieth century, the two World Wars were to round off that process.

The middle classes, however, retained a cultural objection to the trade unions. They worked with the labour movement as a pressure group, and they conceded its political status without ever admitting the trade unions into their cultural world. The anti-union feeling was thus rooted in cultural ground, rather than in explicit politics. And that is why the Boulting brothers and Richard Attenborough and Michael Craig were able to respond to the call for greater realism and get their cameras into the factories before anybody else in 1959. The result was to be two fundamentally anti-union films.

A much better film, which was also on display in British cinemas in 1960, was Karel Reisz' *Saturday Night and Sunday Morning*. Unlike the other two, this was a film of the 1960s rather than the 1950s: more permissive, up to date, and contemporary. It was also witty and well written, and based on one of the few English working-class novels to receive any national attention. For years and years British critics had been saying where is the British Brando? Well, there was the British Brando, a superb one: Albert Finney. Still a little theatrical perhaps, for Finney was an actor trained in the theatre, but he is better than anything that has ever gone before in British acting in his capacity to get inside the character of a young working-class man. In particular, he was certainly better than Attenborough.

We have slipped out of the '50s. We are in the '60s already, and what we are celebrating of course is the energy of one man—one actor. In the shots of the factory we see the other lot 'who were ground down before the war and have never recovered from it', but obviously we are never going to see a cinema about them. The new cinema that was to emerge captures the new individualism in British culture, but it does not in any way reflect the older sense of community and an opposing tradition of politics that Clancy Sigal had admired on his journey north. So a new British cinema is indeed being born, but we have missed out on an earlier era.

With *Saturday Night and Sunday Morning* cinema had turned a corner; we were into the British New Wave, which was to end in 1963 with Lindsay Anderson's *This Sporting Life*. Unlike *Saturday Night and Sunday Morning*, this was not to be a popular film with audiences in Britain. They found it grim and gloomy, but it was acclaimed by the critics and loved by intellectuals. At last with kitchen-sink, there was a British cinema of which we could be proud.

However, despite these New Wave films of the 1960s and the intelligent, perceptive and sensitive acting of Albert Finney and Tom Courtenay, Rita Tushingham and Richard Harris and the outstanding Rachel Roberts, the caricatured acting persisted. The music-hall stereotypes were still to be found in British films and, of course, as television develops, were to be passed on for quite some time afterwards.

By the early 1960s television was on its way to becoming the national cinema that cinema itself had failed to be. It had its own national institutions—among them *Coronation Street*, which started in December 1960. Not only the stock working class characters but also the *I'm All Right, Jack* approach to industrial relations was kept going in TV soaps and sit-coms. One obvious example is *The Rag Trade*, about a factory, where the shop steward was played by Miriam Karlin. She would blow a whistle and say, 'All out!'. And that catch phrase stuck, just as *I'm Alright Jack* had entered the language.

Television was always to be better than the old film studios: the people running TV had more money. Some valued writing and were more aware of debates around culture and class. There were several broader, wider and more creative currents present, and, from these, more perceptive programmes, such as *Z Cars* were to develop.

The last years of the 1950s and the first of the '60s are not only interesting in terms of the kitchen-sink films, which are remembered as spectacular. In order to see how realism was making an impact in British culture we also need to look at the whole output of British television and cinema as an indicator of how attitudes were changing. What we were to get at last was indeed greater realism in the portrayal of working class peoples' lives. But it was a realism that was only occasionally dealing with the full complexities of working-class communities and their politics.

Peter Stead, lecture at 'Images of Labour' Conference, 14 March 1997, edited by Peter Stead, Huw Beynon and Sheila Rowbotham

Notes

1. G. A. Atkinson, *Sunday Express*, 20 March 1927 (Sydney Carroll Collection, BFI Library); quoted in Stead, *Film and the Working Class*, p.99.
2. J. B. Priestley (1939); quoted in Stead, *Film and the Working Class*, p.111.
3. *Ibid.*, p.101.
4. L. Anderson, 'Get Out and Push' in Maschler (ed.) *Declaration*, p.157.
5. Penelope Houston, quoted in P. Kael, 'Commitment and the Straitjacket', *Film Quarterly*, fall 1961.
6. Pauline Kael, *ibid*.
7. David Kingsley, quoted in Stead, *Film and the Working Class*, p.181.
8. Richard Attenborough, quoted in Hill, *Sex, Class and Realism*, p.199.
9. Norman Cecil in *Films in Review*, 12:1, January 1960; quoted in Stead, *Film and the Working Class*, p.184.

4   One Thing Leads to Another

Nina Hibbin

Nina Hibbin was the film critic on the *Daily Worker* and later, from the late 1950s to the early 1970s, for the *Morning Star*. She spent four years as film officer of the Yorkshire Arts Association before becoming director of the Tyneside Cinema. In the early 1980s she and her husband retired to a remote spot on the North Yorkshire coast to sell teas to walkers on the Cleveland Way.

HB For almost all of your life you have been involved in what might be termed 'the politics of representation', and this began, I suppose, with your involvement in the Mass-Observation movement of the 1930s?

NH When I was 15 or 16 I had already joined the Young Communist League. It was all very sociable, but I didn't think we were actually changing anything, and you know my ambition then, as it is now as a matter of fact, was to change the world. I read an appeal somewhere for volunteers to keep diaries and answer various questions about aspects of social life and their own lives and views. The idea was 'to give ordinary people a voice'. Well, at the time that really rang bells with me—I cannot think why it did because it was false, although not so false as it would be now: nowadays there are so many other and more direct ways in which people can express themselves. I can remember writing to Mass-Observation and saying, 'I feel that if I could do my little bit it would wipe some of the blood off the face of the earth'—yes, I can remember feeling dramatic about it. I was thrilled to bits when I was accepted. I answered all the questions and added lots of things of my own, and after a time I realised that I was their sort of pet—a semi-working-class/lower-middle-class contributor. Everyone else was a good bit further up the social scale, so I was often quoted, and began to imagine myself to be indispensable.

Meanwhile my mother had got me this job in a posh London dress shop. I was the office girl. She thought it was the beginning of a great career that would end up with my marrying the boss. But I absolutely detested it—I cannot tell you how much. So I wrote to Tom Harrisson, one of the founders of Mass-Observation: 'Either you give me a job or else I stop writing my reports altogether.' So he invited me in and gave me a full-time job, which was just wonderful for a person of my age and background. It opened out a whole new sphere of life that I thought was entirely closed to me

HB So you were a Mass-Observer, then the War, and then you spent time teaching in Cornwall, Is it that you ended up as film critic for the *Daily Worker*?

NH After the wartime WAAF I was teaching for about ten years and then moved back to London. I was active in the Communist Party, and people at the *Daily Worker* had heard that I played the accordion, which I used to do in the the shelters during the Blitz. They asked me would I mind covering an accordion festival, and they were so taken with the piece I wrote about it they invited me to do more. Eventually the film critic went on holiday, and they said, 'Would you mind filling in for a fortnight?' Well, I thought it was great going to the pictures for a living five or six times a week in the daytime—posh little places, a drink beforehand. The fortnight grew into six weeks and then six months, and I stayed for 15 years. They were very interesting years. I am never quite sure what good I did, but I enjoyed it enormously.

HB You started writing about films in the late 1950s?
NH It was '57. It was soon after the Hungarian uprising and the turmoil in the Communist Party—lots of people had left and lots had changed positions, and it was as a result of all that that I came into it as a professional journalist.

HB I suppose this is a time when British cinema went through changes with films such as *I'm All Right, Jack, The Angry Silence*—both featuring Richard Attenborough—and *Room at the Top*.
NH You have put them in quite a different context from mine because I never regarded *The Angry Silence* or *I'm All Right, Jack* as part of the significant New Wave in British cinema that started in the late l950s and in differing forms went right through the 1960s. My view is that *I'm All Right, Jack* and *The Angry Silence* were rather old-fashioned opportunistic films that took advantage of the new movement in cinema but actually stood against it. The real films of the New Wave were films from within—or trying to be from within—the working class or within some kind of grass-roots experience. I always like to think that a pointer to it was a little film, *The Man Upstairs*. It was perhaps the first to deal with the issues of the time, including the atom bomb, in a serious way. It was not a big cinema film, although curiously it did have Richard Attenborough in a lead role; I always thought it was a straw in the wind. But it was completely overshadowed in the same period—1958 as I remember—by *Room at the Top*, which seemed to me to be a big breakthrough, although at the same time it was only a half-way house. It dealt frankly with class and social barriers, corruption in high places and so on but unlike the real New Wave films it had big stars—Simone Signoret and Laurence Harvey. It was a runaway success in America as well, so it opened the way for a whole lot of other things to come.
   The shift came mainly because of what was happening in the theatre through Joan Littlewood—she was a tremendously important influence—and the kitchen-sink thing at the Royal Court with Arnold Wesker, John Osborne and other young writers who were transforming London theatre. And then some of the Royal Court people—Tony Richardson, Lindsay Anderson and Karel Reisz—began experimental film-making with a documentary style they called Free Cinema. Eventually, through the breach made by *Room at The Top* they were able to make ground-breaking films such as *Saturday Night and Sunday Morning, The Loneliness of the Long Distance Runner*, both based on books by Alan Sillitoe, *A Taste of Honey, This Sporting Life* and lots more.

HB *Billy Liar* too?

This Sporting Life,
1963 (Rank/
Independent)

NH Yes, that was John Schlesinger. He put another angle on it with films like *A Kind of Loving* and *Darling*, and Julie Christie as a new kind of lead woman. I liked his work, though, you see, there's politics for you—he certainly wasn't on the left, but he is humanist, and I suppose that rather vague word sums up a lot of what has been best in British cinema.

HB I wondered how you saw the New Wave at the time?
NH It was tremendously exciting. When I saw *Saturday Night and Sunday Morning* I went back to the office and said: 'I want a big headline across my review saying BEST BRITISH FILM EVER MADE. It was extraordinary in its impact and drew crowds back to the cinema. Some of it was because for the first time ever things like abortion and menstruation were mentioned, but it was also because it was based on working-class experience. Sillitoe at that time was writing from the heart of his Nottingham experience—and writing passionately. Tony Richardson as producer had to battle to get the finance, but once it was made it opened the door still wider for a fresh approach to cinema.

HB Did you see it as a reaction to the Attenborough films?
NH No, not really. It was more a reaction to the mid-Atlanticism of the mid-1950s, which was just 'make any film that has got a British woman and an

American man as stars and perhaps an Italian or two and maybe a German as well and a story that crosses the continents'. There was so much of that. It was the industry's idea of how to halt the decimation of cinemas and film-going at a time when TV was a major challenge. The industry itself became more cynical than ever. I think it was a reaction to all that at one level . But it was also a reflection of the lively political movements that were coming up in the 1950s—all the sit-downs and protest marches against nuclear weapons and German re-armament and so on, all those protests, and the Aldermaston marches. All of this was finding expression, first in novels, then in the theatre and finally in film, not in a documented way but as a reflection of the public mood. It was a wonderful period, but it had its own built-in destruction.

The New Wave film-makers had to battle for finance, though the films were not expensive (in black and white, in modern dress and mainly shot on location). And there weren't big-star salaries to pay, although many, like Albert Finney, Torn Courtenay, Julie Christie and Rita Tushingham, became big as a result.

But then Tony Richardson wanted to do *Tom Jones*. Now you could see why he wanted to do *Tom Jones*, how it fitted into that scheme of things. It was a criticism in its own time of social mores or whatever you call them. But it had to be in colour and in costume, and by then Albert Finney was a star. At the time British Lion, which was the biggest funder for British film and headed by Michael Balcon, just felt that they couldn't finance it. I spoke to Michael Balcon, at the time about it, and he said with hindsight he should have sold the office furniture and the ink stand just to get behind it. But he didn't and it was an American company who took it up. That was the beginning of a too familiar pattern. Whenever British cinema begins to get its own head, America comes in, and the industry welcomes it because it is investment. But they forget that the money is being taken out of the country, and that it's diluting the kind of film that the English cinema—I mean British really—has been so good at.

HB How does this fit then with this slightly later period, which begins with films like *Kes*, and which, I believe, had great difficulties in getting a screening?
NH The political movements of the late 1960s were building up to a climax, and bright young directors such as Ken Loach and Peter Watkins were in their very differing way developing urgent, on-the-spot techniques for presenting urgent social problems or relevant historical events in new docu-drama forms. Towards the end of the 1960s they began making an impact on cinema, Watkins with *Privilege* and Loach with *Kes*. I had heard rumours of this marvellous little film that nobody wanted to screen, and it wasn't until Loach and his producer Tony Garnett wrote to some of us critics that, after much resistance, we were able to persuade the Critics' Circle to organise a screening. Of course once they saw it they agreed it was stunning, and that was one of the main things that got it shown. And of course it's now a classic.

HB These were, I imagine, a small proportion of the films you used to see?
NH Oh, yes, because I suppose the vast majority of films were American films.

One of my all time favourite American films, which again didn't get very much of a reception, was *The Chase*—Arthur Penn's film. I thought it absolutely brilliant. After the press show I wandered around London in a daze. When I went back to the afternoon film nobody seemed to be talking about it, to such an extent that I thought, 'I've made a mistake.' So I went and saw it again, and I just thought it was terrific. There's a case of a film that has got such power and dynamic, an entertaining thriller with strong social criticism underlying it. It has been shown several times on television since, and I think it still stands.

HB Toward the end you said you got a bit fed up with your work as a film critic. How did that come about?

NH I'd been seeing films, thousands a year, for 15 years, and I remember distinctly being in the cinema one day seeing a perfectly acceptable film called *Kotch*—good cast, good script, and it absolutely meant nothing to me at all. I just thought, 'Why am I sitting here? I could be teaching little children or writing a book. [laughter] I could be doing anything, and here I am sitting thinking about what to have for supper tonight because I'm finding this film hasn't got any relationship to me at all. Why am I spending my life doing this?' As soon as I asked myself that question I was out.

HB That is when you moved to Bradford?

NH What happened was that our daughter had just finished school and was going to University, which meant that we were no longer chained to that particular corner of London. So we began to apply for jobs outside of London, and I was lucky enough to get one first, which was Film Officer of Yorkshire Arts Association, so we moved up to Bradford, where it was based, and my husband, Eric, very soon became the Office Administrator within the Association and so we worked together on that for four years.

HB What was that? What did that involve?

NH Well, that is rather funny because nobody knew exactly. There were very few Film Officers at that time, so I began to draw out all kinds of ideas myself about opening up film appreciation, film-making and film education. I thought there should be a greater variety of screenings, more places where people could make and study films, and a film culture that embraced amateurs, students and professionals. Eventually these ideas all came about, even to setting up a Media Centre. It was a wonderful place where we had a whole studio, a sound room, cutting room and so on—mainly throw-outs from Yorkshire television, who were very kind to us and gave us lots of stuff. It was mostly on video, of course, but people made films there too, which was good. I understand it is now flourishing in Leeds and very different from the rather tatty place I set up in the first instance.

HB Were there things that you really liked about what you did in Bradford?

NH Yes, because we really made waves. Lots of the ideas other people brought to me, but I had the know-how to get things moving. I knew where to get the money. One I really loved was *Second Sight* and it was brought to us by two ambitious young men who wanted to be in films but were also interested in education. They set up a film-making van that they would take to a school. This was when schools had money, you know—it is very difficult to do this sort of thing now. The kids would shoot the film, and the lads would go back, edit it and bring back the finished film for a school screening—that was lovely. And then there was another time when we had a day in Hull in which we borrowed about 20 video cameras. That was when video cameras were very heavy and not readily available—they were huge things. We had a couple of 'video doctors', because they were always going wrong. We invited people to go out in groups all over Hull to film whatever they fancied, all the morning and half the afternoon. In the evening we screened what everybody had filmed that day. It was magic. We were funding short films—very low level funding—but I am quite proud of the fact that a number of people who did work with us then have gone on to be serious film-makers.

There was a big gap between the students and the amateur movement which was largely untouched by the film establishment. But with the help of a film tutor at Leeds University we set up a weekend in which amateurs and art students showed their films to each other, which was dynamic because neither had seen the other kind of film-making before. And some of them were dire but in totally different ways. I enjoyed my association with the amateur movement. I was often asked to be a judge, and I remember once my fellow judge said to me, 'Let's think. Marks out 100—we'll give 20 for definition, and 20 for focus, and 20 for composition and so on.'

I said, 'No, we won't'. 'What do you mean', he replied. 'We'll give 80 for creativity and 20 for technique,' and that is what we did. I was pleased with that, because that was the kind of influence that I was trying to exert.

Life in the Yorkshire Arts Association was terribly pressurised—nobody was pressing us, but we were just pressurised. There were such a lot of exciting things to do, and there was no limit to our hours. We just seemed to be working all the time, and the phone was always ringing. I set up all kinds of things including a film library for films that people had made. Eventually I got fed up with it. I think four years is a good time to build something up, consolidate it and then go, let somebody new have fresh eyes on it and take it forward.

HB So you moved on to Tyneside?

NH I was persuaded to apply for the job of Director of Tyneside Film Theatre, which in some ways I wish I'd never done because it was so hard and so harrowing, but it was also very rewarding when it came out well. The cinema had been closed for two years — there had been a fire. The last thing that had happened before it had closed was that there were about five or six people in the cinema watching this film, and they suddenly realised that although it was in black-and-white it was becoming coloured round the edges, there was a glow, and they realised it was on fire. Apparently someone went up into the projection room and found the projectionist wasn't there: he was actually in the pub. The cinema was closed for two years, and then I was persuaded to take it over. Eric came with me and worked as office manager for nothing for the first three months.

When we got there, it was to discover a strange warren of a building, with a heap of keys that nobody knew where they belonged to. We couldn't find the lavatory for three weeks—we had to go to the public ones! When we found them, we couldn't find the keys to them. And there was no habitual audience, so it was really very difficult to see how to get it moving again. But by a stroke of luck (for us anyway) a cinema that had been showing *Lawrence of Arabia* for six years closed down finally, and the projectionists came over in a group and asked, 'Would you like us to work for you?', to which I replied, 'Yes, please.'

One of them said, 'Are you the Nina Hibbin who writes in the *Daily Worker*?', and that really made my day. So we had this wonderful group of three first-class projectionists who had brilliant ways of extemporising when the old equipment let us down. On one occasion when the rewinder wouldn't work one of them rushed home and got his electric drill and came back and held it on the bench while we rewound the film with it. It was extraordinary the things that they did.

Then we had an opening that was an imaginative disaster. I thought we'd open with Chaplin, a compilation of Chaplin films. I got some local talent, who were really very good actors, to go all round the town being Chaplin and the girl. They were lovely, but it didn't attract many people into the cinema. But, eventually, by scanning the audience and trying all kinds of things, we got to find out what worked and what didn't.

Even in that period when cinemas were closing down right and left Tynesiders were always keen film-goers, if they got the right combination. So we worked out a scheme where we had double programmes—no adverts, but the films—one for the fans and one for the buffs. I couldn't very often do it in just that pure way, but when I did do it, and when it worked, it worked marvellously. We sometimes had people queuing up round the block. We had an upstairs cinema that we inherited as a club. It hadn't got a public licence, and it was very esoteric, really film buffs getting together in their threes and fours to see a film that only two wanted to see anyway. So I thought of the idea that any organisation in the town could become members of the club. Their members could be our members for one night, and they could show their choice. Soon we had a lot of local organisations, ranging from the Elvis Presley Fan Club to the Greek Classics Department of the University, showing their own films and bringing their own people in—and as a result they got to know the cinema. There was a film called *Juvenile Liaison*, which was banned—it could only be shown in the club. Some social workers came and said that they would like to see it, but they had not got a club, so I said, 'Form one.' Then the police heard about it and said, 'We'd like to see it as well', so the single screening that I had arranged came into seven screenings, which were packed. Then everybody began to make their own clubs. We had the Russian Language Film Club and the Gay Film Club, the Roundheads Film Club and the Cavaliers Film Club. Yes, we had about 32 different clubs, some existing and some made specially for the club scheme.

Downstairs in the foyer of the big cinema I had a suggestion box asking people to let me know what they would like to see. We would get requests like 'All-night Godard' and other avant-garde ideas. Then, one day I reached into the suggestion box and out came '*Kung Fu* or your windows get done in.' I was pleased, and thought, now we've got to the town as well as the students'.

HB I remember you telling me that you sometimes had suggestions that you could not understand and that puzzled you.

NH The one I remember best had to do with Derek Jarman's *Sebastiane*. I think somebody had written, 'Please, please, please, *Sebastiane*', which was a typical way of asking for things. I pinned up a reply saying, 'You, and who else? It is after all a gay film, and it's in Latin and how am I going to pair it with anything else or bring in a wider audience?'. Then somebody wrote: 'It's got a Brian Eno soundtrack.' As soon as I knew that, I located a wonderful Brian Eno short, and I put those two together, and it made a smashing evening. It was cross fertilisation. I enjoy it for its own sake. I like centres of energy and putting two centres of energy together and making them fizz.

HB I believe that your policy of showing 'popular' films was not always appreciated by the Northern Arts Film Panel.

NH At first they were extremely critical of what I was doing on the basis that I was showing too many popular films. I had to go to one meeting to plead for my annual grant, which I really resented because I was more or less head-hunted in the first place. So, anyway, one really nice guy on this committee, thinking he was siding with me said, 'What Nina is really doing, you see, is showing the popular films like the *Carry On*s in order to get people into the cinema, and then they get introduced to film-makers like Bunuel and Bertolucci and so on' and they all began to nod—they had seen the light. And I said, 'I'm afraid that is not what I'm doing, that is only half of what I'm doing. Because while I would be really glad if the people who come for the *Carry On*s begin to learn about the Godards and whatever, I'm equally concerned that the people who come in for the Godards should begin to appreciate the popular films—the *Carry On*s and all the rest of them.' Well, I got my grant, and once it became really successful there was no question.

HB What was it about the *Carry On* films that you thought relevant?

NH I'm only using *Carry On* as an example here by the way, but I liked them right from the start when I was a film critic, especially the early ones, because I thought that they carried on a working-class tradition of humour in a very unisex way. Men and women all wanting to have a go, and the women were often the strongest characters. There was something very feisty about the way people carried on that I thought was great and often very funny. I thought that there was an extraordinary snobby approach to them, which was much the same as when I was a kid and the cognoscente sneered at Laurel and Hardy. Now everybody thinks they are marvellous—it is just that you had to be dead or passé before you are appreciated. It's the same with the *Carry On*s now. Everybody has an affection for them

HB You also showed less popular films if you like—you talked about Bertolucci very early on.
NH That was a real event—I was showing all kinds of films, because over the four years that I was there we really had built up an audience that understood that they were going to enjoy themselves whatever level of film they might see, and so we were able to show very popular films and very serious ones. Mel Brooks was very popular in Tyneside, and one of my most successful double programming was *Young Frankenstein* and *Frankenstein*. So I was able to show a Mel Brooks one week and a Bertolucci the next. One night we were showing his epic *1900*. It was in mid-Winter, and it was pelting with snow, and it was so bad that I was afraid that people wouldn't be able to get home. So halfway through, I made an announcement saying the buses were about to stop because it was snowing heavily, and that anybody who wanted to go, could go now, and we would repeat the screening next Sunday and we would give them a ticket for it. But nobody left—they were so absorbed by it.

HB Did you have a favourite film director at this time?
NH Kurosawa is one of my favourite directors. You feel as if you've learnt some-thing about humanity by seeing his films. I think it is to do with the fact that he sees human beings both as individuals with existential lives and as social beings, and that self-fulfilment is essentially a social thing. Gradually all his films have developed and retained this theme. He takes the whole environ-ment and shows how human beings can and can't relate, and there are very fine points about what you can and can't do in relation to nature, which I think is very affecting, I use the word 'affecting' but they are also very unaffected. They are very direct and clear. I've heard him speak, and he spoke like that as well, with great passion and simplicity.

HB Is that what you think is important in the cinema— the capacity to express political and social ideas so powerfully?
NH I'm never quite sure of that actually—I think it is so much more complex. I'm not sure that I ever regarded cinema as a political tool, but maybe as an ideological tool, which is a bit different. To begin with, I don't like the way that films are discussed in terms of genres, because if you think about, say, Hollywood through the 1930s, 1940s, 1950s and 1960s, there were two differ-ent streams of film. There were films that were sheer entertainment and gloss, and there were films that really did have serious social ideas in them. And that cut across the genres. You could have a Western that did that, or a Sci-Fi, and I wanted to look at films in that way rather than through genre. So I don't think

that films just reflect society. They reflect it and in some ways they influence it. A continuous giving and taking thing, not just a two-way but a multi-way process, where all kinds of things are fed into the cinema and come out of the cinema, and are reflected and re-reflected and so on.

HB There is the gloss and the social commentary—but one of the things that you have always believed is that the cinema is also entertainment, really.

NH There is not much point in being serious and not being entertaining, and I've never seen any division between being entertaining and being serious, or having a serious undercurrent. Indeed, most of the most successful films do have a serious undercurrent. Take *The Full Monty* as an example—one of the most entertaining films from British cinema for ages, pure entertainment—and yet it has got a very serious undercurrent. I don't agree with it entirely, but it is valid in its own terms. If a serious film isn't entertaining then you don't go and see it, and that is one of the mistakes that very solemn film academics forget.

HB In saying that you see film as entertainment, I wonder if you have also thought of film having the capacity to change people?

NH My own life was changed when I saw Chaplin's *The Great Dictator* in 1940, and promptly joined the WAAF. I think they can change individuals. But I'm not convinced that films change society much. Well, some have—Ken Loach's TV drama-doc *Cathy Come Home* did change the law, I'm not sure that it changed the suffering of homeless people, but it did something, and it added 'Cathy' to the vocabulary. I think generally social change is a very complex interaction in which film plays a part. If a film doesn't hit your experience, it isn't going to change you. If it does hit your experience, it might just carry you forward to want to do something else, so it is an extremely complex thing. I don't want to over-emphasise the importance of film, but rather the importance, for want of a better word, of a culture of creative experiences generally. But film is important because it is accessible in a way that a lot of things aren't, including, at the moment art, fine art. Poetry, too, is sometimes inaccessible, whereas it ought to be among the most popular forms.

HB So what is it about film that you think is important?

NH To begin with, it was the art form of the twentieth century; it is a really popular art form, that was, and remains, addressed to working-class audiences— the only one that has come up in that way. There was the music hall as well, I suppose, but the cinema was very much of the twentieth century. And in the twenty-first, it's going to change rapidly because of the internet. Something I can't put properly into words. relates to this question of technology. One of the reasons for film being popular, has to do with the fact that it is an art form, a cultural form, that uses the most advanced technologies. And that is what being working class is partly about—understanding how things work; working with machines and technological processes. It's the same with the internet and the Cybercafes—the internet is going to transform the way we live. I can't really see people reading off it, but I think it is going to be the art form, if you like, or the communication form of the twenty-first century. And it is very democratising. They just can't control it—it's great.

HB Is there something about this idea of popular art that works so intensively on our visual senses that is perhaps revolutionising the ways in which we think and communicate? For example, the twentieth century has also been termed the century of visual cutlure, in which books have been replaced by cinema.
NH The best films reach people in the deepest part of their consciousness, or even unconsciousness. You could have a theory of film criticism about where it is hitting you. Is it the mind, the heart, the genitals? How are people connecting to it? You could build a whole theory around the depth in which the film and the people meet each other and exchange. Film operates most effectively on the emotions.

Different audiences create different films. They really do. For instance, I showed Pontecorvo's *Queimada!*, about the colonisation of the Caribbean islands' to quite a lot of different audiences. When the black revolutionary killed the British diplomat—Marlon Brando—at the end, the audience of local people and students would usually reel back with shock. It was a terrible thing to happen. They could see that he was a duplicitous kind of character. but there was a certain respect for him, and you could feel the shock in the cinema. But when I showed it for the Iranian film society, they all stood up on their seats and cheered when Marlon Brando was killed. It was a different film altogether.

HB Then you left Tyneside and set up this innovative café.
NH We retired to a cottage on the highest cliff on the East Coast. People were passing by, and sometimes they asked for a drink of water or directions. So we thought let's have them in. We had got planning permission and all the things that you have to do in order to make your living room into a place in which people can come and have a cup of tea. Believe me, there is a lot of bureaucracy that goes into that! We did that for 20 years, and I think for 15 of them I really enjoyed it. It became predictable the last five years. Well Eric, my husband, really ran the café. He did the cooking and the washing up, the pricing and everything. I was the waitress and the chatter-upper. I enjoyed that because I'm a gregarious person.

HB You met a number of your friends through that.
NH That was our social life, and we made lots of friends through it. One couple had only recently got together when they first came, soon after we opened. Now they've got three children, and they still come, so we now know all their children as well. Lots of my women friendships started with them coming into the café. And there were one or two people, creatures of habit, who used to appear once a week or once a fortnight, and still do, because they can't break the habit. So I let them come, even though the café no longer functions.

HB Since you have left, cinema has become more popular again.

NH Yes, it is a different kettle of fish altogether now, and I don't think that I would need to run a cinema in the way that we did then, I used to call it amenity cinema, by the way. I didn't like the word 'community'—I preferred 'amenity'. Today, though, you don't have to lure people to the cinema. Maybe you lure them to this cinema rather than that cinema. But there is still the very big problem. Despite the fact that we have got a very good multi-screen in Stockton, the Showcase, it still only shows the most popular films, and sometimes it's *Jurassic Park* in three of them or whatever. So still some of the minority films hardly get seen at all. I must tell you a funny thing. You know, one of the most harrowing films Ken Loach ever made was *Ladybird, Ladybird*. about a woman whose children were taken away from her one after the other by the social services. I did think it would come to Stockton at some time or other, But what they often did with these films, (and still do, if they show them at all), is to show them once or twice at nine o clock at night, and then claim that nobody wanted to see them. So I phoned them up and asked 'When are you going to have *Ladybird, Ladybird*?' And the manager said 'We're waiting for the school holidays.' He thought it was a film based on a 'Ladybird' book.

HB Did they ever show it?

NH No, and there are other films that weren't shown that should have been, and that still aren't. I think that with all those screens, one could be a subsidised screen of some kind, and show a minority film. That would make more sense than many of the Regional Film Theatres, because they shouldn't be needed. They exist because the multiplexes aren't doing their job. But it would be better if the subsidised cinema was in a complex where people were already going to see films within a popular film context.

HB When you were doing Tyneside Cinema, people were predicting that television would wipe out cinema.

NH It was earlier than that, the 1950s. By the 1960s and 1970s, the challenge was to bring it back again. Mine was one sort of isolated way of doing that, if you like, but gradually it came about in other ways—mainly by the cinema doing visual things that couldn't be done in any other form.

HB Meaning special effects?

NH Yes, because although it would be a shame if cinema were only special effects, I think it did have this function of bringing people back into the cinema—though they are now very fed up with special effects, and domestic dramas are having a come back. So there you go—one thing leads to another, which is what I was doing all the time.

HB That would be a good title for your piece—one thing leads to another

NH Yes [laughter].

Nina Hibbin
interview by
Huw Beynon,
11 September 1999,
edited by Nina Hibbin
and Huw Beynon

Section III

MAKING SENSE OF THE WORLD

Sheila Rowbotham

Tony Garnett and Ken Loach entered television in the early 1960s, a period of economic prosperity and political conservatism, that was none the less simmering with an inchoate sense of impending change. The Angry Young Men novelists were challenging the hold of metropolitan upper-middle-class culture; the theatre was being radicalised by writers such as Arnold Wesker and Harold Pinter. Both from working-class families, Loach and Garnett identified with this mood of cultural rebellion.[1] Television was changing too, and the media was a matter of public debate. ITV's challenge to the BBC had raised questions about standards in broadcasting, and the 1962 Pilkington Report was to lead to the creation of a third television channel in 1964 (BBC 2).

Sydney Newman, who came from ITV's popular Armchair Theatre to head the BBC Drama department in 1961, was interested in drama that related to contemporary social issues and prepared to encourage an experimental approach that broke with the stiff conventions of BBC 'plays'. The crime series *Z Cars*, on which both Tony Garnett and Ken Loach worked, was started by John McGrath and Troy Kennedy Martin and proved a breakthrough. It combined drama, documentary and social comment in a tough view of the police that was in marked contrast to the cosy 'bobby' in *Dixon of Dock Green*.[2]

With Tony Garnett, James McTaggert and Roger Smith in charge of the Wednesday Play from 1964, viewers watched BBC drama transmogrify. Ken Loach directed *Up the Junction* (1965), based on Nell Dunn's account of living in Clapham. He and Tony Garnett then worked together on *Cathy Come Home* (1966), which mixed fiction and the use of factual material to reveal the problems of homeless families.[3] Carol White, who played Cathy, also starred in Ken Loach's feature film *Poor Cow* (1967) as a new kind of '60s working-class heroine. Loach and Garnett's television play *In Two Minds* (1967), which evolved into the film, *Family Life* (1971), also focused on a young working-class girl's struggle for psychological freedom from her family. *Kes*, written by Barry Hines, was to be their most successful film. Appearing in 1969, it told the story of a young boy's love for his kestrel and used non-actors. Thirty years later it had retained its popularity, being among the Top Ten 'favourite British Films' in the British Film Institute's poll in September 1999.

The industrial conflict of the late 1960s and early 1970s was caught in *The Big Flame* (1969), a television play written in a documentary style by Manchester playwright Jim Allen about the occupation of the Liverpool docks.

In the historical series *Days of Hope* (1975), on which he and Loach collaborated again, the industrial unrest that led up to the General Strike in 1926 was depicted; the parallels with the tumultuous early 1970s were apparent. *Days of Hope* appeared at a turning point when the optimistic faith in radical change was beginning to shift into a more pessimistic gear. It raised the theme of betrayal that was to appear in much of Ken Loach's later work.

The 1980s, with Margaret Thatcher in power, were to be a bleak period for both film-makers. Tony Garnett spent some time in North America, while Ken Loach's attempts to document the right-wing attack on the trade unions and the internal conflicts between the left and the right in the trade union movement (*Questions of Leadership*) on television were to be blocked. He also found himself at odds with the prevailing ideas in radical film theory that were dismissive of the combination of naturalism and social criticism in his films.[4]

It was similarly difficult to raise funding for feature films. However, in 1988 Channel 4 arranged for low-budget films to be made that could be shown on TV. Also in the late '80s the British Screen Consortium, along with European sources of finance, began to back British features. Ken Loach was able to make *Hidden Agenda*, set in Northern Ireland, in 1990. It won a Special Jury prize at Cannes that year. *Riff-Raff* (1990), *Raining Stones* (1993), *Ladybird, Ladybird* (1994), followed, all dealing with contemporary social issues. In *Riff-Raff*, which was produced by Sally Hibbin, he returned to the subject of what was happening in the work place. *Riff-Raff* was also a love story, albeit a political one, as were his films about the Spanish Civil War and Nicaragua, *Land and Freedom* (1995) and *Carla's Song* (1996) and the Glasgow-based account of life at the rough end of Britain in the 1990s, *My Name is Joe* (1998).

Tony Garnett meanwhile had returned to British television. Engaging with the challenge of working within popular idioms, he has produced several extremely successful drama series. These include *Cardiac Arrest*, *Between the Lines* and *The Cops*, which have taken a critical look at conditions in the National Health Service and the police. He also continued to produce feature films, including *Beautiful Thing* (1995), with Bill Shapter. Directed by Hettie Macdonald this was about a love affair between two teenage schoolboys living on a Thamesmead Council estate in South London.

Sally Hibbin, who became the producer of Loach's, *Riff-Raff*, *Land and Freedom* and *Carla's Song*, had already co-produced *A Very British Coup* for television. A football supporter, she has also covered racism in sport in her television work. From a younger generation, she shares Garnett's and Loach's commitment to working democratically, their interest in communicating in direct and accessible ways and their desire to express aspects of experience that are being denied.

In 1997 she went back to work for television, producing *Dockers*, a fictional film based on the Liverpool dock dispute of 1996. It was shown on Channel 4 in July 1999 and made in collaboration with the Initiative Factory, the organisation formed by the sacked dockers to create alternative employment. Directed by Bill Anderson, it was partly written by the Dockers' Writers Workshop, helped by Jimmy McGovern and Irvine Welsh. Mark Lawson hailed it in the *Guardian* as 'a play of debate', adding that 'in both production method and rhetorical temper' it heralded 'a new kind of political drama'.[5]

Notes

1. On the background to the late 1950s and early 1960s see Hewison, *In Anger,* and *Too Much*, pp.1–39.
2. S. Laing, 'Ken Loach: Histories and Contexts' in McKnight, *Agent of Challenge and Defiance*, pp.11–18.
3. On the background to TV in the 1950s, see Corner, *The Art of Record*, pp.73–89; on *Cathy Come Home* see McKnight, *ibid.*, pp.90–107. On the Wednesday Plays see Cook, *Dennis Potter*, pp.23–32, 60–61.
4. J. Petley, 'Ken Loach and Questions of Censorship' in McKnight, *Agent of Challenge and Defiance*, pp.106–18.
5. M. Lawson, 'Work Experience', *Guardian*, 5 July 1999.

5   Working in the Field

Tony Garnett

I don't bring to this subject the detachment of the critic, the perspective of the historian, or the analysis of the political theorist. I just work in the field, as it were, head down, ploughing my own lonely furrow and dimly aware of what else is going on. So my personal account will, of necessity, be partial in both senses of the word. My working life, almost exactly, coincides with the period under review. I began working in television and films as an actor in the late 1950s. The choice of London University allowed me to spend most of each term appearing on the telly. I was rarely seen in the department. On one of my rare visits my tutor caught me in the corridor and said, 'I saw you on television last night , it would be nice to see you in a seminar occasionally!' But I didn't go very often.

Those were the days of *Dixon of Dock Green*, *Probation Officer*, a soap set in a glossy magazine called *Compact* and *Emergency Ward 10*. I appeared in all of them! Plus some B-movies, the names of which I have forgotten. Each part was virtually the same—teddy boy, angry, aggressive, minor criminal or just cheeky working class. I played them all as James Dean! My generation of actors in this country modelled themselves on either Marlon Brando or James Dean, depending on their build. So, of course, Albert Finney was Marlon Brando. So was Richard Harris. Tom Courtenay and I were James Dean. These parts were written to send a frisson of fear into the homes of respectable people. But I was always caught by Sergeant Dixon or contained by my probation officer. It was the drama of reassurance. The country was going to the dogs even then, with youths threatening the very fabric, despite the fact that they hadn't thought of joy-riding. It's been going to the dogs ever since. As Adam Smith said, 'There is an awful lot of ruin in a nation.'

The representation of the working class was from the outside; created by people from the educated middle class, London and Home Counties biased and mainly based on second-hand stereotypes rather than on first-hand observation. As an actor I felt like one of Shakespeare's rude mechanicals. The posh did the important things in iambic pentameters, and I spoke the prose. The working class were patronised as criminals and comic relief. Or they were to be seen in war films: brave, loyal, chirpy Cockney foils to an heroic officer who always got the girl. And, just like blacks in North America, working-class actresses—they were still called 'actresses' then—did a good line in maids and charladies. I don't believe that acting outside your social class in this country

Tony Garnett was initially an actor. In the 1960s he produced several influential programmes for television including *Cathy Come Home* and *The Big Flame*, with Ken Loach, while their feature film *Kes* has become a classic. In the 1990s he produced several successful TV series, *Cardiac Arrest*, *Between the Lines*, *The Cops*, and *This Life* and the feature film *Beautiful Thing*.

Z Cars, 1962–78
(BBC)

before. We were quite unashamed about going for a big audience. We had a very sexy opening sequence—the music was composed by a big pop group of the day called Mannfred Mann. If we were going to put on a very difficult piece of writing, say by David Mercer, the week before we'd put on a comedy and the week after a thriller. It was very important to us to be in the mainstream, to get that audience to make a date with us.

Dennis Potter wrote his first pieces for the Wednesday Plays. Other writers included Jimmy O'Connor and Nell Dunn. We were looking for people who had something to say. I learnt so much from Roger Smith—he would look everywhere for writers. That's been one of the things I've been trying to do all my life—take the mystique out of writing, film-making and acting. We wanted news from the front, people who had an experience of an aspect of life and were desperate to say something about it. I've always thought that if a writer can create a believable world and make characters come off the page, we can teach them how to do the rest. If they can't do those two things they should stick to their day job, because you can't teach them that. Instead of going to the established television writers, many of whom we thought were hacks, we tried to find new ones. So Dennis Potter wrote a play, *Vote, Vote, Vote for Nigel Barton* out of his own experiences standing as a Labour candidate in the 1964 election. And Jimmy O'Connor, who was just out of jail, having spent ten years doing a life sentence for a murder he did not commit, wrote a play for us about a boy who was going to be hung. And we took it all the way through, and we hung him. This play went out during the debate on the abolition of capital punishment as the bill was going through Parliament.

We did another piece, *Up the Junction*, written by Nell Dunn. In one of the central scenes a character called Ruby is having a backstreet abortion on a kitchen table. Because Ken Loach and I were very into Brecht at the time, I got my GP to talk, with that quiet doctor's authority, about how many deaths there were from illegal abortions, cutting his voice across all the screams of Ruby on the table. That went through as David Steel's Abortion bill was being debated. Fortunately we were a very successful show: the '60s were a confident time; the BBC management was cool, and we were allowed to do these things.

Drama at this time used to be done in the studio with multiple electronic cameras. I hated this as an actor, and I hated it as a producer, which is what I was then becoming. I fought a campaign at the BBC to be allowed to make films on location. It was very important to me, not just a matter of empty aesthetics or purely technical. As far as I am concerned the aesthetics, the techniques and the politics are all one argument.

We had nearly worked Ken Loach to death on the Wednesday Plays and he and I got personally very close, and he became my main collaborator during the next few years. It was vital to both of us to go out and observe the world as it is with a camera, rather than imagining what it might be like and recreate that in a studio. I had been very impressed by Raoul Coutard's work in *Breathless* (1960). I didn't think much of Godard, but I liked the way the film was shot. Coutard and Joan Littlewood were the two biggest influences on me at the time. I wanted us to go out with a 16mm camera on the shoulder and just grab these films. The BBC film department at Ealing didn't want us to do this: they thought it was 'lowering standards'. Those 16mm cameras were for news, not drama. Drama was posh. Anyway I fought the battle, and we won. Indeed within two or three years no one wanted to work in a studio anymore: writers, directors, everybody wanted to go out to make films, leaving the expensive BBC studios in danger of lying empty.

The Lump was written by Jim Allen. Jim had been in the Merchant Navy and had worked on building sites and down the pit. He was a self-taught writer who had begun by reading Jack London's novels. He had got himself a gig doing the odd episode of *Coronation Street*. I heard of him and got him down from Middleton to London. We met at my office in the Television Centre, and it was a very strange afternoon because Jim and I were prowling round each other. I was trying to get him to talk politics, and he was refusing. Finally, towards the end of the afternoon, we actually met properly when he said, 'Well, I thought I'd never get a job if I came down here to the BBC and talked politics.' And I replied, 'Well, I was getting to the point where if you were going to refuse to talk politics you wouldn't get a job!' But in the end we came together, and he wrote a script about workers on the lump, which was quite prescient because there was to be a lot more of that going on in subsequent years. It was directed by a documentary film-maker called Jack Gold. It was the first film with actors that he'd ever tried, and he did a good job.

Ken Loach and I went on to do *Cathy Come Home*, which was written by the journalist Jeremy Sandford. He and his wife, Nell Dunn, were living in

Battersea, and they found that some of their friends were disappearing. When Jeremy Sandford investigated, he found that they had become homeless. And he just followed them through the homeless experience, into sheltered accommodation, making a lot of notes. He had a terrible title initially *The Abyss*. The BBC turned it down, and he came to me, and we made it. Ken Loach and I both have very mixed feelings about the film itself and about its actual impact. After all many more people are homeless now than there were then, while the people mainly responsible for making *Cathy Come Home* have got very nice houses to live in. It was a reformist film in many ways.

There's an unsung hero called Alfred Bradley, who was living in Yorkshire at this time. Alfred, who worked for BBC sound radio, was a wonderful man—selfless, generous and one of the most valuable people in my business because he loved writers. Everybody in my business lives off the writers; if it weren't for them we'd all be out of work—everybody, John Birt, the lot of them. To get up and face a blank sheet of paper every morning is hard work. It's the only non-technical job you can't con your way through. I know because I've done it. I've earned my living as a writer, but I find it easier to make other people do it. Alfred encouraged a lot of young writers, and he tipped me off about a young man who was living just outside Barnsley—Barry Hines.

Barry, who was teaching at the time, had written a book, a first novel drawing on his own experience. It was very much a young man's novel, about a lad from Yorkshire who wanted to become a professional footballer. He came down to the Television Centre and I asked him if he would like to write a Wednesday Play. He replied, 'Well, I've never written a play before.' I told him that it didn't matter and would he like to write one anyway? He answered, 'I would, very much, but I've got this book going round in my head, and I've got to write it.' So I told him I respected that but if he wanted to write a Wednesday Play when he'd written his book, he should get back to me. In the meantime, when he'd finished his book, could I read it?' He replied, 'Yes.'

I had enormous respect for Barry's integrity, because his wife, Margaret, was not working, they'd a baby still on the floor, and a mortgage. God knows what he thought he was going to earn from his book, because those sort of novels earn nothing. There was quite a big fee for a Wednesday Play on the table—and he didn't take it, because he had a book in his head.

Anyway, he wrote the book and sent it to me in a typed manuscript. It was called *Kestrel for a Knave*. I looked at it and I thought, 'This'll do'. There was a strong central image going through it, which was an unself-conscious and unpretentious metaphor for the whole piece, and it was just beautifully written. I sent the book to Ken Loach because I thought he would be good casting for it. He liked it, and so the three of us put a screen play together—not that difficult because Barry Hines had written it so visually, and it was more or less a cut-and-paste job. The film was subsequently called *Kes*; the story of a boy in Barnsley who finds a kestrel and trains it.

We went up to Barnsley to make it. If Barry Hines had written the book about Dagenham and set it in the Essex marshes, that's where we would have gone.

Ideologically it was an absolute article of trust and faith on our part to go to the actual place Barry had written about. So we went to the local school, for instance, to find the boy to play the lead. We only had a problem in casting one of the characters, the sports teacher. Neither I nor Ken could think of anybody who could do it credibly. I like working collaboratively, I don't believe in the factory assembly-line way of making films, and it was Barry who suggested, 'Well, there was a chap who used to teach in my school, he's a bit of a show off.' This teacher would finish a day's teaching, get into his car and drive to Nottingham where he was a wrestler in the evenings, under the name of 'Leon Arras (France)'. We found out that he was also a member of the Variety Artists Federation, which was affiliated to Equity. This meant that we could have him. I'm still a member of Equity, but I've had terrible rows with the union policy of a pre-entry closed-shop policy. I believe in a post-entry closed shop. Anyway this fellow played the part of the sports teacher and subsequently went on to quite a career as an actor—his name is Brian Glover. When we finished the film, nobody wanted to show it. Finally, after a big campaign we got it into the cinemas, but we had to fight against the distributor who said it ought to have sub-titles south of Nottingham. Anyway it seemed to go down OK once we got to the public.

The Big Flame was another film we made at the time. I don't know how we got this on to the air in 1969. It was about the Liverpool docks; after a strike the dockers end up declaring a soviet. We had to film on the docks. That was made more difficult by my friend Ken Loach, who is absolutely trusting and showed the docks management the script. It took a lot of lunches and booze to persuade them that we weren't really doing that film, we were doing another!

In the early '70s we did a series called Days of Hope, an attempt at an historical piece. We tried to tell the story of the labour movement from 1916 to 1926, the First World War to the General Strike, through the lives of three or four characters. There was some good work in it, including Ken's of course. But I have very mixed feelings about it. I'm worried about doing films that are based on true events, because, as soon as you start making a film it becomes fiction. I have had many disagreements with David Puttnam over this fact/fiction thing. We're like chalk and cheese. David loves to make films that put 'a true story' on the screen, and I'm very uneasy about this. One's relationship with the audience is, I think, compromised. But, despite these problems, I think Days of Hope made a contribution to the discussion about labour and class, particularly in the light of the events of the last few years.

A mini-series, Law and Order was also done in the 1970s. The director was Les Blair, the writer G. F. Newman—again it was the first thing he had ever written for the screen. It was a four-parter about the judiciary, the prison service, some criminals and the CID. We had an immense problem because the BBC weren't prepared to believe that corruption in the Met was anything other than the odd bad apple in the barrel, and we were saying in the series that it was systemic—you can't be in the CID without being bent, period. They told us we were wrong, but since then, of course, there has been case after case, the Bridgewater Four just one example.

Really I had a lot of freedom in this period. Of course there were constraints: you had to be careful about Northern Ireland, you couldn't piss on the Queen. But compared with the situation now, it was really quite liberal. I had a contract to do four films a year: two on BBC 1 and two on BBC 2. There was a young film-maker called Mike Leigh, and I thought I could give him and Les Blair a kick start. When the Head of Plays, the head of department, asked me what I was doing, I told him, 'I'm doing a couple of films with these two lads.' 'What!' he exclaimed,'Who's done the script?' 'Well, there's no script,' I said. When he wanted to know what it was about I replied, 'They just work it up with the actors, and you don't know until you make it.' So he asked 'Who's in it?' 'Nobody you've heard of!' But I was allowed to do it. Nowadays if you want to do a big show on the television you get the controller of the channel or the network centre telling you that unless you have a particular actor you can't make it, and they're even interfering in the choice of directors. This is part of a huge, huge change.

Towards the end of the 1970s I just felt burnt out. I was exhausted from producing non-stop for all those years: all the battles to get things made and all the political battles on the left. I knew there was going to be a sea change, and I needed to have a think, so I went to work in North America. When I came back in the 1990s there was not only a different environment in the country—that hardly needs spelling out—but a different broadcasting environment too.

Previously I'd worked on single films and mini-series. In the '60s it had still been possible to create a national event with one film—the kind of event that everyone is talking about the next day. But with the proliferation of channels, the remote control that allows easy grazing from one channel to another, along with computer games and pcs, this has become very difficult. The best chance is to do it cumulatively, through a long-running series. I became a late convert. I've realised that this is TV's natural form—the equivalent to a nineteenth-century episodic novel. The difficulties and the opportunities of these long-running series now fascinate me.

A lot of television drama consists of genre pieces, and, if you want to get a big audience, one of the tasks is to put new wine into old bottles. I thought I'd like to do a cop-show, and I wouldn't mind doing a doc-show. They are the mainstays on the box, that's where the people are—in front of those shows. But I didn't want to do one just for the sake of it. Then a writer called John Wilsher—J. C. Wilsher—walked into my office and said, 'How about a series about the police investigating the police?' I knew instantly that it was a bloody good idea; as soon as he spoke I thought, Why didn't I think of that? In fact I'd seen an American movie, *Internal Affairs*, on the same theme just the week before on a plane, but it hadn't clicked. Shit! I thought, That's great. We can have crooked cops on the screen every week. So we did this series about the Complaints Investigation Bureau, *Between the Lines*.

With the doc-show we did the obvious and put an advert in the *British Medical Journal* asking for writers. There's a long tradition of doctors writing in this country; I don't know why so many doctors are good writers. Out of the

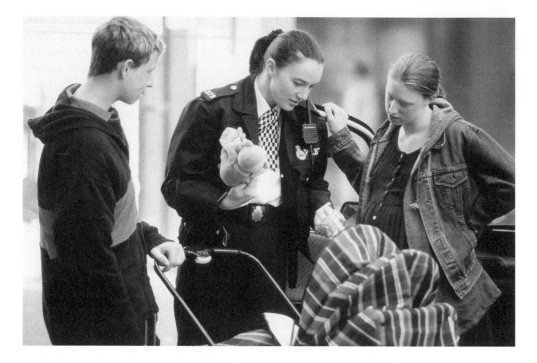

hundred or so replies there was a handful who sent us stuff that looked promis-ing. We picked Jed Mercurio, who was then a houseman at a hospital in Birmingham; I don't know how he found the time to write at all working all those hours. However, my colleague Margaret Matheson and I could tell he was fuelled with fury about what was happening to the NHS and junior doctors. He also had this wonderful black humour, and we thought, It would be wonderful if we could slip this on to the Beeb! Let him loose! He wrote some acerbic, strong angry stuff. It was called *Cardiac Arrest* and ran for three seasons.

The Cops, 1998 (World Productions/ BBC)

There is a completely different broadcasting environment from when I started to work, and they are going to continue. We ain't seen nothing yet, as they say. For instance, though most of the work I do is on location, they are now squeez-ing the budgets so much that every time a show I have on the air is renewed they say, 'Could you do it cheaper next year and get another million viewers?' There is a continuing pressure to speed up; in *This Life* we had to get nine minutes of screen time a day single camera and there is now a tendency to build a multiple set on location, which I find ironic but am forced into.

In British television, particularly in the BBC, there used to be a doctrine of 'producer power'. I'd done about 30 films before anyone asked me who was going to be in any of them or what they were about. It was assumed that produc-ers could be trusted to do the right thing. If they had doubts or feared trouble, they were meant to refer upwards, but they made the decisions. One of the biggest changes—and it isn't accidental—is that there has been a centralisa-tion of decision-making. Now as a producer you have to be a seller. Thirty years ago there were hundreds of sensibilities at work, all making their deci-sions about what went on the air. Now when it comes to long-running drama series or sitcoms, it will be around three people who can decide what goes on.

This century has been dominated by petroleum: seven big companies, known as the seven sisters. Towards the end of the nineteenth century Rockefeller had a few oil wells, but he knew that owning oil wells wasn't the important thing. You had to get the oil to the customer: it was distribution that was important. So he made a deal with the railways, and everybody else who had an oil well had to go through his deal with the railroad. The next century will be dominated by information technology, and there may indeed be seven sisters, or more likely a few big brothers, dominating them, Murdoch, Time-Warner, to name but two of them. They're fighting it out now.

Of course it's going to be difficult. They're not going to hand it to us on a plate, any of it. It requires capital to make films. It is possible to make them outside the system, but the price you pay is that you only get them to a hand-ful of people. That's fine, but I chose to go another route. The only thing I'd say is that although going into a dark room and sitting with a number of people to watch a flickering light being projected on to the screen is a valuable expe-rience for some people, increasingly that commodity, film, is going to be reach-ing people in diverse ways. Maybe in a cinema, or probably at home. You have videos and laser discs. You're going to be taking films off the internet on to your television screens. Now with flat TV screens coming in and the whole busi-ness being digitised, the technical quality in the home is going to be very high in the next five to ten years. I don't give a shit where it is seen. Indeed I'd like it to be in a whole range of situations. I'd like people to decide themselves how they are going to experience film. So the first problem is how do you get it made, and then how do you get it out?

I've always tried to work in the mainstream. Nowadays it has become much more difficult; I need a mainstream show on the air to get the confidence of the broadcasters. Then I try to do Trojan Horse drama. That's just one way and not the only one. Radical film-makers are working in very different contexts and let's hope that all roads lead to Rome. I don't see it as simply an either/or. It's not a question of 'Do we find alternative ways around it to communicate with each other? Or do we work in the mainstream and try to infiltrate and get things on the air whenever we can?' We've got to do both and take whatever opportunities come up with the new technologies. Of course it isn't easy; it's never going to be easy. But the opportunities will come up.

I think that my generation of the left blew it. We indulged ourselves in the '60s at the end of the boom. In the '70s, when Keith Joseph was embarking on his long march through the universities, all people did was throw tomatoes at him. When Margaret Thatcher was sitting at the feet of Hayek in a drawing-room in Chelsea, much of the left, in its fissile way, was becoming atomised and scolding each other. When Arthur Scargill was strutting with his hubris after the famous victory over Heath at the Saltley coke plant, Ridley was quietly preparing his plan to destroy the miners. We all know what happened after that. Blair has taken Thatcher's agenda, though it's better to have a Labour government than to have any kind of Tory government.

But there is something in the air now, something is stirring. What I'd really like to know, though it may sound naive, is:- what is the working class? Once it was organised in trades unions, and now less so. The workplaces were larger and more homogenous, and now less so. You were defined by your job, and your job defined a social classs, now less so. Society is going through a big change. The old joke about librarians being the lumpen intelligentsia seems to have acquired some reality now. Look at the wages and lack of job security of university lecturers and researchers, of people working in banks and the financial services, broadcasting and journalism. In white-collar jobs throughout the economy, layers of management are being excised. All this may have been done in a Thatcher-like way, but clearly the causes go beyond her. There's been a paradigm shift: the revolution in technology, free movement of capital and globalisation. Do we broaden our definition of the working class? What of the unworking class, the unemployed? What of the shifting demographics, an ageing population—some of whom are very well pensioned thank you and a lot of whom are very poor? Should we be questioning who is included and excluded? Is there a credible, contemporary definition of what we mean by the term 'working class'? In the modern Labour Party hardly any of the leading figures now have ever done a day's work in the wider economy. They tend to be professional politicians, lawyers, trade-union officials or university lecturers.

I am solidly middle class now. I have been most of my adult life, despite my political views and my social background—which is why I constantly search for news from the front, brought by writers whose voices are authentic and unmediated—and they're difficult to find. The images of the working class in the mass media are put there by the middle class, as indeed are the images of the aristocracy. That's why both the working class and the aristocracy so often come over as clichés, as stereotypes, not as rounded and unique human beings. They are both patronised and sentimentalised. I don't give a shit about the aristos, but if you are on the left the way the working class is represented obviously has political importance

Those of us who were film-makers on the left used to think, rather romantically, during the 1960s and '70s, that TV at its best could allow the nation to speak to itself. In the TV of the future, with its fragmented audience, the working class will not be speaking to the working class, not even when mediated by sympathetic professionals. In certain aspects, the working class is being represented less and less, and this tendency is going to persist because of the way TV works. Increasingly most TV is becoming commercial. The programmes are there to deliver audiences to advertisers—that's their function. But not any old audience. Gross numbers are not so important now, it's the demographics that are important. If you want to sell fancy cars, or upmarket consumer durables or luxury drinks, you don't want the poor, the unemployed, the struggling single parent, or even the average wage earner watching. You want a programme wrap-

Beautiful Thing, 1995
(Film Four/World
Productions)

ping around your ad that will attract the well-off. It is the ones with disposable income who are the target audience for your goods and services. This does not mean that the working class will not be represented at all on these programmes, but it does affect the filter through which they are portrayed, the point of view, the stance taken.

It would be wrong to confine consideration of the screen images of the working class to dramatic fiction and serious documentary. You don't have to be Eisenstein to know that if you impose the right images you can create any impression you want. Even on the news, shoot a group of dockers on the stones, by a brazier on a windy day, and you can easily make them seem like an undisciplined rabble. Follow this by a well-lit, low-key interview in an office with a management suit or a junior minister, and you start to think those dockers have sacked themselves. There are images of the working class on the news, on game shows and on Kilroy, on Cilla Black or Jeremy Beadle, and these are just as manipulated, mediated and created as any I create in drama. It is all fiction in the sense that the producers make it up, pick and choose the material and the participants, and then edit the results. So my advice is, Don't trust the people from the telly.

In drama most television images of the working class are in soaps, and that's what most working-class people watch. When it comes to cinema, more people in the world, given the choice, prefer Hollywood movies by a large majority. With the lottery money, many British films will be made with the cinema in mind. Good luck to them, but precious few will get distributed or audiences of any size. It is very snobbish and misplaced to see this kind of cinema as exclusively important.

Personally, having worked in films like this a lot, I have become irritated by the self-regarding little world of the European art film, with its film-makers, festivals and critics. It is almost as if they pull back from the vulgarity of reaching large audiences: if it is popular it can't be good. What brought me to television in the 1960s was the chance to reach millions of people on the same occasion. I wanted to occupy that platform. For the time being at least, my current focus is still mainly in TV. I like its vulgarity and its immediacy. I like the challenge of having to ask, 'What can I get my cousin Norah to watch?'

I work in fiction. I help to make dramatic fiction—I have never used the phrase 'drama documentary', which was probably invented by some journalist. I have experimented with other forms, but most of my life has been in a particular, narrow, interpretation of dramatic fiction and in a socialist-realist tradition. When I am working with writers I say, 'Research it and research it and research it!' Then we make it up. That's what we do because we work in fiction. I think there was a confusion because we attempted to create a style that was borrowed from the documentary tradition. When there is a willing suspension of disbelief, people will often say, 'Oh, I like your documentary,' but it is scripted, acted and put together as a fictional narrative. One of the things that Ken Loach and I have spent a lot of our lives doing is questioning the nature of performance. The kind of work we do depends on acting not seeming like acting. I hate 'writing writing', and I hate 'acting acting'. A young actor once went up to Spencer Tracy and said, 'Mr Tracy, I'm an act-tor too.' And Spencer Tracy replied, 'Yeah! Well don't ever let them catch you doing it!'

We all see ourselves and each other being represented on television. You can't raise consciousness unless you confront reality, and I still think it is important to struggle for true representations. That is achieved through constant struggle and goes beyond any particular political agenda. Dramatic fiction, if it rings true, can help us feel what it is like to be someone else. It can make us feel less alone, and it can be the invisible glue that binds communities and social classes. We all live by stories, by myths; we all need a narrative to hold our lives together. The question is: which narrative? That is why history is so fought over. Tell us a story, tell us a true story. Well, I shall attempt to go on doing so.

We have to be thinking about the future. We can't just bury ourselves in nostalgia. I'm spending most of my time now with the next generation, making shows with kids in their twenties. They are going to have their own ways of working. Goodness knows, they come out of difficult-enough circumstances. They are teaching me, and I am trying to teach them. We have to encourage them and trust them and help them, but not by imposing our old methods. We have to love good work out of them because they are the generation who are going to have the energy to carry it forward. There is an enormous energy coming into the industry, an enormous energy. And that gives rise to hope.

Tony Garnett, lecture at 'Images of Labour', edited by Tony Garnett and Sheila Rowbotham

6 The Subversive Who Surprises: Ken Loach

Sheila Rowbotham

Ken Loach worked in television from 1964, directing three episodes of *Z Cars* before working on the Wednesday Plays. *Cathy Come Home* and *Kes* are his best-known works from this period. He made the historical series *Days of Hope* with Tony Garnett in 1975. In the 1990s his feature films *Riff-Raff*, *Raining Stones* and *Land and Freedom* have won prizes in Europe. He has also made documentaries about miners and dockers and trade unionism.

Ken Loach's track record is impressive: over 30 years of films for television and cinema that have become markers of radical resistance, making him a standard bearer of left film-making. In the 1960s *Cathy Come Home* highlighted the predicament of the homeless; *The Big Flame* imagined dockers occupying the docks; *Kes* was a searing reminder of how class permeates the education system. During the 1990s, an era smugly inoculated against rebellion, his films have dealt with challenging and unfashionable topics: the role of British intelligence in Ireland, dangerous working conditions, revolutionary movements in the Spanish Civil War and in Nicaragua.

In person he is disarmingly mild mannered for a man whose life's work has been a defiance of the powers that be. Nevertheless he is contemptuous of the unspoken taboos that have resulted in what he describes as a 'miasma of phony discussion that never touches the core of any issue'. The present cultural mood is very different from the late 1960s and early 1970s when he directed *The Big Flame* or the historical series *Days of Hope* for television.

Finding himself going increasingly against the grain, he remains emphatic that his duty as a communicator is still to get 'into the centre of a point, not to beg questions, not to leave an assumption unchallenged.'

This quest 'to record actuality' is a continuing thread from his days in television working on the pioneering TV series *Z Cars* and then on the Wednesday Plays. He, and a talented group that included Tony Garnett, John McGrath and Troy Kennedy Martin, struggled to create 'a new grammar' for television drama. His own background was in theatre rather than cinema, and he drew on the radical dramatic impetus of Joan Littlewood's Theatre Workshop. Like her, he sought 'to capture people's experience', and also like her he wanted to celebrate it. Celebration amid adversity is evident in the most personal ways. Cathy, the homeless single mother, defies her circumstances with her desire for love and pleasure; Billy in *Kes* cherishes the injured kestrel. In *Raining Stones* a beautiful confirmation dress becomes the symbol of the recalcitrant human spirit.

Commitment to self-expression is there also in a more overtly political belief that film should provide a democratic space for suppressed voices. His 1996 TV documentary, *The Flickering Flame*, presented a rare opportunity to hear the case of dockers and their wives in the midst of the Liverpool docks dispute. As he says, 'People who are in the middle of a struggle are very articulate, because they have to shape the thoughts in their minds over and over again.

They have gone through the arguments to themselves, they know what
it is about. They have formed the
ideas, and they have defended them.
They have chiselled them out, and
they have found a language for it.'

He believes that TV and broadcasting should be about 'finding
exactly what people have got to say
rather than trying to confuse them into
inarticulateness'. Instead the media
usually 'works against people being
articulate' by transplanting them into
an alien setting, where they face
unstated assumptions that cast them
in predetermined roles.

'A television studio is a very hostile
place. You can be an articulate person
but not be able to express yourself in
a TV studio. The lights are very harsh,
and you're blinded. You are in a very
strange environment, talking to somebody who is accustomed to a sound-
bite politician. They won't ask the core
questions; they will ask the ones that
are superficial. So you have to change
the question in order to make your
point, and that's a skill in itself. If you
put people in a situation where they
feel at ease they will talk absolutely

clearly. All you have to do is listen and ask the question that is central to the
issue.' Even outside the studio the odds are stacked against working-class
people, especially workers in a dispute. 'People in a situation that they are not
usually in can become their own stereotypes. For instance they become the
shouting voices on the picket line; they all try to butt into one another because
the reporter will go along with the microphone and point it vaguely at six
people, and whoever shouts the loudest gets heard. Then you cut to the studio,
and it's the management, or whoever, sitting talking calmly one to one.'

Cathy Come Home,
1966 (BBC)

His aim is not to replace one stereotype with another: 'If you just have a
glorified picture of a worker with his fist in the air, it is so far removed from
anybody's day-to-day experience that you can't relate to it, so you can't get
anything from it.' It is not the clichés or the generalisations that communicate,
but 'that struggle to be articulate, to find a way forward and to grope for an
understanding that is moving in the end. That is actually the essence of drama—
it is where the hope is.'

Riff-Raff, 1990
(Paul Chedlow:
BFI/Parallax/Channel 4)

In the early 1980s, with Thatcherism at its height, Ken Loach attempted to demonstrate the unheroic underlay of trade-union democracy in four films for television, *Questions of Leadership*. They were never shown. Frank Chapple, the wily right-wing leader of the Electricians' Union, objected vehemently when rank-and-file members pointed to hidden obstacles to internal democracy in the union. The films were deemed defamatory, despite Loach's offers to cut specific offending material.

They catch the interior world of organising that is so rare on film, confirming Ken Loach's conviction that film can bring out meanings that would otherwise be obscured. Instead of 'just putting people in a room and saying "talk", you cut out the repetition, and you make one point answer another, so there is a logical development to it'. Viewed retrospectively, they give a fascinating insight into the labour movement at a crucial juncture just before the more documented onslaught that was to hit the NUM in 1984–5. The Conservative's targeting of a group of confident and strategically aware rank-and-file trade unionists is all too clear—the breaking of the NUM was just the mopping-up operation.

He is regretful still that the trade-union films were suppressed. The decision not to show them was indicative of the fearfulness that was to pervade the media. One consequence of this timidity has been that whole areas of thought and debate have been marginalised. As a result, 'That whole body of experience and ideas has no existence in our political and cultural life; it can only exist as an alternative.'

Ken Loach might be mild-mannered, but he is not the type to go easily into exile. In response he changed tack, coming up with the feature films of the 1990s that contrived to be independent of the American market by being relatively low budget. They tell stories in familiar idioms, but with a difference. *Land and Freedom*, for instance, is not the normal historical-drama-with-love-interest. It shows how messy political choices can be, and it contains a convincing and extremely dramatic 15-minute debate about collectivising the land. Like many of Loach's enactment's of political conflict this has a more general meaning. 'It is an age old problem. Do you try and build your lives with people who are fundamentally hostile to you, or do you go for broke when people are prepared to have a fight? It recurs in one form or another with every dispute, every strike.' He presents us with the problem not a dogmatic set of answers.

His fascination with the process of politics coexists with a refusal to abandon mainstream culture. He retains some of the early 1960s optimism around *Z Cars* and the Wednesday Plays about the possibilities of radical communication through the mass media. It has, however, been tempered by experience over three decades. He is all too aware of what left films are up against—a Hollywood-dominated cinema that is 'mainly about the consumption of commodities which come with the popcorn'. Not only is there funding in the first place to get together but distribution remains a persistent dilemma: the box office is stacked in favour of the Hollywood blockbuster. To counter this he would like the Labour government explicitly to back the distribution of films from Europe that present alternative cultural perspectives, both in terms of content and in production.

When he was learning his trade in television the director was meant to be 'serving the writers'. It is an approach that has stayed with him right through. His working relationships with Nell Dunn, Jimmy O'Connor, Barry Hines, Jim Allen and, most recently, Paul Laverty have been creative, ongoing collaborations, in which 'one project arises out of another'. The process extends to the actors, including those who are not formally trained but whom he selects because they possess an inner understanding of their part. They help shape the script.

He insists it is all quite simple, 'I will give them a script in advance, and they will have a good sense of how one line will develop into another. Perhaps we will mark it through before we shoot. Then we'll start shooting and really work on it as we go. The essence of the writing is in charting that development between the people in the scene. So that is what it is my job to get on film. If there is something that is supposed to take somebody by surprise, or make them think twice before they answer, then I'll drop that in out of the blue. It may not work, but the thing about film is that you can always do it again. They may need to do it two or three times to get the sense of how to play it, but they can still live off the surprise that they had when they first heard it or saw it or experienced it. But if you read it in a script six weeks before you shoot, when you come to shoot there's a lot of skin grown over it; it is kind of dead.' This desire to surprise his actors also of course takes his audience by surprise.

His search for the unguarded revelation of motivation, that inquisitive presumption of the communicator 'to catch somebody's response' is the intangible element in his work and its strength. It is undoubtedly one of the reasons his films do find a wider audience.

Ken Loach presents himself as the artisan film-maker, trying to 'scrape off the layers of paint to get to the nub of experience'. On the one hand, he says film is not particularly important politically: 'It's just something I do.' On the other, he acknowledges that a film can 'reverberate, resonate, make something vivid and more accessible'. And, however limited, the reach of a radical film-maker, is likely to be broader than the general run of left culture.

Most of the time Loach takes what he calls 'the worm's eye view'. He feels as if he just keeps 'banging on', but there is an intimation of playing for high stakes. 'We have to write our history, keep it vivid, not let it be forgotten. You would never think that the US had a history of labour struggles. It is like those pads you had as a kid, you pull it down, and all the writing disappears—just gone completely'. He quotes Milan Kundera's phrase, 'The struggle of memory against forgetting.' He does not belong to a group, a school or a genre, yet his work has helped to sustain a critical and committed film culture in Britain against the odds. Thirty years on he is unashamed to be subversive: 'Cinema should enhance you—it should really be a place of enrichment instead of exploitation.'

Ken Loach interview by Sheila Rowbotham, originally published in *Red Pepper*, February 1997

7 Letting Voices be Heard

Sally Hibbin

I grew up going to the flicks; my mum, Nina Hibbin, was the film critic on the *Daily Worker*, so cinema was always part of my background. My first job was researching the history of cinema on a magazine. After three years there I figured I knew quite a lot about film, but I realised I had never really seen anything being made. Some mates were doing a Fares Fair commercial for the Greater London Council's campaign for cheaper transport in the early 1980s, and I asked them if I could watch them shooting it.

They all knew about film-making, whereas I knew quite a lot about organising. I had been active in the National Union of Students, where I suppose you get used to making deals and compromises, getting the best you can from a situation. Compositing resolutions at the conferences taught me how to negotiate. Then I used to help organise the Communist University, a vast yearly educational event during the late 1970s and early 1980s. I not only learnt how to negotiate through left politics, but also used to try and get the Communist University to make a profit! These all proved to be transferable skills, and I ended up organising the Fares Fair film, sorting out the money and the legal work.

Shortly afterwards the group was commissioned to do a documentary about youth unemployment by Channel 4, which was then in its very early days. I became the producer. We went on to do more stuff for the Greater London Council (GLC) about training, jobs and the police, as well as a cinema advert for them when Thatcher was trying to abolish the GLC for being too independent of central government. Several videos for trade unions, charities and campaigning outfits of one sort or another followed. We formed a film co-operative, Parallax, and I would do everything from casting though accounts to driving the minibus—a great way to learn about filming. That's how I started. I still don't have any technical skill.

When I read *A Very British Coup* I thought it was a really interesting novel and tried to get the rights for it. They had already gone to another producer, and they had a treatment with Channel 4, but it didn't work. I went to them and said, 'Let me find another writer and see if we can do it as a film.' After a bit of toing and froing we got it, and Alan Plater wrote the script. I left Parallax for a year really, to produce *British Coup* with Ann Skinner at Skreba Films. We couldn't finance it as a feature film so it had to go back to television in the end as a three-part series. *British Coup* obviously tried to offer an alternative vision

Sally Hibbin produced videos for the Greater London Council in the mid-1980s and then co-produced *A Very British Coup* for television. In the 1990s, through Parallax films, she has produced several films with Ken Loach, including *Riff-Raff*. She returned to television to produce *Dockers*, which appeared in 1999. A dockers writing group helped to create the script.

A Very British Coup,
1988
(Skreba/Channel 4)

of politics to Thatcherism and right-wing Labour, but it was not exactly commenting on the times, because a Labour government of any kind then appeared almost like science fiction. British Coup was more an aspiration of things that might be.

When I had finished it and returned to Parallax, the GLC had been abolished, and it was much harder to do the stuff that we had been doing. In the early 1980s, even when we weren't working directly for the GLC, a lot of the organisations who had commissioned us were financed by them in one way or another. But after the GLC's abolition by the Tory government in 1986, this all came to an end.

I was doing several jobs and not earning much money when, some time after *British Coup* went out, Ken Loach suddenly phoned me up and asked if

I could take on the new film he was directing called *Riff-Raff*. He told me he needed somebody more Establishment than himself! Or someone who was capable of talking to the Establishment anyway, to try and get some money together for his project. It was quite funny really, because he rang me at home when I was in the garden. So I was talking to him sitting on the stairs with my walk-about phone for about an hour. As soon as I put the phone down, I rang my mum up to say, 'Guess what?'

'What's the project called?' she wanted to know. I could only reply that I didn't know, that I had asked but I hadn't listened to the answer. So she said, 'Who wrote it?' and again though I had asked I couldn't remember. I realised I'd been having this long conversation with Ken, asking all the right questions, but I was so sort of knocked out that he had phoned that I hadn't taken in any of the answers.

Obviously I knew about Ken as a film-maker: *Cathy Come Home* and *Kes* had made an important impact on me when I was growing up. As a film critic, my mum had really championed *Kes* and I'd seen more or less everything Ken had done. I had met him occasionally over the years, and we were on a nodding acquaintance. In fact I'd taken *British Coup* to Ken to see if it was some-thing he wanted to do. He had said no, because he was far too busy with *Fatherland*, but he had put me in touch with Alan Plater. Then we happened to bump into each other at the London Film Festival screening of *Fatherland* when I was very up about *British Coup* because we had got the money and the go-ahead to do it that day and I was bouncing about that.

After our phone call I was bouncing even higher, and it went from there really. We got the go-ahead from Channel 4 to make *Riff-Raff*, which was to be the first film I made with Ken. When he first approached me, Ken had already devel-oped the story and found Bill Jesse, who was the scriptwriter. Bill was work-ing on a building site by day and trying to write scripts at night, so he knew the territory he was writing about and had a lot to say on the conditions in the industry under Thatcherism.

Riff-Raff took us a long time to get financed; the budget came down and down and down. Eventually we almost made it as a sort of glorified documentary with an art department. We put the production offices actually on the building site itself in portakabins! But it actually worked. Both Ken and I wanted to do the film differently, so that its content would be integrated in the way it was made. We carried this manner of working on into the later films as well. Ken's approach is very political, and this translates into how he makes films. He's very much about a no-frills kind of film-maker, whereby the money gets itself on to the screen and not into the auxiliary aspects of film-making. By being low budget you keep control over what you want to do, editorially and in terms of casting and so on.

One of the interesting things about working with Ken Loach is that he allows the people we are working with to have some kind of self-expression of their culture and way of living within the film. That is not to say his films aren't scripted—they're actually quite well scripted—but the casting process involves bringing people into the film to play roles to which they have some relationship in real life. They are not coming from the outside, but from inside the characters. This is partly what gives them such a rooted reality. It also helps create the humour.

I think one of the strengths of *Riff-Raff* is that wonderful scene where the older, left-wing trade unionist, played by Ricky Tomlinson, who himself had a militant past as a shop steward, is pontificating about the exploitative conditions and the capitalist system. His mates, meanwhile, are much more to the point, saying of their young workmate who is homeless (Robert Carlyle), 'But he only wants a squat,' which is classic, isn't it! The political worker's trade-union stance is part of the film, but it is treated lightly. Though in the end, of course, the Ricky character is proved tragically right—health and safety is a life-and-death problem, not just sloganising.

I loved the way *Riff-Raff* shows London. It was shot in my home patch, in Tottenham, and it showed the city as the London I know, which is a mix of people from different parts of the country. London actually seems to have a minority of Londoners living in it, and that richness of diversity is what makes it engaging.

We were making *Riff-Raff* right at the end of the Thatcher period. By the time it appeared she was gone. Ken often said that during Thatcherism he made documentaries because there were too many important things to say to make drama. Maybe the change, end of an era, did help to free up his ability to comment. I think it was quite hard really to understand what was happening while we were living under Thatcherism.

When *Riff-Raff* was finished we showed it to a number of British distributors, who all basically said that they didn't think it was a cinema film. They didn't believe it had an audience at the cinema and said we should show it on television. *Riff-Raff* eventually was shown in 1991, but that kind of attitude kept coming up time and time again and was fundamentally a British distribution problem. Nobody in Europe, in France or Germany, Spain or Italy, ever maintained that films like *Riff-Raff*, *Raining Stones* or *Ladybird, Ladybird* weren't cinema films. It was a British film-industry thing.

It is always a long, long process to make a film or even a documentary these days, trying to get the project right, trying to raise the money. You have to feel very passionately committed to a film to want to do it. It was very hard for me to get the finance for *Riff-Raff*. I'd made *British Coup* with Ann Skinner, who was very experienced, and I guess people did not take me seriously until after I had done *Raining Stones* with Ken. When Ann and I were working on *British Coup*, there were only a few women producers about. Interestingly it is starting to be almost a woman's job. However, usually the men are considered to be the deal-makers, while the women are the creators. I am one of the few women deal-maker producers: I do both the raising of the money and putting together the deals.

Even when you make the films you must have access to a kind of network or something to broadcast them. The hold of the distributors still leaves you powerless. Of course people keep trying to find alternative contexts for distributing film, such as, for instance, the group of angry young guys and girls who are doing films and projecting them in raves at clubs. Fanny Armstrong, who made the documentary about the dispute with McDonald's—*The McDonald Two* has not been able to get it on TV but can show it on the Net. But none of these is going to reach a mass audience.

I think one of the problems we have as film-makers in Britain is that we share a common language with America. This makes it far harder for us than it is for our colleagues in Europe to carve out some sort of cultural ground of our own. What we were getting in the early '90s was a sort of equation that said if it had stars in it, and pretty frocks and posh accents it was cinema. However, if it had working-class accents and council estates, if the frocks were not that pretty and you had never heard of anyone in it, then it was television.

Signs of a shift started to appear in the second half of the '90s, when films such as *Trainspotting* and *Secrets and Lies* were to have a big impact. It is incredible really that *Brassed Off* could get made. In the early '90s I think they would have dismissed it as a subject that nobody wanted to see at the cinema: it's got Yorkshire accents, it's got brass bands, and it hasn't got pretty frocks. Nor can I imagine somebody saying they wanted to make a film like *The Full Monty*, about unemployed miners who start a Chippendales-type strip group. None of those films, which contain some wonderful images of the working class, reveal how a culture of class has survived despite everything and really open a door to things as they might be, could possibly have been funded a few years ago.

Behind that sort of change, which you can actually see expressed within the films, is a much greater confidence in British cinema. We have managed to find ways of financing low-budget projects through European sources, which enables them to acquire a degree of cultural independence one way or another from the Hollywood system. This has made it easier for people to produce films rooted in more realistic subjects and to retain more control over making them the way they want.

Ken Loach's films still do a lot better in Europe than they do in England. The British audience for them is pathetically low compared to the European market. However, at least since *Ladybird, Ladybird*, distribution has looked up, and we have managed to achieve something almost sensible. I think we did 15 prints of *Ladybird, Ladybird*, but by the time I produced *Carla's Song* we could do 40, which makes it possible to have some sort of comparison with other films that are made here. Again, this has been made feasible mainly by of the European subsidies that you can get for the distribution of films.

After *Riff-Raff* I executive produced *Bad Behaviour*, which Les Blair directed and Sarah Curtis came out of the BBC to produce. Stephen Rea and Sinead Cusack took the parts of a North London Irish couple—there was a mid-life crisis but no bad behaviour in it really, but there you go: very North London. And then I did *Raining Stones*, *Ladybird, Ladybird* and *Carla's Song* with Ken Loach.

One of the things about which I felt rather proud during the making of *Carla's Song* was the response we got from Strathclyde buses when we were negotiating how to film the scenes on their vehicles. We were having a long discussion with them about whether they were going to give us buses and teach Robert Carlyle, our lead actor, to drive them properly, and whether they were going to lend us uniforms and all the rest of it. We got a wonderful letter from them, saying that they would normally worry deeply about working with film-makers. What they really cared about was for their workers to be portrayed with some kind of dignity and honesty, which, as it was Ken Loach, they were sure would happen. I thought that was great.

When *Carla's Song* came out we got a lot of flak in the reviews about how we had portrayed the Third World, especially from the *Independent* and *Time Out*, I was puzzled by the reaction. Our best review was in the *News of the World*, which saw it as a love story! The more liberal papers seemed to think that we had imposed some simplistic perspective on the peasantry of Nicaragua. I could not work out where that notion came from. Obviously the film is constructed and directors always have a say in how a film is constructed. I'm not arguing with that. But the way in which Loach works, the way that peoples' experiences filter into the film, means that what actually happens up there on the screen does reflect how people see themselves in a real way.

I think this is particularly true of the Nicaraguan ending to *Carla's Song* which was very much guided by how the people chose to portray themselves—at a party, singing, dancing and talking. I continued to be perplexed by the criticism until I did a session at the London College of Printing, and one of the students started talking to me about the scene on the top of the bus in which there is a political discussion about the Revolution. The Nicaraguans saw it quite concretely; one declares,'You know there was this plot of land that once had one family on it, and now it's got fourteen families.'

The student said, 'It's so simplistic, people don't talk like that.' And I suddenly realised that people who did not know Nicaragua or Latin America probably think that is our way of trying to put a bit of politics into the film. It does not occur to them that this scene was completely unscripted, that it was people talking of their experiences of the Revolution and what that meant to them. But then I thought again that where we had been simplistic was in assuming that we could film people in the Third World and that what they do and say would communicate directly to people in Britain. We had failed to bridge the cultural gap between the West and the Third World because we had assumed that what we were trying to do would be self-evident in that film.

The thing that tends to hook me into a project very often is the possibility of giving a voice to something that is not usually heard, either from a certain class of people or from particular individuals. That is why I always end up with the sort of projects I do, such as a recent venture that came out of the Liverpool docks dispute. When the dispute was over, the sacked dockers were trying to plan their futures, and one of the things they did was to set up a workshop that began to talk about creating a play, or something, about the dispute. Two interesting writers who have been successful in reaching a popular audience, Jimmy McGovern and Irvine Welsh, came in to help the workshop as tutors. Gradually the meetings turned into a script that Jimmy has written, as it were,

with the workshop. It has been a long haul. It took a year of these workshop meetings before a second draft had been produced, but the script is terrific. It has a depth and reality that has come out of people's experiences, which is really rather amazing.

Dockers, 1999 (Parallax/Initiative Factory/Channel 4)

It is a Parallax co-production for television with the Initiative Factory, the company set up by the sacked dockers to attempt to create re-training initiatives in Liverpool for the dockers. One of the funniest events at which I have been, I must say, was our script conference with Channel 4, because we have 14 writers, and my co-producers, who are the shop stewards, decided to turn up as well. So we were in the Channel 4 boardroom with the commissioning editor and the script editor, 14 sacked dockers and several shop stewards, Jimmy McGovern and myself, along with a television crew, because there is a documentary being made about the writing of the programme. The commissioning editor, Gub Neal, would make a comment about the script, whereupon Jimmy Nolan, who is a sort of older-statesman docker of the old school, would make a left-wing political speech for ten minutes. Gub would make another statement, and then Jimmy Nolan would make another political speech. It was very funny. But it worked, and a mutual respect grew from it.

The dockers' film has brought me back to television, because, despite the breakthroughs in the British film industry, the lack of financial backing is discouraging. If you are going to spend two years trying to raise the finance for a film, a year making it and then trying to get it distributed, you have to be passionate about it. I feel a fraud speaking about images of class, because I can honestly say it is not something I have ever really thought about in working on a film. It is interesting to hear other people analysing how they think film-makers portray class. But it doesn't seem to me that is ever an issue you discuss when you're making a film—or at least not within my area.

I don't think film-makers are driven by debates about representation. The focus is much more likely to be on what story you want to tell, what you care about, what is worth going through hell for. I know the stories about which I get passionate tend to be those that are rooted in some aspect of contemporary culture that you otherwise would not see. And of course there are aspects of class experience that remain out of view. On the other hand it is often said that the thing that holds British cinema together is that it is all fundamentally rooted in class, be it Ken Loach, Merchant-Ivory or revivals of classics. These very different films unexpectedly share something in common—they are rooted within specific localities and class backgrounds.

I think that is essentially what differentiates us from Hollywood. Even when Hollywood engages in 'real life' in films such as *Working Girl*, it doesn't do it in that deeply rooted way that British cinema does. It doesn't base itself within a particular culture. I think this rootedness and cultural specificity is our biggest distinction. This is what actually makes our films attractive and enables them to travel, whether they are about the working class or the middle class or about 'no-class' people who are disenfranchised from the system in one way or another.

What puzzles me is how history is still largely perceived in British films that continue to focus on the frocks and the big houses. There is actually very little working-class history, like the *Days of Hope* series on television in 1975, which gets filmed. The kind of history with which I was brought up and learnt from my parents hardly ever seems to come across.

So while I don't relate to the question of images of class in isolation, I think there is an important issue about what stories you choose to tell and why you want to make a particular film and why that story seems important to you. Very often, as I have said, for me that is about trying to find a way of giving a voice, or allowing a voice to be heard that is not otherwise heard within cinema and television. This has an obvious relevance to class. In Britain we live in a terribly divided society, where a lot of people don't have any consciousness or knowledge of what vast chunks of our society are like. And maybe one of the problems we have is not just *about* making films about the working class, but how you actually find a voice that bridges the cultural gap between classes.

Sally Hibbin, lecture at 'Images of Labour' and interview by Sheila Rowbotham, 18 December 1988, edited by Sally Hibbin and Sheila Rowbotham

'WAYS OF SEEING'
Sheila Rowbotham

Ways of Seeing[1] was the title of John Berger's famous 1972 BBC2 series and book, in which he combined a social and historical perspective with an analysis of images in art. Berger's work resonated at the time partly because there was a widespread unease in left cultural debate about how the modern media was capable of manipulating subjective emotions. Many radical artists and filmmakers, convinced that *how* you did things carried meanings, wanted to find ways that challenged the forms of communication in the mainstream. Feminists were very much involved in these discussions because, like the black movement, a challenge to the power embedded within the terms of representation was an integral part of the women's liberation movement. 'Ways of Seeing' were thus regarded as a practical political issue not an abstract question.

An awareness of the power of the image and a wariness about accepting unmediated pictures of 'the real' were present among activists within the new social movements of the 1970s. James Swinson describes how these ideas complemented the politicisation of cultural workers in the media and in art schools during the 1960s. As a result political and material puzzles interacted with the rediscovery of the history of left aesthetic debates.

Theorists such as Walter Benjamin, Ernst Fischer, Georg Lukács, Antonio Gramsci and Theodore Adorno started to be translated, and Marx's and Engels' writing on art was scanned with excitement. Old battle lines quickly began to be redrawn. Was art about the individual's perception or social processes? Was the artist's creativity essentially mysterious or could it be broken down into comprehensible components? Was it simply the product of a social era or did it carry some quality of transcendence that defied politics and history? Could a reactionary artist produce 'radical' art?

Marx's preference had been for realist writers such as Balzac, whose novels Marx believed presented an indictment of French society, despite the writer's own royalist politics. Marx and Engels were never aesthetic sectarians and remained in friendly dialogue with Heine and Freiligrath, for instance, writers who presented ideas about history and society poetically and expressed their subjective inner conflicts in reflective ways that challenged realism.[2]

After the Bolshevik Revolution theories of art were to be furiously contested, and every scrap of Marx's and Engels' writing was studied with rigour. Approaches to art were to harden into stultifying positions of 'correctness', and 'socialist realism' came to be equated, not with a realistic look at society from the left, but an idealisation of the Soviet Union under Stalin.

Though an aesthetic thaw accompanied a political loosening of attitudes in the mid-1950s, some Marxists theorising about art retained the habit of declaring that particular forms were inherently suspect. For example, the Marxist critic Georg Lukács was hostile to the anarchical subversion of surrealism as well as the very different tradition of 'naturalism', which had arisen as a branch of realist writing in the late nineteenth century.

Marxists were inclined to argue that naturalism presented individuals as trapped in circumstances that appeared to be determined not by society but by 'natural' universal forces. As a consequence naturalism was seen as squeezing out contradictory contingency and diminishing human agency—what Lukács described as the 'slyness of reality'.[3] However, the best-known progenitor of naturalism, Emile Zola, had quite explicitly asserted that he aimed to show 'the reciprocal effect of society on the individual and the individual on society'.[4] In practice, several different kinds of naturalism developed, and was to be adopted by many socialist writers in the early twentieth century.

Contestation about the appropriate aesthetic styles for communicating the experiences of working-class people through a critical view of society transferred from art and literature to cinema and television, and in the last two decades many old disputes were eventually to find a new academic home in cultural studies. Confusion has been rife because terms such as 'realism'; 'socialist realism', 'neo-realism' and 'naturalism' have been used historically in rather different ways and have covered various kinds of work. They have also been loaded by internal disputes among Marxists and further complicated by these debates being misunderstood and given new interpretations.[5]

John Berger's mix of Romanticism and Marxism was to be quickly overtaken by theories of communication that aimed to demystify artistic processes. Film theorists sought to uncover the hidden meanings encoded in the forms of the visual media, while radical artists tried to produce work that was theoretically signposted. James Swinson describes how conceptual art began to have an influence within art schools in the mid-1970s. He observes that one problem with the influence of the theories that have spun outwards from this interaction between Althusserian Marxism and French psychoanalysis has been that in the effort to pin down meaning, the space for a spectator to interpret a piece of work has closed up. What began as an attempt to clarify and democratise the processes of communication turned into a project that disconnected analysis of structure from the experience of living subjects.

James Swinson's account shows how these theoretical concerns interacted with debates emerging in feminism, the gay movement and radical black politics. Within the new social movements disputes quickly arose about whether the answer was simply to substitute one set of images with another or whether the whole process of 'looking' had to be questioned. Indeed many issues that had been contested in relation to class were to be taken up in the context of gender, race and ethnicity. From the 1980s these forms of subordinated experience have tended to eclipse the interest in class inequality evident among left intellectuals in the previous decade.

While the film theory that to appeared in *Screen* from the mid-1970s has passed into academic discourse, the links James Swinson traces to political activism have been largely forgotten. An exception is mentioned by Kerry William Purcell: the inspiration of Third World revolutionary cinema for radical black film-makers and also notes the influence of Stuart Hall's writing on politics and culture. Hall's interest in the 'in-between' intellectuals of the diaspora has countered the tendency to shed actuality,[6] though this has tended to be in relation to 'race' not 'class'. Kerry William Purcell analyses how the shift away from class in radical cultural theory was, by the 1980s, accompanied by a profound internal aesthetic questioning of the concern to depict 'reality'. During the late 1990s the pendulum swung back; journalistic criticism started to hail realistic, naturalistic work and pay tribute to Ken Loach's influence.

The contributors in this section argue for maintaining a balance between an awareness of representation and the relationship between visual communication and the external world. Judith Williamson stresses the importance of understanding the impact of specific kinds of representation, without limiting the means of communicating the experience of subordinated groups to specific aesthetic forms. She calls into question the equation of the critical naturalism employed by Ken Loach as *the* radical way of making films. Kerry William Purcell demonstrates how forms of depicting reality have changed historically. He insists that understanding the complexity of representations of the 'real' does not mean moving away from showing how social existence affects the perceptions of working-class people. James Swinson reflects on how in his own life he found himself balancing on a 'knife edge' around arguments about theory and the meanings given to 'the working class'.

The contributors question the assumption that there has to be a connection between the depiction of working-class people and 'realist' forms and show how there have been several modes of portraying the 'real' in the history of aesthetics. From differing perspectives they argue for a new balance between film practice and film theory rather than an oscillation between an extreme of theoreticism and a rejection of the process of theorising altogether.

Notes

1. See Berger, *Ways of Seeing.*
2. See. L. Baxandall and S. Morawski (eds), Karl Marx, *Frederick Engels on Literature and Art*, pp.30–5.
3. G. Lukács, *The Meaning of Contemporary Realism*, p.125.
4. Emile Zola, quoted in D. Knight, 'Naturalism, Narration and Critical Perspectives: Ken Loach and the Experimental Method' in McKnight, *Agent of Challenge and Defiance*, p.60.
5. In relation to film see Thompson and Bordwell, *Film History*, pp.136–55, 293–304; Schnitzer and Martin, *Cinema in Revolution*; Macdonald and Cousins, *Imagining Reality*, pp.48–69; Youngblood, *Movies for the Masses.*
6. On 'In-Betweenness' and films, see Hill, *British Cinema in the 1980s*, pp.215–18.

8 Changing Images

Judith Williamson in Conversation with Huw Beynon and Sheila Rowbotham

Judith Williamson is the author of *Decoding Advertisements: Ideology and Meaning in Advertising*,(1978), *Consuming Passions: The Dynamics of Popular Culture* (1987), *Deadline at Dawn: Film Criticism, 1980–1990* (1993). She has worked as a film critic on *Time Out* and the *New Statesman* and has made one film, *A Sign is a Fine Investment* (1983). More recently she has been a columnist for *The Guardian*.

SR Which British films come to mind as examples of 'looking at class'?

JW In a sense it would be impossible to make a British film in which the people weren't of some class. The characters' social position will be indicated so quickly by how they speak and so on. But in terms of a self-conscious depiction of the working class I would probably think about 1930s documentaries; Edgar Anstey and Arthur Elton's *Housing Problems*, for instance, which was radical in its way because it was one of the first times working-class people actually spoke on film as opposed to being spoken over. Or I would think of films like *Saturday Night and Sunday Morning* and *The Loneliness of the Long Distance Runner*, which obviously have a broad social project but were also part of a radical new wave in British cinema linked to developments in other countries.

HB On television you had *Cathy Come Home* around the same period too.

JW Yes, that was quite staggering at the time. A bleak, documentary-style drama of children being wrenched away from their mother was utterly unlike other things being shown on television then. In its context it was radical in both form and content.

But looking at how classes are represented in film involves not only thinking about films made by left-wing film-makers, but also looking at films and television as a whole. This is a very important distinction. For a start, we're saying 'class' but we really mean 'working class'. Lots of films are about upper- and middle-class people, but we don't tend to see those as 'about' class in the same way. Then there are also massively popular films that people have watched in millions, films which do show working-class people but not in the 'looking at' sense. Take the *Carry On* series: everybody's working class, everybody's got a working-class accent—unless they're putting on a fake-posh one, which comes over as camp. Whatever the 'carrying on' theme, they're essentially in a working-class universe, but there's no political point being made. Then of course there's the whole realm of TV soaps—*Coronation Street*, *Brookside*, *EastEnders*—where practically everyone's working class. Or think of *Only Fools and Horses*, which has been, I believe, the most popular series ever on television. These are working-class characters, you know they go up and down, they are flawed, they are warm. It's not realistic, but it's not an entirely simplistic picture of people muddling through.

If you looked at how working-class characters have entered mainstream British cinema you would find that they have often been treated with humour. There's a long tradition in drama of lower-class roles providing the comic element. Shakespeare is the obvious example—you have court characters enacting intense tragedies and people like Falstaff creating the comedy.

HB Gangster films like *Get Carter* also show working-class characters.
JW Yes, crime and gangster films.

HB You have things like *Minder*, about people duckin' and divin'. The criminal types are given Cockney accents. Yorkshire has ended up being the Hovis adverts.
JW Working-class characters are often stereotypical.

HB *Four Weddings and a Funeral* and *The Full Monty* were both popular in the States. Perhaps we export stereotyped versions of what the British middle class and the working class are like.
JW I'm certain that we do. The upper-class British are all Hugh Grant-type characters, and the working class are cheeky-chappie types like Robert Carlyle.

SR That has always been the case, hasn't it? You had the quality classics and Gracie Fields in the '30s.
JW Yes. It isn't as if there were no working-class characters in films; it is not like the discussions about race. There were almost no black characters at all in British films for a very long time. Thinking about class is more comparable to thinking about women in films. Of course there have been a few, like war or gangster films, in which women did not appear. But on the whole women have been in films. The issue is *how* they are portrayed. In what kinds of ways have they been represented? For example women were traditionally given roles that did not create the main action in a plot. But this is not the same as an invisibility. These things are often lumped together, but I think they are quite different issues. To not have seen yourself on the screen is quite different from seeing yourself represented in particular kinds of ways.

SR You don't get Driffield or Plymouth working-class people. It is usually London or the North, isn't it? And it's a funny thing how often they are Catholic. There can't be such a high proportion of Catholics in England, but they are often there in films.
JW There is a tendency to look at a particular band of working-class people. Traditionally if people were Irish they might be Catholic. It shows what kinds of labour are still thought of as being 'working class'. Very precise views of class appear.

SR Which means of course that not only are the new kinds of service work missed out but also the whole development in the South East of light-manufacturing industry from the 1930s. The jobs working-class women began to do in the factories of West London, many of which have been pulled down now.

JW It's true that only a particular kind of labour is usually focused on. Millions of different jobs that people do all over the place never seem to feature. Masses and masses of working-class experience isn't there in film.

SR Do you think that recent British films have begun to look at the lives of working-class people in different ways?

JW There are these newer films like *Trainspotting* and *Nil by Mouth*, which present a bleak view of urban working-class existence centred on drugs. I think *Trainspotting* made a big difference: it started a particular genre of films in which the interest was partly based on the fact that they were about something quite hip—not just urban poverty but a kind of young, street-wise poverty. *Trainspotting* wouldn't have been such a big hit if it had been a film about those people's parents. It intersects with drug culture and a youth audience as well as showing a particular group of working-class people.

SR *The Full Monty* captured something very contemporary about what is happening to men. It communicated to people very directly who were not necessarily relating to the class experience.

JW What I found most interesting was the fat guy who puts the clingfilm round himself. Women are supposed to be the ones worrying about their weight. But he feels really bad about it. You rarely see that.

SR I started wondering about how the imagery of class related to the social changes I have been living through in the last 20 years, because I find it so hard in the medium that is more familiar to me, words, to convey the impact of the transformation that has occurred. I am aware of not being able to write about what has happened to the working class—I mean, not just the external facts. I haven't read much either that seems to be able to articulate how it has affected people's consciousness of themselves. But if we can't *say* what's happened, if we can't *see* it, how can we begin to understand?

JW I agree with you. I think it is very hard to get a grip on what kinds of changes have been taking place, and what's going on.

SR While I sense that visual images are crucial, I can't say why they seem so significant. I'm more used to thinking about words, and I find it very difficult to express why it seems so important for a social and cultural experience to be visually there—to be seen.

JW They *are* very different. Words can express something from inside while a photographic image inevitably shows something on the outside. An image isn't a form of personal expression in the same way that words can be. Imagery, particularly social imagery, tends to be symbolic rather than expressive. Obviously that doesn't mean images don't communicate, they just do it differently. You can suggest a subjective experience in a film, for example, by using point-of-view shots and close-ups. But these are not what you think of as 'political images'.

HB There were sets of images that were associated with steel workers and miners—the banners, large numbers of men marching. As industry has dwindled it seems that there are no similar sets of images that can be called on. That is quite challenging and interesting to try and think about, but it is also very disorientating.

SR On the media it's now often assumed that there are a few really rich people and an underclass, with everyone else in the middle. But this seems far too simple to me. The gradations between those classified as 'the middle' are hardly being examined.

JW It seems to me that people commenting from the outside think there has been this massive change because there is not so much heavy industry. But people's self definition has remained working class even if they are not working in a steel foundry. I've never met anyone with a working-class accent who claimed to be middle class. The one thing that makes a difference and puts someone in an ambiguous relation, often a very agonising position in relation to class, is education. But the fact that people are working as clerical workers or technicians doesn't make them portray themselves as no longer working class. What they mean, though, is not the same as '*the* working class' used in the Marxist sense. There is a big difference between how people actually go about their lives and 'the working class' as it has been seen on the left.

SR There are strands of working-class experience which were never really seen as 'working class'. I lived in London during the 1970s and '80s where there was not the same kind of heavy manufacturing industry that existed in the North. But there was light manufacturing. It was the women who worked in those kinds of factories who were active in a whole range of equal-pay strikes in the '70s. Then in the 1980s there were strikes in which women in the public sector, including many Asian and black women, were trying to defend their jobs against privatisation. There were also lots of hospital campaigns and community struggles that involved working-class women. There have always been differing and changing kinds of class experience, but some aspects have been historically more visible. This activity among working class women is still largely an unrecorded labour history, and the images of these kinds of labour struggles are mainly still photographs that are sitting in archives, largely forgotten.

I can think of very little visual record on film. The Women's Film Group in the early '70s did *Women Against the Bill*, a film opposing the Industrial Relations Bill, in which a group of trade-union women talk politics over tea, and there is also Marc Karlin's *Night Cleaners* of course. Yet this recent past has acquired a new significance now because changes in the structure of employment have meant that the kind of casualised jobs the contract cleaners were doing are no longer marginal.

JW But other kinds of changes have also taken place. If you look at how

Utopias, 1987
(Lusia/Channel 4)

people actually go about their lives not everything has got worse, despite the fact that there is terrible poverty and anyone on social security is much worse off. There's much more racial mix in London than when I was growing up. People's backgrounds in the tenants' association on my council estate are much more varied than they were 20 years ago.

HB That is an important part of a more general change. People have moved houses and jobs. I suppose what puzzles me is whether this means that making a cinematographic account of working-class people is becoming so much more difficult?

JW Only if you set out to portray '*the* working class'. Otherwise there are any number of dramas you can make. There is no inherent problem about portraying working-class people. But the handy *symbols* of class, people marching, certain types of housing, are less clear now.

HB But without images of a working class in struggle, you are left with images that seem to me very stultifying. You can show intense poverty or people's misery of course. What is difficult is how you depict the present world where you have new kinds of occupations and different kinds of memories, which have been part of these major industrial conflicts.

JW Obviously because I am a Marxist, I see a relationship between people's experience as part of a class and what happens under capitalism. But I think too that there has always been a gap between the idea of 'the working class' as labour, and the day-to-day lives of working-class people.

Thinking about the films that people on the left set out to make about what they see as happening to 'the working class' is not the same as looking at how class comes across in films in general and examining the patterns in which different film-makers will tend to portray working-class characters. There is a significant difference between, on the one hand, films that show people who happen to be working class, and, on the other, the project of left-wing film-makers to show what is happening to 'labour', in the sense of labour against capital. These are very different enterprises, and it's important not to conflate them.

People don't start to make a Hollywood film thinking, 'How can we make a really right-on realistic portrayal of how the working class is suffering?' They might say, 'Oh, I see a scenario—young man falls in love. I know, we'll make him a factory worker, you know blue collar tough.' They're not trying to put a message across. None the less Hollywood has been quite happy to have cute blue-collar heroes played by Tom Cruise or Matt Dillon. You have a film like *Working Girl* with a major star, Melanie Griffiths, in the key role. The plot was on one level unbelievably reactionary and patriarchal: the Big Daddy figure who owns the company comes in to make everything alright in the end. But the film also portrayed a working-class heroine sympathetically, especially her isolation as she moves away from her tight-knit background. The whole movie was on her side. Hollywood is able to make a film that has the audience all rooting for the people below—the workers—without setting out to make a film saying 'We are now going to show how bad things are'.

The British film industry has worked in a completely different way from Hollywood. We have a stronger tradition of making films to make a point, especially on the left. People want to 'do' something about what's wrong, and there's a sort of slippage that confuses representation and reality. left-wing film-makers want to think that what they do affects material reality. But a film is a film. You can influence people, perhaps leave a symbol within the culture, as *Cathy Come Home* has done. But this is not the same as making a material change. You have to be clear about the difference, otherwise I think you denigrate the organising and campaigning that does actually affect what happens in the material world.

In film terms the problem with having a strong agenda is that there is a tendency for the agenda to become more powerful than the characters or the stories. I find this a problem with a lot of Loach's work since *Cathy Come Home*. Of course *Kes* is the glorious exception; there's an incredible sense of the boy's pain and isolation, of his interior world.

There is a difficulty inherent in trying to show any social group through a fictional character—having to stand for an oppressed group is a burden. It makes the way characters are represented incredibly important. There is a burden of representation hanging on people's backs. If the working-class characters in a film are just there to demonstrate how bad unemployment is or how exploited people are at work, there's often no great reason why anyone would be interested in them as people. Ironically, this is itself a sort of class inequality in cinematic terms. I mean no one is going to say, 'Hey! Let's make a film about middle-class life. I'm going to use middle-class people, they live in subur-bia, now what can we do with them?'

These are similar to the issues of representation that some of us have been hacking through in relation to women. Equally you could compare it to the repre-sentation of black people. There is often a kind of preciousness. *Secrets and Lies* is a very funny film, but Mike Leigh didn't dare make the black woman in it comic. All the other characters are hysterically over the top, completely surreal characters, they seem almost mad, and then, right in the middle of the film, you have this black girl who is incredibly thoughtful and normal. Everybody else is caricatured.

Often when I see films with a message I just think why not make a docu-mentary? Why not say what you want to say really clearly rather than make characters say things? I felt that with *Dockers*. It's a good document of what happened. I know it's a true story. I watched it all the way through, but if I hadn't been someone already with a political investment I doubt that I would have.

SR It had very high viewing ratings.
JW I'm interested in that story because I'm somebody who is interested in seeing a film about a labour dispute. And I was also interested in how the film had been put together. But it was hard to believe it was now. It could have been the story of a dispute a long time ago in a sense.

HB Why do you think that?
JW You don't get much sense of the changes that casualisation involves. You get a glimpse—the shifts, the young wife working in the supermarket and the young family. But you didn't get much flavour of how it was being experienced from the inside. You didn't get much about what it was like to be the younger people.

SR The story comes from the perspective of the older people and particu-larly from the older women.
JW But because you were behind the older people, that made it, in a way, the story of old labour. Also the drama was all external. It was telling a story of a particular kind. You could imagine the writers saying, 'We'll have the guy do this or say that.' But it didn't use the kinds of mechanisms that show people having subjective experiences. In that sense it was like a documentary. There's not much space in the film to draw out things that people are feeling, emotions that are, I believe, political, but also complex. The imagery was absolutely tradi-tional in its evocation. I felt the whole repertoire was familiar from left-wing dramas about labour disputes.

SR But a lot of people outside the old left obviously did relate to *Dockers*. It's almost as if certain groups of workers—the miners, or the dockers—have come to symbolise something about the country as a whole. Something that can't other-wise be spoken about. They stand for the honesty of labour, connection, and a time when things hung together, when people lived in proper families.

JW That is true; the miners and the Liverpool dockers came to stand for community, solidarity, for the old labour movement. And I supported them as much as anybody. But I also think, if we are honest, the left desperately needed them, as symbols, mascots almost. Nevertheless, the brute fact is, they didn't win. It says so much about our time—they didn't get their jobs back, they got a Channel 4 drama!

I don't want to knock *Dockers* for what it does, which is to tell the story of the dispute. It's pointless to criticise something that is really quite effective in what it is for not being something else. But the theme could have been opened up into something much more special. Being on strike, after all, is a really weird experience. It fucks up your head. You're tied to this situation but don't have a job anymore. You can't get into the place where you work. It can be wonderful—but it's also unsettling.

What I'm trying to find a way to say is that if you use stock images, if you have images that are meant to clock particular responses from people, which is how most movies are put together, whether you are right wing or left wing, you are not expressing how things have changed. You are not asking any questions.

People who believe you must go and sort things out through film are inclined to cling to images which are expressive in a known symbolic way rather than a perhaps fresher, less obvious way. It just doesn't mean the same now to have an image of a whole lot of people marching behind a union banner. It gives one a response that comes from memory almost—from a memory of it having this massive meaning, a memory of a time when it represented real power. But since the miners' strike I think it represents almost a nostalgia, a loss. You don't have to be a right-wing person to see this, just a person who has seen how things have changed.

Perhaps a film like *Brassed Off* worked because it dealt so explicitly with that nostalgia, through the figure of the band leader: he stands for an older tradition of working-class culture and pride that the younger characters don't find relevant or aren't quite in touch with. And at the climax, when they are, and they win the contest, it's the older man who becomes cynical. In a way *Brassed Off* consciously speaks about the sense of loss that *Dockers* simply speaks with.

SR Do you think that the economic and social changes mean that the signals through which people have come to understand working-class experience are less evident? The inequality and injustice are still there, but there is a lack of a visible way of communicating new forms of class?

JW Again it depends on whether you are talking about a film about an industrial dispute, where the people will be defined by their work, or about a romance or whatever that is not setting out to talk about 'labour' but has working-class characters. They would have slightly different means at their disposal for representing class.

What we've mainly been discussing so far is representation in the sense of *people* being representative—a character standing for a whole social group, figures in a film representing some issue or point. Part of this is the question of who is represented, and are there social groups excluded from representation?

But what we're moving on to now is the other sense of representation—how does film actually work, *how* does it represent people? In other words, we're not asking what does a particular character tell us about class, but what *in the film* tells us that character's class? What are the signals which indicate that someone is of a particular social group?

Film has basically two interlinked means of giving us those signals: plot, and image (by which I really mean image-plus-sound). These dimensions are like the two axes of a film: there's the movement of the plot going along telling a story, and then there's the physical experience on screen and soundtrack of what we see and hear. Obviously the axes intersect all the time—the story is going to be told *through* images—but still there's a difference of emphasis. So if it's a story about an industrial dispute, and you see people working on a production line, and the boss shouts at them, and they down tools, it's pretty clear what their job is and their class position. Equally if it's about someone living in a council flat going to sign on. The events themselves give you the information. On the whole, films that set out to be 'about' class usually build it into the plot, the story itself hinges on some class issue. In this context, you could ask what are the new stories to be told? What new situations could be dramatised to reflect changing social circumstances? But supposing a film isn't specifically about work, or unemployment, or social conflict—suppose it's a love story or comedy and doesn't even specify someone's job: then it will be down to the image to sketch out social position, and it will have to be shown rather than told.

This is where there's a big difference between class, and gender and race, the other categories we've talked about. It's usually fairly easy to see if someone is a woman in a film, likewise with race—colour is fairly self-evident. Class is more complicated. You can't just have a picture of some bloke standing there in a T-shirt and jeans and know what class he is. He has to open his mouth to speak for a start. You can hear his accent, though even that is vaguer in certain areas and age groups. Unlike gender or race, class is not something that is visually apparent without some sort of other clues or accoutrements being made visible. Those signals are dropped in very quickly in a movie to pinpoint a character's social position.

This makes the mise-en-scene—the setting the scene—extremely important. Basically, to show class in visual terms, you have to rely on things like clothing and interiors. The audience can tell in seconds which class interior they are watching. They can see whether someone's house is middle class, working class, or aspirational, like the characters in Mike Leigh's films. It will be subtle things like what the living room is like. What knick-knacks are on the mantelpiece. Whether there are net curtains, or what the wallpaper is like. Mike Leigh is a good example—the cut-glass thingies on the television set, the way the curtains are draped. These are all familiar signals of class.

Demographic changes and social shifts in people's behaviour, in fashion, taste and style play a part in altering the representation of class. I am not saying that changing representations are at all the *same* as the actual social changes. But certain indicators of class begin to look crude and old fashioned—curlers in working-class women's hair or the man in the cloth cap, for example. The signals have shifted, and it is interesting to think through *how* they have changed. It is not a matter of just looking at social history through film, we're looking at a changing representational history as well. Obviously, representing someone's class through accent, demeanour or scene setting can be very problematic, particularly if you pick older kinds of signals or signifiers, because you can so easily become stereotypical. But that's fundamentally how it's done.

Film-makers showing the lives of working-class people also come up against the audience's desire to look at 'nice' things, elegant interiors, décor and clothes (I mean 'nice' in quotation marks because, of course, it's only a matter of taste). A big element in the history of cinema-going has been people looking at things they did not have themselves. In its heyday the cinema of the '30s and '40s was like a big shop window. Hollywood films have always been incredibly good at providing this pleasure in looking, and it has been a big part of what kept people in the cinema watching a film. If you don't want to go along with the pleasures of accumulation you encounter a fundamental difficulty about what you show instead. I don't know what the answer to this is. But film-makers who want to show something different, say the small living room of a council flat, can easily find their images look patronising. Like those pictures in the Sunday supplements where they use a wide-angled lens so the whole thing ends up looking mad and distorted, weirder than it needs to be.

SR Women have been historically associated with the pleasures of consumption. The Hollywood films aimed at women, like soaps, dwell on emotions. A false division seems to be set up between masculinity, work, reason and realism on one side and femininity, consumption, feeling and melodrama on the other.
JW Melodrama genres, which is essentially what soaps are, have been mainly aimed at women and are, indeed, more watched by women. So it seems to me a genuine observation, though slightly old fashioned. It doesn't mean that one would therefore see that as based on some biological inevitability of women watching melodrama. It is simply what has happened socially. If you are thinking of form, however, an equivalent masculine form would be adventure and war movies, which are not melodramas but a kind of block-buster realism—drama action. They're also aimed at emotions, though of different kinds.

The interesting thing about soap operas is that they are both melodramas and realist: they combine both forms. They are melodramatic in terms of plot— you know there are an unconvincing number of long-lost children who have vanished at birth and jinxed relationships. But they are realist in their form and presentation, in the actual filming.
SR There has been a long argument on the left about the implications of using certain forms. Marxists have argued for realism, though historically a

lot of left theatre, which sought to attract working-class audiences, has been melodramatic or naturalistic.

JW There has certainly been endless debate about this on the left. Brecht attacked the way that in bourgeois theatre it was as if you were watching a drama through the fourth wall. In the 1970s various people in radical theatre and film took up his ideas and rejected the kind of naturalism you got in bourgeois drama because it made the means of production invisible, that is, it treated the actual process of making the play or film as transparent, like a window. But when you watch any kind of film, no matter how naturalistic, you are not just seeing what is happening in the world. It is mediated.

The opposite of the Brechtian position was the kind of film-making that Ken Loach got into—a sort of naturalism where you try and get people talking normally and doing all sorts of things naturally. There is no attempt to do things that are seen as phoney like remixing the dialogue to make it clearer. Loach's style tries to make something more immediate, so that things just 'show through'—no fancy stuff, nothing extraneous, nothing is to be jacked up. It's a kind of anti-aesthetic which I personally find makes some of his films quite grim to watch.

SR In the early '60s there was a very strong emphasis on 'authenticity' in radical culture.

JW There is a problem about collapsing together an idea of authenticity in terms of content, people's experience, their emotional situations or their stories, and the idea of authenticity in how you use the medium. A medium is not an 'authentic' or natural thing. To be in the room with someone is not the same as being in the room with someone with a camera. There's a medium in operation. You can't erase that.

HB Do you think that specific aesthetic forms carry different political meanings in various historical periods?

JW I'm not saying that a film should be this, that or the other, in the sense of suggesting there is some ideal model. Though I feel personally if you are using a camera, why not make an image that is nice to look at rather than one that is less nice to look at. Documentary photography and films of the 1930s, for instance, had a very strong aesthetic. They photographed something like back-to-back housing in ways which made it striking, the images are visually powerful. There is a social message, but that doesn't mean the images can't have their own style. Realism can be quite a stylised form and highly organised in terms of its look and its sound, often with a fantastic aesthetic. It's not pretending to be natural. Realism and naturalism are not the same.

HB Which films about working-class people would you say combine strong characterisation with a visual aesthetic?

JW A good example historically would be Italian Neo-realist films—Rossellini's *Open City*, early work by Visconti, or perhaps a better-known example is de

Sica's *Bicycle Thieves*, or *Umberto D*. They show working-class lives and poverty, yet they're beautiful films: they have a visual strength, and they tell these powerful stories in a semi-documentary but highly aesthetic way. They are all about class and exploitation and urban experience, but the stories are not just vehicles, you engage with the characters. In *Bicycle Thieves*, for example, you are looking at an underclass in a very ravaged society, but the film is not simply a means of talking about poverty. It's melodrama, top melodrama, heart wrenching. You do get deeply engaged with the boy and the father and the bicycle, or with the little dog in *Umberto D*—it's not just a 'message'. Then French cinema can be very socially incisive, showing class at play from all sorts of angles. Chabrol, for example, has made riveting films about the bourgeois milieu. Bunuel's work is a savage indictment of class oppression.

In Britain, I could think of examples like *The Loneliness of the Long Distance Runner*, which was formally an extraordinary film, almost surreal actually in its attempt to show an internal experience. Other British films that I think speak about class with a really powerful aesthetic are Bill Douglas' trilogy: *My Childhood*, *My Ain Folk* and *My Way Home*, or pretty much all of Terence Davies' work. Neither of them has been mentioned in this discussion up to now, but they are working-class film-makers speaking for themselves, not trying to speak for other people, and it makes a quite different tone. Their work is so strong visually, it shows harrowing class experiences, but it's not didactic. It shows something from the inside.

A more recent example—a really amazing piece of work—is Lynne Ramsay's *Ratcatcher*. It's a vivid, subtle, but unsentimental picture of a boy's life on a Glasgow council estate during the dustmen's strike. The aesthetic is utterly unlike Loach-style naturalism—it's a disturbing story in a harsh situation, but the images are both simple and mysterious in an almost surreal way. It's absolutely haunting.

SR Along with realist and naturalist forms there has also been radical work which was influenced by Surrealism, attempting to show how several possibilities are carried in the everyday. Because they are trying to reveal elements of experience that can't be seen, that are not already mapped out, these films might present dreams or fantasies.

JW Yes, and I think that kind of form is more likely to emerge if the film-maker is not *only* thinking of class. That's part of what I am saying about showing interiority. I think if you set out to show class as an issue and make your characters stand for something you are less likely to be focusing on inner fantasies. There can be something not real, something patronising in a conception of 'the working class' as a symbol. The films are about a needed dream of the middle-class intellectual rather than about actual working-class people, and their own dreams and desires.

I don't think you can speak 'for the workers', for other people. If one has things to say one should say things as oneself. That doesn't mean that you

Ratcatcher, 1999
(Pathé)

can't make a space for people to say things: you can let people speak in a documentary, give them a chance to explain themselves, or show inequalities that you think are appalling. There's a subtle difference between allowing people space and speaking *for* people and it often shows in how things come across.

If you want to give people a voice, documentary is a fantastic mode. You can have people talk about what they are doing. Whereas making a fictional version of something for the same purpose feels phoney to me. You are trying to force what you want to say into a story that will somehow speak.

It's probably clear which kinds of films I prefer, but that's not the issue. I'm asking a more general question, really, about why it is that this mix of drama and documentary has become more or less the only kind of left alternative film in Britain? There's a massive and very varied tradition of left-wing photography and film-making which is realist to draw upon, and then there's also the realm that we touched on of the fantasy or surrealist work, which I think is an equally valid way of exploring things.

One of the amazing things about film is that you can show anything— fantasy, dream sequences. There's absolutely no limit on what you can show. The only limit is what *you* set out to make. I think one of the limits left-wing film-makers often impose upon themselves is that they are making films for like-minded people. That can have an inhibiting effect. It also means that criticism of them tends to be stifled, within the left-wing context, and I don't believe that helps produce an open atmosphere conducive to imaginative work.

In contrast, less agenda-led films can sometimes be freer to take dramatic personal situations or even wider social situations and engage you as a viewer, sometimes make you see something you hadn't seen or thought before, or feel sympathy with someone you wouldn't have related to before. I think that's a good rule of thumb, whether a film really pushes you or surprises you, rather than simply reaffirming what you think. That's what makes a film radical, rather than simply 'right-on'.

Judith Williamson interview by Huw Beynon and Sheila Rowbotham, 10 August 1999, edited by Judith Williamson and Sheila Rowbotham

9   Reimagining the Working Class
From *Riff-Raff* to *Nil by Mouth*

Kerry William Purcell

Kerry William Purcell did an MA in Visual Culture at Middlesex University and went on to research the treatment of class in British films during the 1980s. He has written on both film and photography and, through Revolutionary Eye Productions, is working on a film about the Russian photographer and art director Alexey Brodovitch.

[If] the works that prove enduring are precisely those whose truth is most deeply sunken in their material content, then, in the course of this duration, *the concrete realities rise up before the eyes of the beholder all the more distinctly the more they die out in the world* [my italics].' Walter Benjamin [1]

Representations of working-class life have been circumscribed by a set of characteristics that have changed little over the years. Seen essentially as 'belonging' in the North of England or the East End of London, the working class have been repeatedly portrayed as employed primarily in heavy manu-facturing industries and/or living within close-knit families and communities. It is a mise-en-scene that is immediately recognisable in British film and televi-sion, but one that has always been a restrictive means of narrating everyday working-class experience. Even when a large-scale industrial economy existed, such images were limiting and partial, missing many of the complex and contra-dictory nuances of a life bounded by socio-economic inequality. However, when set against the changing conditions of class relations in the 1980s, these conventions were to become perceptibly less appropriate.

Under the successive Conservative governments of Margaret Thatcher the social, cultural and economic forms, through which British working-class life has traditionally been lived, experienced and shaped, underwent widespread transformations.[2] One of the lasting consequences of these transformations has been that while social and economic inequalities—such as poor living conditions, ill health, insecure and laborious jobs, low pay and restricted life chances—grew markedly through the 1980s, the recognisable class distinc-tions with which these inequalities have traditionally been aligned became increasingly hidden.[3] By rendering a particular language of class outdated and inappropriate, the dominant ideological and authorising narratives of the New Right and Thatcherism were successful in manufacturing the misperception that, as the principal social-economic group within society, the working class itself was no longer relevant.

Throughout the 1980s, the historical and alternative points of reference that have been markers of class consciousness were assailed and reduced. By the early 1990s it was evident that the process of working-class recognition was far more problematic than it had seemed even two decades before. Consequently while significant numbers of working class people were to suffer as a result of the intensification of social inequality, it was to prove extremely difficult for them to find a language to identify what they were experiencing or to trace the reasons for the material changes occurring in their day-to-day lives.[4]

However, what has occurred has been a reconstruction of the nature of working-class life, not the erosion of class inequality itself. As Stuart Hall correctly recognised class 'relations do not disappear because the particular historic forms in which class is "lived" and experienced at a particular period change'.[5] Ultimately class is still a 'difference that makes a difference'.[6]

The character of this reconstructed class experience is, however, not easy to understand in the midst of a period of confusion. Cultural and political imagery can provide a particularly valuable way of making visible and manifest what has been invisible and obscure. The late 1980s and 1990s have seen a series of films that have attempted to articulate the dramatic shifts that have been occurring. Films such as *High Hopes* (1988), *Making Out* (1989), *Raining Stones* (1993), *Brassed Off* (1996) all respond in differing ways to the significant transformations in class experience that have occurred.

I intend to take two films from the 1990s—*Riff-Raff* (1990) and *Nil by Mouth* (1997)—as case studies and explore their contrasting representation of the changes wrought upon working-class life by Thatcherism during the 1980s, drawing on the work of two contemporary photograhers, Paul Graham and Nick Waplington. However, the first question that has to be addressed is why there has been relatively little discussion of class in recent cultural theory?

The relationship between the 'real' and images of the 'real' in film is obviously far from straightforward. Indeed this relationship provoked a whole series of debates around realism in film during the 1970s and '80s. It is not my aim here to reproduce a history of these 'screen theory' debates for they can be found elsewhere.[7] It is relevant to note, however, that the analysis of films and filmic language in relation to their particular socio-historical framework has been relatively neglected within contemporary film theory. This disregard has been partly underwritten by a wider drift in left theoretical discourse away from questions of class and class experience, characterised most clearly in 'postmodernist' analysis.

It is, however, important to examine how imagery of the real is related to the wider historical moment. This is especially evident in approaching the issue of working-class representation, because images of class, as the result of specific signifying practices, emerge in the last instance, like class inequality, as the product of history itself. The process of reimagining through culture is thus vital, not simply in terms of the imagery of class but also in relation to the actuality of class experience and possibilities of class recognition.

The Invisible Ink: Notes and Reflections[8]

There has been a notable and unfortunate silence on the left in analysing the problem of working-class recognition. This is not only because the 'postmodern' strand in the left has turned away from the concrete questions of class. At the opposite theoretical pole, other parts of the left have tended to hold on to a narrow and inadequate definition of class, one that is primarily limited to static forms of status and employment.

In challenging this static view, E. P. Thompson stressed the need to understand the relational nature of class dynamics; instead of focusing narrowly on the single issue of work, he looked at how the social, cultural and economic experiences of class interact and function in everyday life. Following a period when working-class life has undergone some of the most dramatic changes since the Second World War, Thompson's call to understand the broader dynamics of class inequality has become all the more urgent. As Jeremy Seabrook and Trevor Blackwell have observed, Thompson's 'imaginative insights into how it felt to be a dispossessed handloom weaver, or a redundant field labourer, need to be equally applied to the making and re-making of the contemporary working class.'[9]

The formation of the working-class then is not a once-and-for-all event. Capitalism repeatedly transforms the means of production, and consequently static definitions of class that continue to rely on a particular type of work as the primary point of reference are bound to result in an analysis of class that slowly loses all pertinence.

An important theoretical development over the last two decades has been a pronounced preoccupation with language, culture and 'discourse' in radical thinking. The emergence of this field of enquiry in fact owed much to those writers on working-class life, like E. P. Thompson and Raymond Williams, who shifted attention away from a narrow and restrictive definition of 'culture' and embraced a broader conception of culture as the 'everyday'.

While much of the early work on working-class life continued to address the inter-relationship between popular culture and its socio-economic context, we have witnessed over the past decade a loosening, then severance, of the economic from this correspondence. At a time when capitalism has become more, not less, active in (re)constituting class relations, we have seen on the 'postmodern left' the growth of an idealism that perceives language as not simply infused with socio-political intonation, not merely shaping our social and cultural knowledge of the world but also operating as our only form of knowable reality. The end result is critiqued by Ellen Meiksins Wood: 'Society is not simply like language. It is language; and since we are all entrapped in our language, no external standard of truth, no external referent for knowledge, is available to us outside the specific 'discourses' that we inhabit.'[10]

The stance is not so new. As Marx and Engels famously remarked in *The German Ideology*, this is to 'detach the consciousness of certain historically conditioned spheres of life from these spheres and evaluate it in terms of true, absolute...philosophical consciousness.'[11] They go on to say that simply to perceive language as distinct from the socio-historical sphere in which it 'means' is to fail to comprehend language as 'manifestations of actual life'. To see language then as the only knowable life itself is indeed to forsake the realm of real history for 'the realm of ideology'.[12]

It is evident, of course, that our understanding of reality can only be formed through particular languages or theoretical frameworks (whether or not we are conscious of those frameworks). As the Marxist linguistician V. N. Voloshinov pointed out, however, the 'understanding of any sign, whether inner or outer, occurs inextricably tied in with the situation in which the sign is implemented...it is always a social [and historical] situation.'[13]

Only the more extreme corners of left 'postmodernist', 'poststructuralist' or 'post-Marxist' thought are likely to dismiss utterly any reality outside discourse. Yet the tendency of their approach has demonstrably been to turn away from the social and material. The idea that society is structured 'like a language', that our 'subjectivities' and 'identities' are formed by, and confined to, the endless play of 'difference', that any claims to a wider external reality are at best fantasy, at worst 'oppressive' and 'totalitarian', are all common currency in much postmodernist thought.

The repercussion of this influential theoretical current in a period, when the thorny referent of class was going through a series of radical transformations, has been that it became easier to deny, outside of language, any knowable reality beyond the discursive, rather than endeavouring to address the changing experiences of a society divided along class lines. This philosophical stance might offer a displaced political radicalism, but it is surely not a coincidence that it should concur with the widespread collapse of political horizons on the left. A pseudoradicalism of whether, as Terry Eagleton has noted, 'the signifier produces the signified or vice versa' became a lot more exciting for many theorists than the messy job of trying to figure out what was happening to a working class under attack.[14]

As Ellen Meiksins Wood recognises, however, it is precisely when the issue of class re-enters the equation, that, 'the "politics of identity" reveals its limitations both theoretical and political'. She asks,[15]

Is it possible to imagine class differences without exploitation and domination? The 'difference' that constitutes class as an 'identity' is by definition a relationship of inequality and power, in a way that sexual or cultural 'difference' need not be. A truly democratic society can celebrate diversities of life styles, culture, or sexual preference; but in what sense would it be 'democratic' to celebrate class differences?

Terry Eagleton remarks how the habit among postmodern theorists of situating class at the end of the 'gender-race-class' triplet is merely an afterthought, which fails to understand that belonging to a social class, unlike one's gender or ethnicity, is in itself 'to be oppressed, or to be an oppressor.'[16] Ironically, the approach that relegates class to just another 'difference' among many other competing identities and interests, parodies the language of Thatcherism and reproduces Thatcher's own indifference to the specific needs and claims of groups like the miners, teachers and print workers who rebelled during the 1980s.

When class is being categorised as 'difference' and real life itself viewed as nothing more than a set of competing 'discourses', it is not surprising that postmodern theorists have suspected attempts to ask what historically specific forms of representation might tell us about periods of social transformation. While it is obvious that in cinema there is not a simple link between representations and their referent—beyond the physical reaction of light on film— the assumption that particular signifying practices are purely arbitrary and unmotivated carries its own over-simplifications. Gilberto Perez has observed in his book, *The Material Ghost: Films and their Medium*, that the, 'recognition of arbitrariness will supposedly lead to the realisation that things can be changed. But changed towards what? Not changed for the better, for there can be nothing better, only more arbitrariness, if all our conventions and systems of expression, all our human transactions can only be arbitrary.'[17]

Maintaining the approach that the forms of expression are arbitrary thus leaves us stranded in a conventionalist no-man's- land, fortified from history. It means we are not able to contest/contrast dominant images of the real with aesthetic strategies that could be better suited to the particular socio-historical moment. When faced with explaining transformations in filmic imagery of social change—why, for example, a historically variable 'form' such as 'realism' may strike a chord in one particular period and ring false in another—a conventionalist approach is left with nowhere to go.

In contrast, the concept of 'Third Cinema' has started to revive an historically sensitive grasp of cinematic language. The term originally came from the revolutionary cinema of the third world, a project that defined itself as distinct from Hollywood and European 'art' cinema. Interest in the diaspora in relation to Asian and Afro-Caribbean experience in Britain has contributed to its revival in a new context. Third Cinema has proved especially useful in addressing representations that seek to respond to moments of socio-historic change. Echoing the quote from Voloshinov earlier, Paul Willemen notes in his introduction to *Questions of Third Cinema* that, because of the 'realisation of the social nature of discourse, the Third Cinema project summons to the place of the viewer social-historical knowledges...[that are] relevant only so far as they form part of the particular social historical processes addressed.'[18]

For Willemen, the idea of a Third Cinema functions not simply as a category for films of the 'Third World' but also more broadly as a mode of cinematic production and viewing that enters into a dialogue with the historical use of film and 'the entire cultural networks within which the experiences of making and viewing are located.'[19] Willemen recognises that a Third Cinema practised by critics and writers has been slowly developing in the West and distinguishes an emergent form of criticism that seeks to understand films and film-making 'in relation to the historical processes, institutions and struggles from which these texts and currents received their formative impulses'.[20] Operating beyond the critically (and now cinematically) redundant dualism of an 'Art'/'Hollywood' cinema, the utility of Willemen's approach is rooted in a way of showing and seeing that recognises an audience's need for historical analysis with a specifically cinematic discourse.

Willemen cites John Hill as one proponent of such a critical approach. Hill's study of British realist cinema, *Sex, Class and Realism: British Cinema, 1956-1963*, demonstrates that applying a historically sensitive approach to film enables you critically to address the differing 'aesthetic strategies' necessary to specific moments of socio-cultural change.[21] Hill examines a specific period of British social realism and discusses its response to a particular phase of working-class transformation. Hill thus acknowledges the importance of assessing the pertinence of a film's particular aesthetic approach to the period under view, along with the issues it is attempting to address.

In looking at how films have responded to moments of social and historical change, with reference to Raymond Williams, Hill pinpoints how a change of content has frequently not been accompanied by new forms to match the new subject matter. He notes the '"injection of new content": new characters (the working class, juvenile delinquents), new settings (the factory, the housing estate) and new problems (race, homosexuality)', observing that these did 'not, in any major sense, entail the "invention of new dramatic forms"'.[22] Hill demonstrates the consequences of this aesthetic lag in representations of class amid the changes wrought by social and cultural shifts in relation to films in the late 1950s and early 1960s. He shows it restricts what meanings can be made and what contentions can be fought about the newly developing experiences of working-class life.[23]

Hill's approach is not only useful in illuminating the films of this earlier period but also has a wider theoretical relevance. There is a vital dialectical tension at the heart of film-language. Understanding this tension involves the active recognition of film as a form that both produces and is in turn produced. Criticism thus needs to acknowledge how the very means of representation are forged and shaped by social-historical processes. This is particularly evident in periods of extensive historical change when a shift in 'content' labours upon the shift in 'form' required to convey these changes.

The implications that follow from this approach are crucial. Understanding the inter-relation of form and content makes it possible to grasp the impetus that impels the development of 'new' ways of seeing. If our representations and contentions of the 'real' are to be anything more than just theoretical parlour games, and 'realism' is to be something more than just a stylistic gesture, it becomes important, in discerning specific images of working-class change, to question how the quantitative shifts in society in particular periods necessitate qualitative transformations in our imagery of class relations.

I intend to examine Ken Loach's *Riff-Raff* and Gary Oldman's *Nil By Mouth* in relation to the contemporary restructuring of the lives of working-class people. By selecting these two films I wish to show how they mark a possible transition in the reimagining of working-class experience. I consider that Gary Oldman's *Nil by Mouth* signals a 'break' in the quality of British realist cinema. Not only is it responsive to the social shifts of the 1980s but it also attempts to offer an cinematic form commensurate with these changing experiences. However, I see *Riff-Raff* as representative of a form of aesthetics developed within an earlier historical context, which, when faced with the transformations of working-class life, fails to respond with a filmic language applicable to the changed set of conditions.

Riff-Raff

Through his desire to address the inequalities of class relations and reveal the political structures at work in determining everyday life chances, the film and television works of Ken Loach have frequently stood alone. During a career that has spanned over 30 years, Loach's films have always attempted to instigate debates responsive to those political and historical subjects traditionally ignored by the dominant media. From the issues of homelessness in *Cathy Come Home* (1966), via the need to expose government policy in Northern Ireland in *Hidden Agenda* (1990), to representations of the past that question the present in *Land and Freedom* (1995), Loach's work has always aspired to examine the true costs of social and political change.

The success of his work has been his ability to respond to these social and political issues with a form of film-making sensitive to the historical moment. At its most successful this awareness has been characterised by a filmic language composed of a fictional narrative mediated via a documentary form, an approach that has been termed 'documentary-drama'. Over the years Loach has gradually honed this style of film-making, identifying the objective of such an approach as simply attempting to convey an 'authenticity of experience'. As he has outlined:[24]

The aim is to find the most economical way of doing something rather than the flashiest, the most dramatic, the most cinematic or the most stunning...If you can be fairly accurate about the way people are and what they are up to that's always interesting and relevant. Providing you are true to people you don't have to invent theories or construct an aesthetic for what you do. Just go and be accurate and that will be contemporary by definition.

While this way of working proved successful throughout the 1960s and 1970s, when faced with the urgency of responding to the emergence of Thatcherism, Loach perceived the drawn-out process of a fictional narrative as more of a hindrance than an aid. Thus, true to his belief in finding the most economical method of working, the intensification of attacks upon working-class life compelled Loach toward a purely documentary form. He made films such as *Questions of Leadership* (1983) on the trade-union movement and *Which Side Are You On?* (1984) about the 1984–5 miners' strike. The directness of Loach's approach was critically appropriate for such a period of social and political transformation. However, while it enabled him to tackle issues 'head on', given the increasingly hostile political climate and the contentious subject matter of his work, he was to discover that, akin to previous films, it was 'just as hard, if not harder, to get them transmitted'.[25] As a result of this and, as he put it, a lack of 'very good ideas',[26] the 1980s proved to be somewhat of a fallow period for Loach. It was not until

Riff-Raff, 1990
(BFI/Parallax/
Channel 4)

the forced departure of Thatcher towards the end of 1990, when the transformations in working-class life that had occurred while she had been in power were
stabiliising, that we see Loach returning both to regular work and, more significantly, to the particular style of documentary drama, that marks his film, *Riff-Raff*.

Riff-Raff centres on the figure of Stevie (Robert Carlyle) who, newly arrived
in London from Glasgow, is homeless and has just acquired work on a building site run by rogue contractors. The opening shot of rats scavenging through
the rubble sets the tone for Loach's explication of the desolate landscape that
resulted from successive Thatcher governments. The building site is populated
by a collection of economic migrants; as Larry (Ricky Tomlinson), the politically conscious Liverpudlian, is quick to remind his fellow workers, this is the
wretched reality of Norman Tebbit's infamous declaration about 'getting on
your bike' to find work.

On arriving at the building site, Stevie is quickly sorted out with a squat by Larry, Mo (George Moss) and Shem (Jimmy Coleman), who gain entry to an empty council flat. At the building site, the hunt for profits requires the men to cut corners, and we witness several dangerous incidents. When Stevie finds a stolen bag dumped in one of the skips, he goes to return the bag to its owner, Susan (Emer McCourt). After an initial hesitancy, Susan invites Stevie in. It transpires that Susan is a singer, and Stevie goes along with his work mates to see her sing at a local pub, where Larry defends Susan against hecklers. Susan goes back to Stevie's flat and later moves in.[27] At this point the incidents on the building site are becoming progressively more life threatening; when one of the builders leans on a piece of scaffolding, it gives way. After talking with the other workers Larry agrees to go and speak to the foremen about the dangerous working conditions. Larry secures a guarantee that all the hazards will be rectified but subsequently is given the sack himself.

Stevie and Susan's relationship is becoming more erratic when Stevie has to go away to his mother's funeral. Upon his return he discovers Susan using heroin. Stevie recounts a story about his brother and brother's wife who became addicted to heroin and then tells Susan to leave. Finally, as Larry had predicted, one of the builders seriously injures himself by falling to the ground because of faulty scaffolding. This spurs Stevie and Mo on to 'get their own back'. In the final scene they torch the building they had helped to build.

This synopsis fails to reveal what is, for Loach, one of his most humorous films, and there are many scenes that, having no direct bearing on the narrative, are just played for their comic value alone. It is characteristic of Loach's approach that such scenes are not, however, extraneous to the film as a whole, but are frequently what constitute its 'authenticity'. The random episodes thus attempt to underwrite the validity of the fictional narrative.

Yet, it is precisely in such scenes, not all comic, that through Loach's desire to foreground the sources of socio-economic injustice, he maintains a political distance. Rather than developing an understanding of working-class life out of the consciousness of the characters' experiences, *Riff-Raff* removes the film image from its object of interest by receding into a form of political recounting. This makes the film incapable of conveying the struggles of the characters' lives in a convincing way. This can be seen most clearly in the character of the left-wing trades unionist, Larry. While Stevie is the central character in *Riff-Raff*, it is Larry who frequently signposts the political implications of the various situations in which Stevie finds himself.[28] When Stevie is offered a squat, this prompts Larry to speak about Thatcher's corrupt housing policy; when Stevie, Mo and Shem are hassled by youths on a council estate, Larry remonstrates against the waste of youth in the country; when Larry connects the gas in Stevie's flat he inveighs against privatisation; and, when the workers complain about the conditions on the building site, Larry proclaims the dire situation of the building trade.

Larry offers up the socio-political explanations that provide a way of comprehending what is happening to Stevie. But this means of explication removes us from connecting with Stevie's predicament in a more intimate and affecting form. Stevie thus is sidelined by Loach's wider aim of communicating a political vision. The result is that the film ends up offering an objective undestanding without any convincing subjective equivalent.[29]

The consequences of such a heavy-handed approach are that Loach attempts to make the links between the social repercussions of Thatcherism and Stevie's struggle on behalf of the audience. From the glaringly obvious metaphor of rats rummaging in the rubble, to the final unconvincing scene of Stevie and Mo torching the flats, we are prompted at various points in the film to connect the workers' struggles with the wider political inequalities that shape their lives. Loach identifies the structural contradictions at work in his characters' lives, but he offers them up in such a way that he short-circuits the possibility of any real recognition between his characters' experiences on the screen and those in the audience. Ultimately, a concerned observation lies at the heart of *Riff-Raff*, a remoteness, that, as David Thomson in his *Biographical Dictionary of Film* has declared, means 'it is easier to respect Loach than enjoy him.'[30]

For all of Loach's ability in locating the objective structures of social and economic inequality, *Riff-Raff* struggles to convey these through the subjective experiences of its characters' lives.[31] By its failure to make the necessary connections between the class experiences common to both their lives, Loach's handling of the relationship between Stevie and Susan just serves to highlight this discrepancy. While the exploitative conditions Stevie endures on the building site are given a meaningful, if strained, context, a comparative account of his subjective predicament is lacking. In antithesis to this, while we are aware of the frustration that Susan vents at being trapped within the flat, we are provided with no real sense of her relation to the wider determinants of her situation. One consequence is that the heroin incident with Susan simply seems like a flimsy melodramatic device.

The outcome is, in effect, two films. One that offers an accurate view of the economic conditions faced by Stevie on the building site, and another that focuses upon the 'individual' anxieties and problems of Susan. Cut together they ultimately fail fully to articulate how the 'determining pressures of structured processes are experienced and handled by people'.[32] The source of this divergence stems in part from Loach's historically specific application of the documentary-drama form. While the general aim of this approach is to reveal how the wider socio-historical context intersects with the lives of those shaped by these processes, *Riff-Raff* signifies a divergence of this objective/subjective dialectic, and is not able to fuse the world of work with that of private relations.

As society has altered in new and unfamiliar ways, it seems that Loach has failed to respond with a filmic style better suited to the changed set of conditions. The result is a rupture between Loach's style of film-making and the ability to address 'authentically' the subject matter of his films. As John Hill explains:[33]

The great strength of Loach's work has been, with some exceptions, its rootedness in a specific social context...However, Loach's work at the end of the 1980s and start of the 1990s does also suggest that it may have been too dependent upon pregiven aesthetic recipes, and, as a result, failed to re-imagine, in a way which was entirely successful, a political cinema appropriate to the changed circumstances of the period.

The economic and social transformation of working-class life during the Thatcherite period rendered the traditional imagery of class inappropriate. It was one of the 'successes' of Thatcherism that it offered a political imagery of these changes; yet one that 'individualised' the causes of its class oppression.[34] Through this ideological language, working-class identity was frequently displaced and the hidden injuries of a class system transposed into the 'single issues' ('differences'?) of crime, teenage pregnancy and 'regional' unemployment, which were to become so beloved by the media during the 1980s.

These transmutations have affected the qualitative experience of working-class life. While class divisions have become more pronounced, the channels open to the formation of a recognisable class identity have declined. Whereas earlier in Loach's career it may have been enough 'just [to] be accurate' and 'observe people sympathetically', the new developments necessitate a filmic form capable of revealing class experiences that have been denied social and political recognition. One is required that connects with the felt experiences of its audience now. By maintaining both a political distance from his characters' lives, and a historical distance in his visual style, Loach effectively pulls back from an engagement with these class experiences on their own ground: a withdrawal from the present into the past. Ultimately, authenticity means nothing without artistry; as one critic of *Riff-Raff* in *Sight and Sound* observed, '[not] for the first time in a Loach film, the frame does not support the construction: the centre does not hold.'[35]

When faced with the challenge of responding to periods of great social change, any serious film-maker will encounter the problem of the need to rethink their filmic approach. Such a reappraisal is integral to the process of confronting actuality. If this is not done, a departure from the real will inevitably ensue. Gilberto Perez identifies the consequences of evasion:[36]

The remove of the film image makes the things of reality easier to handle, more amenable to the workings of art [and politics], and by keeping things at a far enough remove incoherence may be avoided, but so will genuine engagement with reality. *The risk of incoherence must be run, unruly reality met on a ground close enough to its own energies and its resistance to come into play.* [my italics]

As the opening quote from Walter Benjamin intimates it is only in works of enduring value that, over a period of time, we begin to identify a cleavage between form and content. Over the years, the critical success of, and animosity towards, much of Loach's work has been due to his ability to respond accurately and sensitively to those social and historical issues ignored by other film-makers.

However, following the significant transformations under Thatcherism, Loach has perceptibly failed to reimagine a cinematic form capable of revealing the changing experiences of working-class life today. As these 'realities' have become more apparent, so too has the artifice of Loach's film-making.

Nil by Mouth

Gary Oldman's first film as writer-director focuses upon the lives of an extended family in and around a south-east London housing estate. Centred primarily upon the character of Ray (Ray Winstone), the film, like Loach's *Riff-Raff*, is more a collection of incidental scenes than a straightforward story. But, unlike *Riff-Raff*, the film attempts to offer an intimate and detailed understanding of working-class life in late twentieth-century Britain from the inside.

In the opening scene we find Ray at a social-club bar trying to order some drinks. The opening shot of him fills the entire screen; an imposing figure, he looms ominously over the film as a whole. In the social club are Ray's pregnant wife, Val (Kathy Burke), Val's mother, Janet (Laila Morse),[37] and Ray's friend Mark, (Jamie Foreman). Billy (Charlie Creed-Miles), Val's heroin-addict younger brother, comes into the club and is recruited by Ray and Mark for a job they plan to undertake the next day. Billy and his mate Danny (Steve Sweeny) go off to score some more drugs.

The next day, after Billy, Ray and Mark have unloaded some cases of vodka to a night-club, they head off for an evening in the West End, visiting arcades and a strip club. In the morning Billy, who slept on Val and Ray's sofa, is accused by Ray of stealing his drugs. Billy denies all knowledge of it, and Ray beats him up, biting a large chunk out of his nose. Billy needs more drugs so he goes to see his mother, Janet, at work. Having no luck Billy breaks into Val and Ray's flat and steals Ray's favourite painting. Billy disappears and Ray, Val, and Janet try to find him. Later Billy turns up with some money, gives some to Janet and then goes off.

Fed up and worn out by Ray's constant drinking and violent behaviour, Val goes to the pub with Janet and some friends. While she is playing pool with a friend, Ray comes in demanding that she goes home. When he accuses her of cheating on him, she tells him to stop being so stupid. In a vicious frenzy Ray beats Val up, and as a consequence she loses the baby. While Val is staying at her grandmother's house, Ray, in a drunken state, trashes their flat. He then attempts to re-start their relationship, but Val remonstrates about the state of her life with him. Janet and her mother, Kath (Edna Doré), go out to the social club for Val's birthday, and Kath ends up singing 'Can't Help Lovin' Dat Man' on stage. Sometime later Kath, Janet, Mark and friends are all at Ray and Val's flat waiting to go and see Billy who is now in jail. Ray has redecorated the flat, and it seems that he is off the booze. They all leave to visit Billy.

Nil by Mouth depicts a world circumscribed by generation upon generation of social and economic inequality. It is clearly not a portrayal of an 'average' working-class family home: the intensity of Ray's emotional and physical violence is too extreme to be regarded as representative. What it successfully communicates is a view from within, of the hidden injuries of a class system that limits the scope of each generation's realisable expectations and possible opportunities. Attempting to convey these related, but differing, experiences throughout the family makes for an erratic narrative. Yet, whether we are following Billy on his search for drugs, or witnessing the social isolation of both Janet and her mother, we come to an understanding of the shared iniquities of an unjust society that is politically more powerful through its refusal to moralise or offer up glib metaphors of alienation. Unlike *Riff-Raff*, *Nil by Mouth* withdraws from the temptation of foregrounding—at the cost of a credible grasp of subjective experience—the objective origins of the difficulties faced within its characters' lives. By avoiding this stunted society/individual dichotomy, *Nil by Mouth* successfully reimagines a narrative of working-class life that can render the cost of Thatcherism. The result is a cinematic encounter that, as Nick James says, 'recognises an audience's need for their experiences to find their equivalent on screen.'[38]

While the narrative structure in itself fails to mark *Nil by Mouth* out as distinct from much of British social drama, what makes this film so unique is a shift in the filmic quality we have come to expect from much working-class realism. The estate setting successfully signifies the social and political claustrophobia of its characters' lives through a combination of tightly framed close-ups and cinematic expressiveness. This is something rarely seen in the work of other British realist film-makers honed through the conventional route of televisual apprenticeships.[39]

Oldman's full use of the cinematic medium allows him to articulate fully those class experiences that are inclined to be assuaged by the aesthetics of the smaller screen. Our identification of the experiences and surroundings of the characters emanates not just from the locations but also from a truly filmic attention towards the areas of light, colour and cinematography. This vivid quality of *Nil by Mouth* stems in part from the photographic work of Paul Graham and Nick Waplington,[40] two major influences upon the visual style of Oldman, and the director of photography, Ron Fortunato.

Graham and Waplington are two British photographers who came to the fore as a response to the transformations in the socio-economic landscape of Thatcher's Britain. Graham's work has been characterised by a range of photographic projects on Northern Ireland, unemployment centres and motorway service stations. What was initially distinctive about it, marking these projects out from previous forms of social-documentary photography, was Graham's decision to use colour over the more traditional medium of black and white.

Together with many other British photographers in the 1980s, such as Martin Parr and Paul Reas, Graham's use of colour was combined with a growing interest in representing differing aspects of working-class life. However, unlike these other photographers, Graham refrained from using excessively vivid colours—an ironic device that can be seen most odiously in the work of Martin Parr. As a consequence his work withholds from appeasing middle-class prejudice by fetishising differing aspects of working-class life. Influenced by the

American photographer William Eggleston, and particularly by his 1977 port-folio, *Election Eve*, Graham's subtle use of colour offers instead a poetic vision of everyday life that approaches each subject—from the mundane to the exceptional—with the same level of respect and attention to detail; a way of working that Eggleston defines as 'photographing democratically'.[41]

Such an approach results in photographs of social and political sensitivity that respond imaginatively to the massive changes of the 1980s. The outcome is an understanding of the extent of transformation that a solely realistic style would be incapable of expressing. Graham has developed this symbolic and imaginative use of colour further in his most recent projects. In his work enti-tled *New Europe* and in his latest series of portraits of young clubbers in vari-ous European cities, Graham's distinguishing use of soft, dark and rich colours emotes a sensibility that the American photographer Lewis Baltz has described as being akin to a 'paper movie'.[42]

Fortunato translates this aesthetic in Graham's recent work into the unique atmosphere that permeates *Nil By Mouth*. By appropriating Graham's aesthetic, Fortunato accurately signifies the brutality of the film's setting. Kevin McDrew describes this as a 'colour palette that was keyed by [those] cold-looking exte-riors and the oppressive yellow lights [that are] found in the hallways of London housing blocks and…streets'. The result, in McDrew's words, is, a 'rough, dark, and cold and dreary [look] that would emphasise the bleak environs of working-class South London'.[43]

The effect is reinforced because the film was deliberately shot on a slow Super 16mm film stock and blown up to 35mm. Together, this method of light-ing and use of film stock successfully produce a dark grainy feel to the film, as McDrew says,'like night-time in the middle of the day'.[44] The very method of film-ing thus powerfully communicates how the oppressive aridity of this desolate, sprawling estate colours the lives of Val and Ray and families confined within it.

One scene that demonstrates this can be seen when a bored Billy is wander-ing around the estate, and the camera pulls back to reveal a grey south-east London landscape. Having lived in the area , this is an image with which I can personally identify, but in Billy's life it signifies the limited horizon of 'the next fix', which his heroin addiction demands. Throughout the film Oldman repeat-edly realises such scenes, whereby the camerawork and mise-en-scene combine to provide an emotionally convincing connection with the characters' experiences. The result transcends authenticity: it is a form of realism that, as Nick James has noted, 'acknowledges that British audiences are now more "in touch with their emotions"'.[45]

One area of the film that benefits from such close attention to detail are the interior scenes that frequently constitute the stage where Ray and Val's troubled relationship is played out. Throughout the film we rarely get to see Val and Ray within the same frame, even when they occupy the same room the camera whip-pans from one close-up to another. Moreover, further to enunciate the mutually distinct worlds that they occupy, objects—such as panes of glass—are frequently placed between the camera and the individual. In one such scene, for example, while Ray is in the living room with his mates, the camera swings to a emotionally charged shot of Val, symbolically and physically isolated in the kitchen behind a glass window. Over the duration of the film the accumulation of these scenes actually serve, on a wider level, to express, rather than deny, the common set of conditions to which Ray, Val and her family are exposed.

Nil by Mouth is dissimilar from *Riff-Raff*, in that a close attention to the use of lighting, colour and music—the latter in this instance by Eric Clapton—provides a continuity of experience to the characters' lives. We are offered an expression of the shared predicament they face, but, because *Nil by Mouth* refrains from simply verbalising this, the film supplies a powerful cinematic 'understanding' of the 'lived' experiences of a society still founded upon class division.

The overall look and feel of Oldman's work, and the combination of subjectivity and documentary, especially in his treatment of Kath, evokes the photographic style of Nick Waplington, which he himself refers to as subjective documentary. Waplington has produced two books documenting the lives of two working-class families in Nottingham: *Living Room* (1991) and *Weddings, Parties, Anything* (1996). He amassed a series of images over a nine-year period of their lives, charting the ups and downs of daily struggles.

Waplington knew many of the people in his photos before he even picked up a camera, and the most striking aspect of his work is the tacit admission of his lasting relationship with the people he photographs. Precisely because Waplington is not intruding, people do not stare at the camera in his images. He is part of their everyday lives and, consequently, is present in the images themselves, sometimes literally. Obviously, after a series of exhibitions and the publication of two books, Waplington has moved beyond the limited social environment in which he grew up. Yet, it is clear that the people in Waplington's photographs are still very much part of his own life—even if, as his photographic projects widen and develop, it may become more difficult for him to return.

Technically, Waplington's work in the *Living Room* series is characterised by large-format colour photographs made on a 6 x 9in camera. The outcome of using a 6 x 9 within the confined spaces of a family home—a camera traditionally utilised in panoramic studies—is to infuse the everyday banalities of family life with a signification that makes the epic everyday and the everyday assume an epic meaning. Indeed, John Berger has compared Waplington's work to the baroque. As in the baroque, his images 'turn the earth-bound into the celestial, and…make human figures appear as at home in the sky as on the ground'.[46] Similarly the format of Waplington's images contrives to fix the viewer in a position that is more typical of landscape photography—we find ourselves looking through the images rather than at them.

Yet, paradoxically, the space opened up by Waplington's images is regularly closed off by both the ellipsis of photographic framing and, more significantly, the positioning of people/objects in front of the camera. In many of Waplington's photos—I keep wanting to say the families' photos—children, adults and furniture partly eclipse the photographic space, everywhere playing, crying, and engaging in the familiar dynamics of working-class family life. Waplington's work is thus marked by a heightened realism which tacitly avoids the commodification of working-class life. Like Graham, he portrays the subjects of his project as 'conscious of the dynamics of their lives, not slaves to them'.[47]

It is by claiming the innovative imagery manufactured by Waplington and Graham that Ron Fortunato's cinematography provides the viewer of *Nil by Mouth* with an understanding of its characters' lives from the centre. Like Waplington, Fortunato and Oldman's shots of the oppressive and confined spaces of Val's and Kath's council flats are intensified by the use of a wide-angle lens and repeatedly placing objects between the subject and camera.

Contrary to Loach's belief that the use of wide-angle lens objectifies,[48] the application of this visual style in *Nil by Mouth* results in the viewer being positioned both within and without the experiences of the characters. Watching the film is to be aware of the relationship between the characters' state of existence and their connection to the wider society, while at the same time being cinematically situated within the unbearable conditions of their everyday survival. It is a 'paradoxical combination of intimacy and distance'.[49] Oldman's film provides a view that is simultaneously disconnected and immediate: a way of seeing that 'corresponds' with the intensely isolated experiences of a working class systematically excluded from the wider society.

The playwright and film-maker Trevor Griffiths has stated that if you are attempting to 'create a form that will accurately reflect contemporary experience—it is going to be [a] flow rather than solid structures'.[50] *Nil by Mouth* offers such a form. In a period where much of the traditional imagery of class frequently seems antiquated and unilluminating, Oldman's film advances a method of articulating those experiences originating from the contradictions of a social system that, in its smug indifference, continues to normalise the impoverished existence of millions of people. Its value lies in its ability to give shape and texture to these experiences. It constitutes a form of cinema attuned to the objective—subjective determinations that make up the daily struggles of working-class life.

In contrast the imagery Loach uses in response to these contemporary experiences arises from an approach developed in the process of imagining working-class life in the 1960s and 1970s. This is perceptibly inadequate in the context of the changed relations of contemporary Britain. In *Riff-Raff*, the disparity between the historically specific conventions Loach utilises, and the contemporary experiences of working-class life he wishes to address means that Loach's only recourse is to compel the characters to spell out the political message that the film fails to make cinematically.

This is not a criticism of all Loach's films but, of those that have failed to reimagine a form pertinent to the changed political circumstances of the 1990s. While Loach's films are always worthy of our attention, there has been a tendency on the left to hold each new 'Ken Loach film' in reverence. Whereas there is certainly a necessity to support those increasingly rare films that attempt to articulate the processes of class experience, simply to eulogise them is to leave untouched the issues raised. As capitalism gathers pace in its search for profits, the historical terrain upon which working-class life is founded is shifting. Before class relations can ossify and while in this state of flux, the need to engage with how differing films are attempting to reimagine these changes has never been more urgent.

Notes

1. Benjamin in M. Bullock and M. W. Jennings (eds), *Walter Benjamin, Selected Writings: Volume One*, 1913–1926, Harvard University Press, Cambridge, MA, and London, 1997, p.297.

2. 'The bourgeoisie cannot exist without revolutionising the instruments of production, and thereby the relations of production and all social relations,' K. Marx and F. Engels, *The Communist Manifesto*, Penguin, London, 1985, p.83.

3. See Hudson and Williams, *Divided Britain*; Campbell, *Wigan Pier Revisited*; N. Danziger, *Danziger's Britain: A Journey to the Edge*, HarperCollins, London, 1996.

4. 'The modern poor are not the visible homeless and alcoholics rummaging in litter bins. They are those like Amy and Trisha and their children, who appear "normal", whose poverty is enclosed and internalised. Meeting her, you might never guess that Amy has repeatedly tried to end her life,' Pilger, *Hidden Agendas*, p.104; 'It is the working class who still bear the brunt of unemployment. Among the young people I met class is rarely an issue...the poverty of their aspirations, to Aneurin Bevan's phrase, has been replaced by a wealth of expectations that are rarely attainable,' Danziger, *Danziger's Britain*, p.6.

5. Hall, *The Hard Road to Renewal*, p.212. See also S. Hall and M. Jacques, *The Politics of Thatcherism*, Lawrence & Wishart, London, 1983; B. Jessop, K. Bonnet, S. Bromley and T. Ling, *Thatcherism: A Tale of Two Nations*, Polity, London, 1988; A. Gamble, *The Free Economy and the Strong State: The Politics of Thatcherism*, Macmillan, London, 1991; M. Hayes, *The New Right in Britain: An Introduction to Theory and Practice*, Pluto, London, 1994.

6. D. Coole, 'Is Class a Difference that Makes a Difference?', *Radical Philosophy*, 77, May/June 1996, p.17.

7. See R. Lapsley and M. Westlake (eds), *Film Theory: An Introduction*, ch.6, Manchester University Press, 1991. See also Lovell, *Pictures of Reality*; Cook, *The Cinema Book*.

8. 'The events surrounding the historian and in which he takes part will underlie his presentation like a text written in invisible ink,' W. Benjamin, quoted by P. Willemen, 'The Third Cinema Question: Notes and Reflections' in Willemen and Pines, *Questions of Third Cinema*, p.11.

9. J. Seabrook and T. Blackwell, *A World Still to Win: The Reconstruction of the Post-war Working Class*, Faber, London, 1985, p.31.

10. E. Meiksins Wood, 'What is the Postmodern Agenda' in Wood and J. Bellamy Foster (eds), *In Defense of History: Marxism and the Postmodern Agenda*, Monthly Review Foundation, New York, 1997, p.5. As Marx and Engels understood it, the development of such views is more an outgrowth of the academic divisions of labour than a recognition andunderstanding of language as the 'manifestation of actual life'.

11. K. Marx and F. Engels, *The German Ideology*, Lawrence & Wishart, London, 1996, p.119.

12. *Ibid.*, p.118.

13. Voloshinov, *Marxism and the Philosophy of Language*, Harvard University Press, Cambridge, MA, 1986, p.37.

14. As Terry Eagleton has noted: 'Talk of whether the signifier produces the signified or vice versa, valuable though it doubtless is, is not quite what stormed the Winter Palace or brought down the Heath government,' *The Illusions of Postmodernism*, p.13.

15. Wood, *Democracy against Capitalism*, p.258.

16. Eagleton, *The Illusions of Postmodernism*, p.57.

17. G. Perez, *The Material Ghost: Films and their Medium*, John Hopkins University Press, Baltimore, MD, 1998, p.22.

18. 'The term Third Cinema was launched [in the 1960s] by the Argentinean film-makers Fernando Solanas and Spanish-born Octavio Getino,' P. Willemen, 'The Third Cinema Question' in Pines and Willemen, p.5. John Hill has used this concept in a critique of Ken Loach's work. See J. Hill, 'Finding a Form: Politics and Aesthetics in *Fatherland, Hidden Agenda* and *Riff-Raff*' in McKnight, *Agent of Challenge and Defiance*.

19. Willemen, 'The Third Cinema Question' in Willemen and Pines, pp.27–8.

20. *Ibid.*, p.14.

21. J. Hill, 'Finding a Form' in McKnight, p.139.

22. Hill, *Sex, Class and Realism*, p.59.

23. As Terry Lovell has stated: 'Realism as a critical instrument of working-class politics and sensibility must be flexible in its strategies, and must always consider questions of form and technique in relation to particular audiences as well in relation to content,' *Pictures of Reality*, p.67.

24. J. Hill, 'Interview with Ken Loach' in McKnight, p.165.

25. Quoted in P. Kerr, 'The Complete Ken Loach', *Stills*, 27, May/June 1986, p.148. See also J. Petley, 'Ken Loach and the Question of Censorship' in McKnight, p.99.

26. *Face to Face* interview with Ken Loach by Jeremy Isaacs, BBC2, 19 September 1994; quoted in S. Laing, 'Ken Loach: Histories and Contexts' in McKnight, p. 22.

27. As with so many of Loach's earlier films there is much action between these key scenes that seems to have no bearing on the narrative at all, other than to confirm Loach's desire to convey an 'authenticity of experience'. One such a scene is where Susan goes to audition for a musical, and Stevie, annoyed at the pompous producers, demands them to clap for Susan's performance. Aside from some abstruse point regarding the class divisions within the theatre world (forgetting for the moment that we never actually get to know anything of Susan's past) this sits awkwardly with those set on the building site.

28. To be fair to Loach he does offset this against those workers who have no time for political discussion and find Larry's remarks tiresome, recognising that they themselves are frequently apathetic towards social change.

29. As when Stevie is walking to Susan's house and we see CLASS WAR sprayed on the wall; or when Larry is caught in the bath of one of the apartments he is building by three Arabic women who have arrived in a stretched limo.

30. D. Thomson, *A Biographical Dictionary of Film*, Deutsch, London, 1994, p.448. This point has also been made in a recent review of Loach's *My Name is Joe*. See J. Hill, 'Every Fuckin' Choice Stinks', *Sight and Sound*, 8:11, November 1998.

31. Ellen Meiksins Wood notes: 'It is essential to recognize that objective" and "subjective" are not dualistically separated entities...related to one another only externally and mechanically, "the one sequential upon the other"...conscious and active historical beings [are] "subject" and "object" at once, both agents and material forces in objective processes,' Wood, *Democracy against Capitalism*, p. 92.

32. *Ibid.*, p.97.

33. Hill, 'Finding a Form' in McKnight, p.139.

34. 'Working-class interests do not exist outside of the political space in which they are defined, or outside of the ideological discourses which give them sense, or outside the balance of forces which define the limits of the possible in which they have to be realised.... Socialism carries no absolute guarantees,' Hall, *The Road to Renewal*, p.179.

35. D. Wilson, Review of *Riff-Raff*, *Sight and Sound*, May 1991.

36. Perez, *The Material Ghost*, p.40.

37. Laila Morse is actually Gary Oldman's sister. Laila Morse is an anagram of *mia sorella*, Italian for 'my sister'. See G. Andrew, 'True Grit', *Time Out*, 3-10 September 1997.

38. N. James, 'Being There', *Sight and Sound*, October 1997, p.6.

39. The exception being Alan Clarke, whose films such as Scum (1979, starring Ray Winstone); *Made in Britain* (1983); *Rita, Sue and Bob Too* (1987) and *The Firm* (1989, starring Gary Oldman) have been acknowledged by Oldman as a significant influence upon his filmic style.

40. James, 'Being There', p.8.

41. W. Eggleston, *The Democratic Forest*, Secker & Warburg, London, 1989, p.171.

42. See L. Baltz, 'A Conversation: Lewis Baltz with Paul Graham, 1995' in *Paul Graham*, Phaidon, London, 1996, p.141.

43. Quoted by K. McDrew in E. Rudolph, 'Colour Timing Comes to the Fore', *American Cinematography*, November 1997, p.115.

44. *Ibid.*, p.116.

45. James, 'Being There', p.8.

46. J. Berger, 'Means to Live' in N. Waplington, *Living Room*, Cornerhouse, Manchester, 1991. This is echoed in one review of *Nil by Mouth*, which stated that 'Winstone's pustulous, sweaty face ... is a landscape itself,' G. Macnab, '*Nil by Mouth*', *Sight and Sound*, October 1997, p.55.

47. D. Hevey, 'Cross-class Orpheus', review of *Living Room*, *Creative Camera*, 315, April/May 1992, p.43.

48. 'I don't like wide lens (it turns people into objects. The size of the room dictates the size of the shots. '*Ladybird, Ladybird*: The Director', *Sight and Sound*, November 1994, pp.13–14.

49. James, 'Being There', p.6.

50. Interview with Trevor Griffths. M. Karlin, 'Food for Ravens' *Vertigo*, 8, summer 1998, p.7.

10 Putting Life into Theory

James Swinson

I come from a visual-arts background—I did a Fine Art BA in painting at Camberwell School of Arts and Crafts in the 1970s. I suppose I am a classic product of the British art-schools system. As a student I was influenced by conceptual art; documentation and montage were to make my work drift towards the moving image. Because I was working with images and interested in issue-based work, I was necessarily engaging with the politics and culture of representation. During the 1970s, conceptual art, like film studies, was being influenced by Althusserian structuralism, while in the same period feminism and gay politics were beginning to question forms of representation.

In the early to mid-1970s I was straddling different camps. I was close to Big Flame, a libertarian socialist group, living in a squat near Brockwell Park in Brixton and involved in community politics. A lot of people I knew were living in collective households, sometimes in squats, for economic as well as cultural reasons. Nearly everyone was on the dole. We used to hold carnivals in the park and organise street parties. People were starting print workshops, doing posters, producing community newspapers, getting hold of very early video equipment and so on. It was an approach to politics that differed from that of the Labour Party or the left sects, and it was to have an important influence on the growth of community arts. None the less there was a resistance to 'art'. People would be very disparaging about my being at art school, which was seen as somehow a bourgeois activity. I remember actually not talking about being involved in creative things and feeling uncomfortable about a certain distaste for anything that was engaging pleasure or having entertainment value. Everything had to have this kind of functionalism or didacticism.

I also remember arguments around language and the working classes. For left tendencies, the model for communicating was often a form of tabloid journalism. The presumption that somehow there was a working-class culture out there that had to be spoken to in very simple terms always used to irritate me. I came from a working-class background, but my parents, Marjorie and Norman Swinson, despite having to leave school at 15, were better read and had a much broader sense of culture than the people talking down to the working classes. It just seemed, well, this does not fit. So I was always having to switch identities.

I started to experiment with video at Camberwell as a student when it was just becoming available as a medium. Video entered the art school as part of

James Swinson taught cinema at Camberwell College of the Arts and now lectures at Central St Martin's College of Art and Design. He has designed record covers, and made rock videos and video installations. His six-part series of documentaries *Acting Tapes* with Mark Nash were shown on Channel 4 in 1986. He has also made a film about the Australian bicentenary with Jane Madsen and John Cumming, *First Time Tragedy, Second Time Farce*, which features the aboriginal opposition.

the Inner London Education Authority media-resources policy; it was not part of the curriculum, I discovered it by accident. I have never had any formal film or video training, nor been to film school or anything like that. Coming from a visual-arts background, rightly or wrongly, gives you this confidence that you can do anything if it is visual.

This is actually a well-worn pathway; when you look at British cinema, several key figures such as Ken Russell and Derek Jarman were at art school. However, in contrast to the strength of the literary tradition, there is a kind of visual inferiority complex in English culture. High art in Britain has always been associated with drama and the novel: they have always been the most accept-able forms of culture, and the visual arts have often been downgraded.

The English art-school system was the first form of tertiary education outside the universities, and it reached out to artisans who wanted to study. The old art schools in the nineteenth century were set up in the industrial centres. They offered a very specific kind of education to apprentices—applied art and design, to give them design skills, because the labour force needed to be skilled. Only subsequently did they take on fine art, which introduced into the art-school system, a more intellectual approach to art.

The people from an upper-class background who went to art school, have often tended to be the kind of dyslexic members of the ruling class. They would be pushed towards the visual media, because they were seen as not very bright or whatever. There continued to be a lot of people from working-class backgrounds who went towards art in the post-war era. This made for a strange mixture. The ethos was that art was about expressing yourself. One result of all this was to be an anti-intellectualism in art schools. Conceptual art, in contrast, opened up the possibility of a contact with ideas through issue-based work and documentation. However, the intellectual inferiority complex within the art schools and the visual arts had left a vacuum that became suddenly filled by theoreticism. I felt I wanted to break out of that. On the one hand I was very wary of the anti-intellectual approach that I kept encounter-ing both in the visual media and in the activist left. On the other I did not believe that wanting to engage with difficult ideas, or representing the world as a complex place, meant that you had to produce work that was incredibly obscure and hard to understand.

The irony was that despite their apparent dissimilarities conceptual art and left activism shared an ascetic attitude towards pleasure. In the late 1970s and during the '80s there was this rigorous control over how conceptual art work was presented; people resented any reading that was not psychoanalytical, an approach I regarded as reductive. The feminist conceptual artist Mary Kelly taught me at Camberwell in the '70s, and I have a lot of respect for her *Post-Partum Document* project, none the less I felt there was a denial of the subjec-tive pleasure taken in the documentation and presentation, and as a consequence a denial of the meanings that the spectator might bring to the work.

While the tools of cultural theory ought to enable you to see the complicated ways in which meanings are generated, it often seemed the opposite—as if 'theory' were being used as a way to control or pin down meaning. I found myself frequently balancing on a knife edge between a series of different kinds of arguments around theory, around pleasure, around meaning.

After I left art school in the late 1970s, I was also struggling to balance visual-art practice and political activism while working as a residential social worker. I collaborated with Mark Nash, who was editing the film-theory journal *Screen*, on a project about the history of the English garden. Mark and I came to the subject through our mothers, who, though from very different class back-grounds, were both fanatical gardeners. When my mum was in service in Leeds the lady of the house got her into gardening and cooking, which were to be her two great loves for the rest of her life.

We started with the English landscape garden in the eighteenth century. The very moment that capital was transforming the landscape, they were building these idyllic little landscapes at the back of their country houses with money from the East India Company. In *The Country and the City*, written in 1983, Raymond Williams looked at the literary influence of the rural ideal and connected this construction of nature with a particular idea of Englishness. We adapted this approach in a visual context.

There are connections between the formal aesthetics of gardens and the structure of film: both are very much about a point of view. Gardens have a kind of narrative structure. Going around classic English landscape gardens was, in a sense, a precursor of the cinematic experience. Another way in which gardening mirrored photography and film was the resistance to it being taken seriously as an art form. Mark Nash and I were to encounter this resis-tance at the Arts Council because they said that the garden was not an aesthetic. So the project was stalled: it did not get money or go into produc-tion. Yet for the last couple of centuries gardens have been one of the strongest aesthetics in Britain, and the English garden is known around the world. Also in contemporary culture, gardening is a mass activity; its popularity is reflected now in all those garden programmes on TV. However, in the late 1970s, garden-ing was dismissed as simply a middle-class activity.

Though Mark Nash and I brought different experiences to the project, we were part of a broader radical counter-culture in film that existed in London in the 1970s. People would be working for virtually no money in collectives, such as Newsreel and Berwick Street Film Collective. Groups like these would raise money in various ways by working as film technicians elsewhere and financ-ing their productions along with getting very small grants. There was a balance between making money commercially and putting it into your own work.

They were to establish a new relationship with the trade union, which was then the ACTT. The film and TV technicians union had always been a very protective kind of organisation, which had made it very difficult to pick up a union ticket. There was a sort of catch-22, where you had to be working in the industry to get a ticket, but you could not get in unless you had one. A number of activists within the union in the '70s, started to argue that the union should broaden its area of recruitment. They were earning their money in the industry, but also had an independent practice outside—Marc Karlin is a good example. They got together and put forward a case for a new union agreement that allowed people to work collectively, and this became the Workshop Agreement.

It was not just the technicians' trade unionism that barred access to much of the means of production; to meet the standards of television, you had to have skills, money and resources. TV's high production values tended to lock out a lot of material until Channel 4's challenge in the early '80s. The remit that was written into Channel 4's constitution around servicing minorities and so on, allowed work to be commissioned that was not made in the orthodox ways. The Workshop Agreement also offered different copyright relations, in which people owned the copyright of their work, and so there was creative control as well.

The Workshop Agreement, which had been developed in the late '70s, was put into place by the early '80s and met the advent of Channel 4, which is what made it financially viable. I think there were interesting contradictions. On one hand, some people got very confused about the nature of the Workshop Agreement and they started to see a potential for a funded counter-culture that would really allow people access to the means of film and video production around the country. There was also a big regional argument—because the film and television industries are so centred in London—and so there was a move to devolve some of those resources to the regions. In the Newcastle area for example there were a number of workshops—Amber, Trade, Swingbridge and Newcastle Media—and a lot of good work was done. Unfortunately the arguments used to justify funding focused on a false north/south divide argument about where the real working classes were. There was an overhang, an old-fashioned representation of the working class in heavy industry and so on, that characterised the approach despite the fact that the majority of workshop members were middle-class graduates.

Around the same time, by the late '70s and early 1980s, some of the new community-arts groups in London started to be funded by GLAA (Greater London Arts Association). This meant that the people who worked in them had jobs: they were paid, and they were extremely vociferous and articulate in forums such as GLAA. They were inclined to have a very disparaging idea of others who were working individually as visual artists, such as painters or sculptors. They saw the visual arts as somehow suspect, something to do with aesthetics or whatever. The purse-string holders were local councils, to whom the community-arts groups could appear more progressive because they would talk in terms of race and class and gender, claiming to serve and represent a constituency that justified funding. In London, from the early 1980s, the GLC took over a lot of the funding of those organisations, inviting applications on the basis of people's relationship with a community. Applications had to have a particular rubric and be written in certain kinds of terms: 'We are a workshop in Vauxhall or something, serving this community.' The visual artists, however, remained fragmented and atomised; they were the real poor relations in that period. It is a very complicated argument, because one is not averse to people being paid, but an enormous division began to appear, and as stuff started to be funded it tended to become institutionalised.

On the other hand, in the late '70s and early '80s, there were very positive results. A lot of money was being made available to moving-image production that had not previously been there so there was this chink of opportunity. Video productions were being supported by left Labour-controlled metropolitan councils; you could put in scripts and pick up funding from Channel 4, while BBC 2 started to emulate Channel 4. The result was a sea change. In the early 1980s there was this fantastic moment when you could watch certain slots on TV, such as *The 11th Hour*, and identify where you could expect to see a whole range of work, including independent productions from the past that had been bought in. They were buying lots of people's work, which created more revenue, and thus meant more work. The sort of films made by small radical groups such as the Berwick Street Film Collective in the 1970s were getting an outlet through TV by the 1980s. One example was *Song of the Shirt*, which Jonathan Curling and Sue Clayton made through Lusia Films. New film-makers, such as Richard Woolley, had their early low-budget films screened. And there were showcases of a lot of avant-garde cinema, for instance Margaret Tait, who had been making short poetic films in Scotland since the 1940s, suddenly got a wider audience. She has had a phenomenal influence on British cinema, but at that stage no one had ever seen her work on television. This was to be an amazingly educative process; people like my mum and dad would be watching all these slots on Channel 4.

You also got a sense of the impact of identity politics: feminism and questions around race and gay sexuality, for instance, started to come up on TV programmes. The commissioning of such work created a tremendous surge of expectation. People felt there was an opportunity to make films and get out on TV, and they began sending dozens of scripts of all sorts. I think most commissioning editors simply did not have any tools for selecting, so they tended to institutionalise arguments about under-representation, saying 'Well, we're getting enormous pressure from women or pressure from the Afro-Caribbean community or the Asian community.' This led to an implicit quota system, and a kind of 'PC' politics emerged about under-representation. Ironically people like myself, who had been engaged in radical politics since the '70s around feminism and the black movement, suddenly found ourselves being placed on the wrong side of the argument by those who had funding to give out.

The problem was to be that the people who were in the position to commission work became conservative about what the average person in the street wanted to watch on television. That is why Alan Fountain, who was genuinely trying to advance and broaden Channel 4 in the mid-80s, got ground down, because all the other commissioning editors were asking, 'What's this inaccessible junk you're putting out on *The 11th Hour*?'

As he would say, 'It's me who has to walk down the corridor on a Tuesday morning.' By the mid-80s, the chink that had opened on Channel 4 was already under pressure and was eventually to close down altogether because of the pressure of ratings and of commercial interests.

By the late '80s the kind of documentary films that Channel 4 would be likely to commission were those looking at single issues or taking a human-rights approach. It is not that this work is not valuable, but it was unfortunately to result in the exclusion of the more sophisticated documentaries that incorporated theoretical arguments or had a visual poeticism in their form. There was a conservatism both aesthetically and in terms of any serious political argument, and this meant that a lot of work would no longer get through.

I was one of the people who enjoyed the moment of opportunity that occurred in the early '80s. Mark Nash and I set up a production company, Zero One, and we put forward a project entitled *Acting Tapes*. The programmes that eventually went out on Channel 4 in 1984 looked at cinema acting. The theories of authorship that had dominated in film studies had settled on the director as the author of the film. Performance as a component creating meaning in a film was virtually overlooked by film theorists, with a few exceptions such as Richard Dyer's *The Stars*, published by the British Film Institute in 1979. But in popular terms people would go to see 'a De Niro movie'. It is only quite recently that they would go to 'a Martin Scorsese movie', or whatever. It was the star that was identified with the film. There was a contradiction: film theorists rarely wrote about the performances as having meaning in a film at all, whereas popular journalism concentrated on the stars all the time. So we were making a kind of bridge between these differing perceptions of film and more generally between the ideas of high and low art that have really presented immense problems for people aspiring to make films that could be relevant to contemporary Britain.

Mark Nash and I decided to do our own voice-over on *Acting Tapes* and when they were featured in a special issue of *Screen* on acting, the editorial board interviewed us both. One of the things that they really settled on was: 'Why did you do your own voice-over?' They had no problem with Mark Nash, who has a middle-class, BBC-style voice, but they had a problem with me. They beat around the bush, but eventually it came out that they felt I did not speak properly because I had a regional accent. Layers of assumptions about class still existed in media institutions in Britain.

In the late '80s I collaborated with two Melbourne-based film-makers, John Cumming and Jane Madsen, to make *First Time Tragedy, Second Time Farce* (Australia/UK 1989). By looking at the Aborigine protest at the bicentennial we made a complicated film that wove an argument around issues of national and cultural identity, and we drew on the creative documentary tradition, spanning the work of Humphrey Jennings and Chris Marker. However, when I tried to sell *First Time Tragedy* I was greeted with, 'Well, we don't do this sort of thing any more.' In fact the only TV sale in Europe that we got in the end was in Ireland—the Irish were still interested in British colonialism in a critical way. By the late '80s, when that film was completed, other sources of funding had gone, and television had become the main funders for documentaries. There was nowhere else to show work unless you got it on television. TV dominated exhibition.

What is interesting about British cultural politics, is the way in which TV not only became such an important funding source but was also the place that people came from. Take the BBC Drama Department: from the '60s, the BBC had had a policy of recruiting directors or editors from Oxbridge, and a lot of the technical posts also started to be offered to more educated people.

In contrast previous generations of camera operators in British film had been working class in origin; they were kind of apprentices. There are lovely stories of those trained by John Grierson from 1933 for the GPO Film Unit. He would recruit these working-class kids, and they would be sent out to places such as the National Gallery to learn about composition. Then they would be given the camera and told to get on with it. Those people persisted right through the post-war period carrying that amazing sense of incredibly skilled apprenticeship work. But then media production came to be seen as a much more intellectual process. People would be recruited with academic back-grounds rather than through an apprenticeship scheme, and this affected the division of labour.

The documentary tradition established by film-makers such as John Grierson and Humphrey Jennings through the GPO Film Unit and the Crown Film Unit has been a strong influence on British culture—you can see connections to the TV documentaries of the '50s and '60s. Grierson also set up documentary units around the world; so if you went to Canada or Australia, there was Grierson again. But the idea of documenting the 'real' is much more complicated than it might appear on the surface. In actual fact the very early documentaries were poetic, highly constructed films. They were very far from the fly-on-the-wall documentary techniques that have become popular again in the 1990s.

This is particularly clear in the work of Humphrey Jennings. He actually started off as a surrealist painter. The European surrealist-influenced avant-garde had taken to film and to photography in the 1920s, crossing the barrier between high and low art. In Britain, through John Grierson, Jennings was to get the opportunity to make films and find another form of expression. Jennings' work exemplifies that idea of the everyday being made extraordinary. It is marked by a kind of brilliant poetics, particularly in the combination of sound and image. He uses music to represent experiences of class, so you have a mixture of classical music with the coalminers' brass bands. However, the importance of the legacy of surrealism was written out for a long time.

One big problem encountered by the radical documentary film—makers who began working in the 1970s was that modernism had missed out Britain in lots of ways. Theatre, for example, was still mainly dominated by classical performance, and actors were being trained theatrically. This created many diffi-culties for cinematic performance in Britain. In cinema there had been two path-ways through: one was the naturalistic theatre of Stanislavski, which eventually worked its way on to the screen via Lee Strasberg and the Actors' Studio as 'the Method' in America. The other was the anti-naturalism of the Soviet avant-

First Time Tragedy,
Second Time Farce,
1989 (James Swinson:
Zero One)

garde, Bertolt Brecht and so on, which influenced European art cinema. In the late 1970s and early '80s radical British film-makers were affected by the developments that had occurred in European Art Cinema, such as Italian Neo-realism and the French New Wave, even though they were often forced to use theatrical English actors, which undermined their cinematic aspirations. The Soviet avant-garde of the 1920s was also to have an important influence particularly on documentary film-making. Marc Karlin's work is the obvious example: his films about nightcleaners in the early 1970s to his '80s series on Nicaragua constitute a body of work that is largely hidden from critical history.

The films made by Marc Karlin and others increasingly came to defy the mainstream definitions of fiction and documentary. When this kind of work started to be commissioned and broadcast by Channel 4 one of the very good things that happened was that they enabled a second wave of radical film work-shops to draw on what they had done. At the same time younger film-makers began to uncover the older legacy that was there at home, in the English tradition of the documentary. Among this second generation, whose films were starting to come on TV and into the public domain by the mid-80s, were work-shops such as the Black Audio Film Collective and Sankofa. Their films were partly commissioned because they came from an under-represented and oppressed minority. However, the work they then actually produced had an intel-

lectual integrity to it and involved a complexity that raised all those old problems about entertainment and pleasure and was itself, in turn, criticised for being
too inaccessible.

In making *Handsworth Songs* around the time of the early 1980s riots in
Birmingham and other British cities, the Black Audio Film Collective adopted
this quiet, complex approach and a kind of essay structure. John Akomfrah
used a lot of the cultural theory ideas that had come out of the Birmingham
Centre for Cultural Studies and, instead of confining himself to an essentialist range of influences in black history, also went out of his way to credit people
like Humphrey Jennings. The poetical aspect of that tradition in British cinema
was thus an influence on *Handsworth Songs*, which appeared in 1987 and is,
I think, a very important film. Akomfrah also mixed real life with archive material; extracts of films alongside scenes of drama were being introduced into
documentaries. There was a lot of crossover and experimentation with different kinds of forms and materials. Akomfrah's work, along with Isaac Julien's
at Sankofa shared the sort of aesthetics that, say, Marc Karlin's films have had,
which make it possible to introduce several levels of complexity. For instance,
Isaac Julien shot his film about Langston Hughes, *Looking for Langston*, in black
and white, and this material that Isaac shot himself met the archive material
almost seamlessly. He merges the two, and the result is that the whole film
has a sensuousness to it. The criticism of that approach was that people said
they wanted more information and content. Again there was this problem about
creative documentary film-making.

Much of this innovative and experimental work has been overlooked, one
reason being the changing trends in cultural theory. From the late 1970s there
was to be a shift away from the initial interest in resuscitating ideas from Brecht,
Walter Benjamin or the Soviet avant-garde. Those early influences were to be
sidetracked and hijacked by the Althusserian structuralist approach. Then interest in psychoanalytical theory led many feminists interested in film theory to
analyse mainly films made from Hollywood. So the thrust of much critical writing was towards gender relationships in mainstream cinema. A bizarre shift
occurred during the 1980s. Some 1970s structuralist theorists, such as Colin
MacCabe, who ended up as head of BFI Production, went through this tremendous transformation. After having produced ideological critiques of Hollywood,
they became these downmarket popularists overnight. They took on this mass
entertainment project, and the biggest irony was that they would suddenly start
confronting you with the fact that your script was too intellectual or too complex.

In Britain now virtually all of the money for film and video production, however
independent you are, directly or indirectly comes from television. And what is
offered is generally a conservative form of populism. So changes in class
might feature, but they would tend to be dealt with superficially and treated as
entertainment in a narrative form. An interesting development, however, is that
video and digital technology is making the means of media production cheaper
and thus more accessible. TV is starting to exploit that in terms of video diaries.
So once again the documentation of everyday life, is becoming a part of the

TV aesthetic, really as a cost-cutting exercise. They can send someone out with a Hi-8 camera or a new digital camcorder to shoot loads of footage. It can be about their lives or deal with an institution, such as an hotel or a hospital. When it is edited together it makes for very engaging television.

In fact this fly-on-the-wall approach that has recently become fashionable is a return to an earlier preoccupation with the rigour of documentation. For instance, during the '60s, ideas about 'direct cinema' influenced people such as Fred Wiseman in America. He would go to a hospital or the army and film there for months. Wiseman is really the quintessential fly-on-the-wall documentarist. He would just roll loads of film and get people to lose camera awareness so that he could capture all the stuff on film. Edited together it became a kind of open critique of the institution. Other examples from the USA would be the classic films of pop concerts, Pennebaker's 1967 *Monterey Pop* and Wadleigh's 1970 *Woodstock*. Both films not only showed what was going on with the stars onstage,but the camera also investigated the mass of people who attended the festivals and consequently left an amazing documentation of the period. Then of course there had been *Cinéma Vérité* in France: Jean Rouch and Chris Marker for instance were also interested in filming directly. They all aimed to reduce the director's mediation of the camera as much as possible by long takes and so on. This was supposed to produce an open film text that the audience could enter and with which it could chose its own relationship. The problem is of course that you can never not be a mediator, never not be selective.

In the early '90s I used the low-budget potential of Hi-8 video to make a 90-minute portrait of a village-development project in South India: *Bonds of Hope*. I also collaborated with the South African artist Pitika Ntuli on an experimental drama—a clash of European and African values in virtual reality. This was funded as a script by the BFI, but the prospects for funding its production were non-existent. In the mid-1990s, after Pitika returned from exile to South Africa, I realised the projects I was interested in producing were no longer fundable. The prevailing conservatism meant that to raise the money for film production you had to make enormous compromises. My art-school background and the intellectual influences on me, combined with my politics, have made me a very uncompromising sort of person in terms of innovation and experimentation with media. When you work for television you face a considerable amount of control over the political content of your films.

However, what has been happening during the '90s and early 2000 in Britain is that while the creative possibilities in documentary film-making have been closing, a growing area has been opening up in the visual arts. The visual arts have become the place where a lot of innovation and experimentation does go on and is welcomed. There is an emphasis on self-help, on artists creating the means of expression themselves. This has become practicable through new technology such as lightweight video cameras for instance.

Remarkable changes have occurred within my own lifetime in the technology available and the impact is most evident in music. From the late 1980s the richness of experimentation in dance music has been made possible by people having relatively cheap electronic equipment. They no longer use those huge and expensive 48-track recording studios—that meant that they had to go to record companies and required the marketing systems of pop music. The same thing is going to happen for all the other visual media, and a real creative and intellectual freedom has begun to open up in this area in London. There are tremendous potentialities for low-budget production, which will enable people to avoid the censorship of the market.

In 1995 I started a part-time Fine Art MA at Central St Martin's, which meant refocusing my interests in a visual-art environment and a personal shift towards doing video installation. *Street* was in the MA Fine Art Show at St Martin's in 1997 and looks at the experience of the city from the street. I was interested in seeing the city horizontally, from above, from tower blocks and the tops of buses, so I installed a video projector and projected these images on to the floor, using ideas around montage to examine how you look at the street. I have gone back really to investigating the relationship between the movie camera and consciousness—in this case consciousness of the city. Looking at street culture is a deliberate attempt to get out of the concentration of cinema on domestic space, on a cluster of characters, or on the family as the centre of drama. It goes out to see what consciousness exists when you are atomised on the street.

When I was working on this installation I put my experience as a documentary film-maker to the back of my mind, but there were some fantastic accidents. For instance once I was filming off the top of a Hackney tower block, and it just happened that I arrived on a late Saturday afternoon when all these African weddings were going on. So there is a phenomenal piece of activity, with people in amazing costumes turning up while the kids are playing in the same space. The notion of public space and how people use it comes through on the video installation. It also demonstrates ideas about hybridity, which have come from the loosening up of identity politics. You can already see the different cultural cross-references in music, and that is now starting to happen visually. I love that bringing together of different things.

I teach Cinema Studies and Cultural Studies at Central St Martin's and Camberwell, so I am very much involved in the relationship between theory and practice in the art-school environment. Cultural theory had a profound impact on art schools in the 1980s. But recently among young British artists there has been a reaction against the dead hand of theory, or against prescriptive theory anyway. As an art educator I am very conscious of the dangers of art students just going right back into an anti-intellectual perspective. It is a case of arguing for theory as being enabling, of convincing them that it is good to read and to confront difficult ideas. I am trying to get over to them that being aware of the philosophical basis of what you are doing actually is part of the creative relationship. You need to have the confidence to take the arguments and use them to guide your work.

James Swinson interview by Sheila Rowbotham, 28 June 1998, edited James Swinson and Sheila Rowbotham

Section V
TESTIFYING TO THEIR TIMES
Sheila Rowbotham

This section consists of statements by four very different radical documentary film-makers. They talk about their own work and about the context in which their films were made. From the late 1960s small left-wing film collectives began to appear in Britain, influenced by the wave of radicalism that followed the student-worker rebellion in France during May 1968. Cinema Action, which Marc Karlin joined in 1969, was set up in 1968 by Gustav Schlacke and Ann Lamche to make documentaries about industrial and community struggles. Early members included David Adelstein, Jane Grant and Dana Purvis, along with Richard Mordaunt, Humphrey Trevelyan and Marc Karlin.[1]

Becoming increasingly unhappy with Cinema Action's approach to filming, Marc Karlin left in 1971 and formed the Berwick Street Film Collective with Richard Mordaunt, Humphrey Trevelyan and James Scott. The group worked on material shot while they had been with Cinema Action and produced *Ireland Behind the Wire*. In the early 1970s Marc Karlin, Humphrey Trevelyan and Mary Kelly began filming the Women's Liberation Workshop's campaign to unionise night cleaners. Instead of a short agitational film, the complex and exploratory *Night Cleaners* was to appear in 1975, followed by a second part, which focused on the life of a black cleaner, *The Seven Dreams of Myrtle* (1976).[2]

These two reflective studies of London night cleaners were influenced by the film-makers' links to the women's liberation movement. It was unusual at that time to look at marginal women workers' conditions, and the films also covered their lives at home as well as their personal dreams.

In *For Memory* (1982), Marc Karlin explored how memory is preserved and handed on, and how dissident recollections are blocked and contained. In *Utopias* (1987) and *Between Times* (1993) he attempted to understand the fundamental shifts that had occurred within the labour movement and the left in the long period of Conservative rule. He also searched out sources for alternative visions of socialism in Britain. A series of four films about the Nicaraguan revolution, made with his wife, the anthropologist Hermione Harris, examined the dilemmas of putting socialism into practice. They were shown on Channel 4 in 1985. He returned to make *Scenes from a Revolution* (Channel 4, 1990).

During the second half of the 1990s he turned towards the conditions of his own work in the media and the difficulties in testifying as a radical film-maker in a period of defeat for the left. His work, which became much more abstract in content, expresses a sense of cultural isolation. *The Serpent* (1997) was a fictional representation of the impact of Rupert Murdoch on the media. While *The Haircut* (1998) protested against the new conventionality of New Labour.

Marc Karlin played an active role in setting up the Independent Film-makers' Association (IFA) in 1974 and was involved in the film union, the Association of Cinematograph, Television and Allied Technicians (ACTT). He also tried to develop an independent means of exhibition and distribution for left films through the Other Cinema. When this failed he encouraged the alliance between the IFA and the Channel 4 Group, which campaigned for a public-service channel.[3] The campaigners' document, *Channel 4 and Innovation: the Foundation*, came out in February 1980 and recommended that 10 per cent of the new Channel's budget should be used to encourage the regionally based film-collectives' work. It became known as 'The Foundation Document'.[4]

Not all their demands were met; however, Alan Fountain's appointment as the Commissioning Editor for Independent Film and Video at Channel 4 secured the independents an unprecedented opportunity to make films that could be shown to large audiences. Part of Channel 4's remit was to provide a space for voices that were not being heard in the mainstream media; while the regional workshops were accepted as a crucial means of extending and democratising film educa-tion. Marc Karlin helped to negotiate terms for the independent film-makers on Channel 4, playing a crucial role in enabling funds to go into radical film-making and the creation of a regionally based workshop infrastructure.[5]

He continued to agitate through the 1990s against the pressure for high ratings on television and for space for contemplative, challenging films. He helped start *Vertigo* magazine in 1993 and supported a new cinema, the Lux in Hoxton, London, which screened radical and experimental work from the late 1990s. Marc Karlin died in January 1999. In his obituary in the *Independent* John Wyver described him as 'the most significant unknown film-maker work-ing in Britain during the past three decades'.[6]

While Marc Karlin had been trained in drama, Murray Martin's background was fine-art at school in Newcastle. After a spell in London learning about film-making, he went back up north in 1968 and helped to form the film collective Amber, with Graham Denham and Sirkka-Liisa Konttinen, joined a little later by Peter Roberts and Lorna Powell. Amber's films have been about the docks, mines, factories and fishing industry of the North East and have charted the changes in working-class communities over the last three decades. They have produced both campaigning films and evocative, romantic portrayals of ways of working and living threatened by economic change. They have also caught personal dreams and pleasures in films such as *Keeping Time* (1983), about a dancing school in North Shields, and *The Writing in the Sand* (1991), which shows an urban family's day out on the windy beaches of north-east England.

Amber made not only documentaries but has also done animation and several fictional films. *Dream On* finally went out on general release in 1992. Later *The Scar* (1998), Amber's film about the effects of strip-mining on family relationships, was shown on television and won four awards, including the Prix Europa Special Prize. Amber is run as a co-operative: money is ploughed back and shared equally. As well as making films, the group has shown films. From the late 1970s to the early 1980s the workshop ran a small cinema and a photography gallery, organising screenings and debates, and also running a pub. Amber set a precedent in joining ACTT as a self-contained 'shop'. They were involved in the IFA, arguing forcefully for unionisation. They have always encouraged the development of independent film workshops in 'the regions' and collective working practices. Murray Martin played a leading part in the establishment of the National Organisation of Workshops in 1984.[7]

Despite the conservative ethos that prevailed in the 1980s, this decade was to see an expansion in radical documentary film-making in Britain. As James Swinson notes in Section IV, the implications of gender, race and sexual orientation were to be raised by a new generation of film-makers. This shift in awareness had its origins in the social movements of the 1970s, but a combination of circumstances instituted the means for it to be expressed through film.

By the early 1980s the IFA had been able to negotiate an agreement with the ACTT. This 'Workshop Declaration' allowed 'franchised workshops' to work with less crew than the union usually required. Not only were existing collectives franchised under the Agreement, but new groups also formed around the country, for instance in Cardiff, Birmingham and the East Midlands. The Workshop Declaration also encouraged 'minorities'. It led to the creation of new women's film groups, the Leeds Animation Workshop for example, and black groups such as Sankofa and the Black Audio Film Collective were able to start up.[8]

The late 1970s demonstrations on race, struggles around immigration legislation and conflict with the police, were to influence the policies of the left Labour Greater London Council which, in the first half of the 1980s, pioneered 'equal opportunities' on the North American model among its own staff and in its funding policies. The GLC also developed a local economic strategy on 'Cultural Industries' and was able to fund co-operative businesses through the Greater London Enterprise Board.

Isaac Julien,[9] like James Swinson, entered the independent sector in this extraordinary period when not only Channel 4 but also the GLC were funding film collectives. Influenced by experimental film-making and the theoretical debates about film, he has sought to express contemporary experiences of black people in Britain in relation to wider questions of culture. Isaac Julien's work has rejected enclosure in 'race' as a 'problem' and the subordinate placing of blackness in opposition to whiteness as the norm. Instead, in films such as *The Passion of Remembrance* (1986), he has explored the implications of cultural disconnection and fragmentation. His films express a creative resistance to constant definion through the fears of others—those with power. Rejecting essentialist definitions, his work is infused with a fluid and lyrical sensuality and a desire to flow over boundaries of space and time. In both *Territories* (1984) and *Looking for Langston* (1989) he uses archive material, showing how the past is perceived in the present. Isaac Julien expresses mixed feelings about the theoretical consequences of the equal-opportunity based funding criteria. It enabled Sankofa to be created and gave him the opportunity to work. On the other hand, equal opportunities and some versions of multiculturalism fostered fixed and abstracted definitions of identity.

By the mid-1980s various interpretations of multiculturalism were having an impact on television. Farrukh Dhondy became Commissioning Editor of Multicultural Programmes at Channel 4 in 1984. Committed to the development of a 'black independent sector', he commissioned Darcus Howe and Tariq Ali to create a radical current-affairs programme, the *Bandung File*, which, from 1985, replaced *Black on Black* and *Eastern Eye*. Bandung's programmes were to combine black, Asian and Third World news and culture, covering a range of international social and cultural issues. The intention was to put points of view in black and Asian communities that were being marginalised.[10]

Tariq Ali and Darcus Howe were not concerned about experimenting with form; their aim was to find the most direct means of communication possible.[11] They proceeded to extend the meaning of multiculturalism by raising cultural debates that would not otherwise have been aired. They also gave the term a radical edge by covering political conflicts and theoretical differences as well as instances of solidarity. As a result Bandung's films constitute a unique record of mainly working-class Afro-Caribbean and Asian communities, during the 1980s and early '90s. Gita Sahgal's work at Bandung focused especially on women in the Asian community, raising questions about how they were represented on television, as well as those about gender conflicts and the efforts of religious fundamentalism to redefine and circumscribe women's place.

Paradoxically opportunities developed for a new generation of radical film-makers at a time when the politics of the country were being moved to the right by the Conservatives. The cultural gains of the 1980s were based on the resistance of the 1970s, but they occurred in a transformed context, which in the long run, was to alter their course and result in unintended implications.

Notes

1. See Dickinson, *Rogue Reels*, pp.35–45, 263–88.
2. On *Night Cleaners*, see P. Wright, 'A Passion for Images', Radio 3 interview with Marc Karlin, *Vertigo*, 9, summer 1999. On the women's liberation campaign see Alexander, 'The Night Cleaners', pp.257–69.
3. J. Ellis, 'Conscience of Radicals', Obituary, *Guardian*, 25 January 1999.
4. Dickinson, *Rogue Reels*, pp.57–8.
5. Ellis, 'Conscience of Radicals'.
6. J. Wyver, 'Marc Karlin', Obituary, *Independent*, 28 January 1999.
7. On Amber see Dickinson, Cottringer and Petley, 'Workshops: A Dossier', pp.16–17; Dickinson, interview with Murray Martin, 1995, *Rogue Reels*, pp.247–62, Caughie and Rockett, *The Companion to British and Irish Cinema*, pp.163–4.
8. See Caughie and Rockett, and Dickinson, *Rogue Reels*, pp.158–9.
9. On Isaac Julien see Hill, *British Cinema in the 1980s*, pp.219–40; Thompson and Bordwell, *Film History*, p.691; Roberts, *The Art of Interruption*, p.156.
10. See Pines, *Black and White in Colour*, pp.168–72.
11. S. Rowbotham, interview with Tariq Ali, September 1999.

11 Making Images Explode

Marc Karlin

Marc Karlin worked as an independent radical film-maker from the late 1960s with Cinema Action, the Berwick Street Film Collective and Lusia Films. His films include *Night Cleaners, For Memory, Utopias* and more recently *The Hair Cut.* He helped to found *Vertigo* magazine and was working on films about Milton and about writing history before he died in January 1999.

I was always interested in films as a kid, the cinema the one place where I could be away from what I wanted to be away from, which was most of what was going on around me at the time. I lived in Paris as a child, and in a working-class suburb, Le Perreux, the Palais du Parc used to have acrobats, jugglers and singers in the intervals between the short film and the feature. The whole thing was an extraordinary event. But what I really loved most about the cinema was the pictures of Hollywood stars—Humphrey Bogart or Ava Gardner in the foyer—they were done in that kind of technicolor colour. I just wanted all of those people in my room.

After school, in the mid-60s, I studied theatre direction in London at the Central School of Speech and Drama. To cut a very long story short, the staff was deemed to be not right for the school, and when they sacked its main members, we immediately resigned. Laurence Olivier came to lecture us—if we were to leave the school we would never work in the theatre again. At this point Stephen Fagan, who is a playwright now, laughed out loud because it was just so stupid. The whole class resigned. This was a total and complete rebellion, way before the London School of Economics. We formed our own drama school which started off in a church hall, where now they have a big building, and it is a leading drama school called Drama Centre London. But I was never that keen on theatre. I used to escape as much as I could to go to the cinema. I had an extraordinarily close friendship with James Scott, a film-maker and painter, and we used to go to the National Film Theatre every night. That is where I learnt most about cinema.

My first film was an interview with an American deserter, Philip Wagner. We showed this interview—it was just an interview—with Philip to the press in a private cinema, and all hell broke loose. At the time Harold Wilson had said, clearly in parliament, that there were no deserters in England. The papers went bonkers.

Philip had deserted from Vietnam and had an extraordinary escape. He landed in England, knew no one and had nowhere to go until he met a woman when it was raining in Piccadilly and she took him in. What caught me about the story was not so much Vietnam, though that was obviously bad enough, but the more personal events. I was a member of the Stop It Committee, which was mainly Americans against the war in Vietnam, but there was a split between those who supported resistance to the war in Vietnam and those who supported deserters as well: Clancy Sigal, for instance, would not support deserters. But I did, so I made this film.

I was dissatisfied with it, so I made *American Choice '68*, where I filmed Philip in Paris, and just as I was beginning to edit May '68 blew up. The only films the lab workers would process were ones about workers. There was a strike of editors, and I was impounded, as it were. I was told, 'OK, if you're with the revolution, this is what you do, you go, do this, do that. You do news-reels for the revolution', and so I was sent to a railway depot. I kind of agreed with this as a sentiment. But to tell you the truth I didn't really understand what was going on.

So I got stuck in this railway depot, miles away from anywhere, and it was hilarious. I fell into a friendship with a railway driver who thought that as the revolution had happened he could meet Simone Signoret through me, because I was a film-maker and she was a leftie. He'd always been in love with her on screen and was desperate to meet her. He felt that was what a revolution should be about. After May I did happen to meet Simone Signoret when she saw my film on the American deserter. She was very helpful, and she praised the film and was really very nice. I told her about this guy I had met who was absolutely in love with her. I wish I had met her before: wouldn't it have been wonderful to have brought him Simone Signoret?

Meeting that driver was the first time I was brought into real contact with a working-class person. I made a film of him, *Dead Man's Wheel*, of which I am very proud. It was screened at the National Film Theatre and apparently is shown constantly in France. I brought him with a crew to the Sorbonne, to the square, and I shot him as he was coming down the road. It was so extraordinary, a complete circus: there were Africans beating drums, magicians and jugglers, and girls with no bras. He couldn't believe what he was seeing: he was a Catholic, a left Catholic, very, very Catholic. He came into the courtyard of the Sorbonne, and because we were a film crew people began gathering round him. He started explaining about his work to the students, miming what he did in the train. Every 15 seconds he had to clasp and unclasp the wheel, otherwise the train would stop. It was to stop him falling asleep and was called 'the dead man's wheel': he explained how ill drivers were, because of doing this every fifteen seconds. It just tortured them. As he explained this, you can see the camera going round the students: they are completely bog-eyed about the worker, May 1968, the possibilities, the world that he came from. It was a hell of an introduction for me, that moment. A moment that you try to expand for years and years—but obviously you can't.

The upshot of it was that this man was caught. He had driven the train to Paris, but he had a family in Lyon. When the revolution happened, the strike, he was stuck in Paris, stuck in this depot, where they had dormitories. He showed me the conditions, just awful. He was so enamoured with what was happening that he left his family for that month and remained in Paris all the time. He just thought the whole thing totally extraordinary. Then the month of May closed its doors, and, like an idiot, I thought, I've got to finish the film. All the other French guys went on holiday—Louis Malle, William Klein, Claude Chabrol—they all went. And I thought, No. So I finished the film.

During May '68 I had met Chris Marker—the monk. He was doing cinetracks with Godard, very sort of messagy films: five photographs, little message and so on. I did find that completely mad. I did not know what they were doing. The idea of seeing a fist, then a photograph of a girl and then saying, 'La force,' and another photograph, 'et' and all that. Marker was doing slightly more poetic ones.

Then Marker formed his film group, SLON, named after the Russian agit-prop group, and made a film about Alexander Medvedkin, who had been on the agitprop film train that went around Russia. The Russian film-makers had laboratories on board and did extraordinary films, a famous example is one of a train in which the coupling mechanism does not work because the people who are building it are in one factory and those producing the coupling mech-anism are in another part. Medvedkin would film the train, then the coupling and bring them together, saying, 'This is what you're doing wrong.' Chris Marker did an interview with Medvedkin and was responsible for getting him out of the cupboard, as it were, under Brezhnev. Marker called him the Bolshevik Chaplin. He discovered his famous *The Last of the Bolsheviks*, a very funny film about collectivisation and the Russian love affair with tractors, that made fun of the rich peasant as the enemy.

When Marker formed SLON, ideas about agitprop films were going round. Cinema Action had already started in England by 1969 when I joined it. There was a relationship to the Russians: Vertov, the man with the movie camera, Medvedkin and his Russian agitprop train; the idea of celebrating life and revo-lution on film, and communicating that. Medvedkin had done that by train. SLON and Cinema Action both did it by car. Getting a projector, putting films in the boot, and off you went and showed films—which is what we did.

In the mid-1970s I did the English version of Chris Marker's *The Train Rolls On*. If Chris asked you to do something you did it: there was no question. I remember one instance when he asked me to go to the Peugeot car factory, where he wanted to make a film about car workers and could not do so because he was known to be a leftie. Peugeot would not allow it, so we wrote a letter saying we were making a film for the Common Market, that Peugeot was an essential car factory and blah blah. This is one of my greatest coups—letter straight back, 'Of course, come.' And, 'Would you like to interview the managing director in Paris?' So we said yes. We didn't put any film in the camera. When we went to Peugeot they put us up in their workers hotel. I complained, so they moved us to a luxury hotel, which was just wonderful. We went into the factory, and I suddenly realised, How the fuck am I going to film something so boring? All they did was boom, boom, boom. Then I noticed that the workers on the assembly line would come up like fish for air. They would touch, and they would open their mouths. The Peugeot people were so canny, because they would put together a Moroccan, Portuguese, French and an Italian, so no one could actually speak to each other because nobody knew each other's language. That was why an excessive amount of touching was going on. I said to the cameraman, 'Look, that's how we film. We don't film the work, because we can show that in twenty or thirty seconds. But we can film these people gasping for air. Or touching, whatever.' That is what we filmed. And then the audience had to imagine, What does it take for somebody to come up for air like that? Or touch? We have seen thousands of takes, news shots or whatever, of women doing chickens, or checking, of people working. But nobody knows what it is. They have not really seen. It has not been shot properly. Those are the questions; when you talk about images of labour, how do you film labour?

There is that story about a factory during the Second World War. The resistance fighter Harry Rée went to the Peugeot directors and said to them, 'You've got two choices. One, the RAF bombs you completely. Two, you allow my men to plant plastic bombs where you're building tanks for Germany, and we let your cars go.' It was total blackmail, wonderful. Peugeot had no alternative and the resistance blew up the part of Peugeot that was building tanks.

Chris Marker had this extraordinary idea in the early 1980s, which I wish he had stuck to: he asked left-wing film-makers and groups to send him their offcuts, because he wanted to make a film about what the left censored. What shots left film-makers did not want for different reasons. And they all sent him stuff. Because Chris was *le maître*, yes? He wrote to me and said, 'Have you got any of this, that and the other?' and I said yes.

Chris had a garage, a huge studio with drainpipes all across it. It was vast, and he put these little rolls of films all along the drainpipes, and then he divided them into countries, so you had Colombia, Peru, Cuba, Africa and so on. I entered this garage to find all these films from all these countries: the whole world was there. Everybody had sent the little bits of film that they had left out of their films. Right at the end there was Chris Marker on a platform with his editing table, and he looked like God. You had to walk past all these films to reach him and sit down. He used some of the stuff. But it was a different film that he made by the end: *Le Fond de l'air est rouge*.

Again I did the English version, a two-and-a-half hour film that Channel 4 showed. It was a reflection on the left, two-and-a-half hours on that and the '60s. In it is the Avignon Festival, which the Maoists broke up. The director of the Avignon Festival, Jean Vilar, was head of the National Theatre, a really brilliant director, on the left and committed to popular theatre; the Maoists nearly killed him. They brutalised the place. So Chris Marker had Simone Signoret reading this extraordinary text on the destruction of the left; it is full of the puns and metaphors that Chris Marker can do.

When it came to the English version, the actress we had cast to read the text, said, 'I'm terribly sorry, I do not understand a word of it.' I asked her if she was interested in politics at all, but she said she was not. How could I get her to play Simone Signoret's voice, giving a letter to the Maoists about how the left destroys and eats its own children? The only way I could think of doing it was to find out if she had any children. She had three. I suggested she remember when they had the colic and just talk as she would to them as she comforted and patted them. She did it and she was superb. She sounds like a wise, political mother figure. It was wonderful, even though she didn't understand a word she was reading.

When I joined Cinema Action there was no question of making documentaries for television. We showed our films in left meetings, where we would set up a screen, do leaflets and so on. It was often hilarious. I remember showing a Cinema Action film on housing in a big hall in the Bull Ring area of Birmingham. It started with machine-gun noises, and Horace Cutler, the hated Tory head of the Greater London Council, being mowed down. The whole place just stopped and looked, but, of course, as soon as you got talking heads, people arguing or living their ordinary lives, doing their washing or whatever, we lost the audience. I learnt something through seeing that.

We were shooting a film about a productivity deal at Vauxhall, in Birkenhead, with the shop stewards. One of them was a Trotskyist Socialist Labour League (SLL) and the other a Communist but they had one thing in common: the two of them were in love with the same girl in Cinema Action, Dana, who had fantastic legs. The ideological battle between the Communist and the SLL was really a total cover for romance, because they were really after Dana. It was just a nightmare. They would wait for us to give them a lift across the Mersey back to Liverpool. The SLL and the Communist shop stewards fought over who was going to be dropped off last. Finally, it just so happened that the SLL man won the heart of Dana, and the Communist guy was left out of it. So we were *personae non gratae* with the official labour movement, which was mainly Communist dominated. It was completely insane!

We wanted to show Third World films to the labour movement and one time we screened a film on the Venezuelan insurrection in 1948. Gustav Schlacke, the German who had started Cinema Action, would come up and lecture these guys in his guttural German-English. The English shop stewards were so amazed, that the guy had the arrogance, the nerve, to do this, that they did not say a word. But after this Dana incident, the official labour movement made sure that we would not get near anyone.

Schlacke had a thing about the materialist dialectic of film. Somehow or other—and I can't tell you how or why—this meant in every eight frames that you had to have a cut. Schlacke justified this with some theoretical construct, but it made his films totally invisible. After a time I just got fed up. James Scott, Humphrey Trevelyan and I started the Berwick Street Film Collective and later on I was to join Lusia Films.

There was a rhetoric of workers doing their own films in the late '60s and early '70s, but it never worked. Now with new technology, families have videos, and they film each other endlessly. However, film-making is a mystery, a craft, that has to be learnt, though you can train people, and it can be demystified. The Ford workers recently made their own video of a strike, but you could give people proper training to do this. What is very interesting is that the Liverpool dockers who were on strike for two years are now working with Sally Hibbin, Jimmy McGovern and Irvine Welsh in workshops, teaching each other.

Night Cleaners, 1975
(Berwick Street Film
Collective)

In the early 1970s there was a women's liberation campaign to recruit cleaners into a trade union and so the Berwick Street Film Collective did *Night
Cleaners*, which we finished in 1975. At that time one of the biggest entertainment corporations was MCA. Their offices, a massive old building, were
in Green Park. Very bravely the cleaners let us in, knowing they could lose
their jobs, but we managed to fiddle it with the cleaning company—I can't
remember what we said, but something totally fictitious about the documentary we were making. In any case we filmed the two ladies, one black, and
one white, with whom the film opens. It was amazing just to see them clean
those offices. They were totally at home with the architecture of it. It was
ghostly, something very strange.

I thought, as did James, that the whole thing was epic in an odd way, much
like the man who was in love with Simone Signoret. It was London, and it was
night. Seeing these groups of women in that setting was really awesome. It
was as if these people owned London, in a very strange way, owned the
offices. They were the kings and queens of that night. I was struck by the
anonymity of those women: they leave no shadow, they are born, they live,
they die, and that is it. People who leave no mark, no trace, nothing, who merge
with the night. And the fact was that a lot of the women were immigrants or
exiles. I have always felt that very deeply: the anonymity, on the one hand,
and the vanity of most of the world, on the other. One only has to think of how
one is supported everyday by armies of anonymous people, literally armies.

There was, at the root of it, a concern about revealing. That is why there is
that very slow shot, a close-up of a cleaner, who has bulging fish eyes. To me
that is a beautiful shot. It is accused of romanticism and all that nonsense, but
I wanted that, I just wanted people to look at that face for a long time, and I
hoped that close-up would mean that people would do that. At the Ministry of
Defence when the cleaners won the strike, I have got a shot of Lizzie, who

looked like a 1920s' filmstar, the joy, the eyes, everything: it ends *Night Cleaners*. I always remember, too, the beautiful close-up of Jean Mormont when the awful union man is speaking. I was in my element, because these women, like Jean, were gorgeous, completely gorgeous. It is interesting to ask why now these shots are impossible. You have to reframe them, to rethink them for people to look at again, to see properly. Or to be given the opportunity to see.

I wanted to make more than just an agitprop film, and of course I got really banged for it. But *Night Cleaners* now is having a second life and is being distributed all over. It was shown at a conference at Leeds University on *Work and the Image* in 1998 by Griselda Pollock, and Sally Alexander, who was in the women's liberation campaign, was there. Apparently, *Night Cleaners* went down a bomb with the new generation. Griselda was totally amazed, as indeed was Sally.

I was not a feminist, I just thought these women were wonderful and lovely—and mothers. It all got mixed up: the record of those voices and the distance between the women's movement and the cleaners, and trying to bridge that, while attempting to articulate the truth made it very painful to edit. And then there was the way they were treated by the unions, who basically could not deal with them. The Transport and General Workers had become so large and so dominated by the recognition of big establishments that they had no idea how to deal with women who worked in a fragmented space, away from each other. I shall never forget the union official saying, 'Well, at the end of the day, you know, you have to measure up whether your dues would add up.' God!

The second night-cleaners' film was *Seven Dreams of Myrtle*, a close-up of a night cleaner from Guyana, Myrtle, who was working at the Ministry of Defence. *Seven Dreams of Myrtle* is the most beautiful thing I have ever done. One of the things that really got me was the way workers were always portrayed in left films in terms of oppression or militancy, as if these people had no personal autobiography at all. It was as if there were no other reason, no *raison d'être*, to film them other than for their militancy—what showed on their badges or whatever.

When I studied theatre direction, I learnt a technique: you ask somebody to describe a dramatic event that happened to them, but you don't ask them to describe the event itself, but only the room or the space in which it happened. By the intonation of what they are saying you realise that something dramatic is happening in this room, though you don't know what it is. I did this in *Seven Dreams of Myrtle*. When, she describes the hospital room during the very painful birth of her child. You see her face changing, accompanied by the sound of her voice. I did time-lapse portraits of her face, with the sound accompaniment. It's actually very beautiful.

For Memory followed. I started writing it 1975 and shot it between '77 and '78. It was done as a co-production between the British Film Institute and the BBC, because Barry Gavin, a really good film-maker, wanted me to make a film independently and for the BBC. This was unknown at the time, but somehow we got it through. In 1982 *For Memory* was the first independent film to be shown on the BBC. It created a great clamour, but after *For Memory* had appeared it was to become more common for independent film-makers to get their work on TV.

For Memory is about memory and history, because I don't have a history, and I have a very bad memory. It was occasioned by *Holocaust*, that stupid Hollywood series that had such a huge effect. The question the film asks is: how could a documentary photograph die so soon—it was then only about thirty years—and be taken over by a fiction? The fictionalisation was so vulgar and so horrible.

I built an imaginary city in a studio, which now looks like Docklands, but at the time I didn't know that of course. I just got architects' models and started literally building a city. I made a camera to move around it, and tried to imagine how the city remembers and forgets. It is not simply that modern cities are amnesiac, because history is all around. As the film says, a citizen can forget, but if there is a danger of too much forgetting he can be pulled by a leash, by a television play, *Henry V*, or whatever it might be. But this is a very specific relationship to history. So it was an essay on a city that forgets and remembers, and how it forgets and how it remembers. The third part was about those who are not allowed in the city with their memories—the socialists. They are outside the city's bounds, and their memories have not yet been incorporated.

One episode was about a historian, Cliff Williams, who collected miners' tools and photographs of the mine at Clay Cross. When he held this exhibition there, you see all the old miners coming back to touch their tools. The second episode was the historian E. P. Thompson at Burford, giving a lecture on the Levellers, who were shot there in the seventeenth century for refusing to fight in Ireland, and the third was Charlie Goodman, an anti-fascist fighter at Cable Street, East London. Charlie made this wonderful mural there, and he guides us through it in the film. So *For Memory* was about trying to get those histories recognised: the Levellers, the Clay Cross miners, the Battle of Cable Street and so on.

After the part on the city, the film starts off in the hospital with people with Alzheimer's disease. There was a photographic project, to give them things to touch, photographs to help them remember and so on. You realised the ruin of memory is so easy:, these people were active, and suddenly they can not remember what happened the last second. They have a long-term memory, but they had no language to capture it; they jumble up the words all the time. The fragility is unbelievable, fragile ruins.

I was interested in that fragility and how those who are outside the city, who have no control, dealt with their memory. I remember in Clay Cross, these old miners, especially one with glasses, very thin, turning up to touch a pickaxe and explaining how he used it. And then, just after him, lots of little, little, children, five year olds, coming up to see us. The camera could hardly get them in, and it just got their tops, looking at their village, Clay Cross, as it was. And Cliff Williams, giving us the lecture on the history of Clay Cross, the pride with which he did it.

Utopias, 1987
(Lusia/Channel 4)

I can't give you a reason why I felt the whole thing was somehow tottering, about to roll. What is funny is that when Edward Thompson is speaking there is a green banner behind him and he. He talks about rosemary being the flower of remembrance, at that point suddenly the green banner collapses. A unique left thing, we are never able to pin up anything properly. Everything's fragile, unless you store it, keep it and communicate it.

I was filming *Utopias* in 1986, around the time Margaret Thatcher said she aimed to destroy socialism once and for all. I was determined to say otherwise, obviously. I wanted to do portraits of different socialisms, take ideas about it and so on, but to put them all in the one boat. *Utopias* was like a banquet table. I liked the idea of having somewhere all these people could be together, where David Widgery, you [Sheila Rowbotham] and Jack Jones, Sivanandan, Bob Rowthorn, and the miner's wife were all going to be there. All their visions of socialism were great. I am totally naive, but I shall remain that to the end, so I just wanted them all at table. Can you imagine it? No: But the film did. I have never understood sectarianism. What I wanted to do was to create a kind of alliance between Jack Jones and, funnily enough, David Widgery, who I always thought wanted to make socialism into a synthesis between the Rolling Stones and the AEUW, though I never worked out how that could be done. But, nevertheless, it was to show the range from Jack Jones to you, as it were, from top to end, and it was on Channel 4 in 1987.

Out of the people who participated in the film, the only person who didn't like it was Widgery. He wanted to be more an upfront, in-your-face, rock'n'roller doctor: It was too sedate for him. It was actually a very successful film, both in terms of audience, and the fact that they showed it twice and all that shit. But, yes, it was trying to make sense of what was happening. Then there was *Between Times*, which was shown on Channel 4 in 1993. I did not have enough time to get the voices right, but it was trying to set up a debate between the *Marxism Today* version of socialism and what you might call the disorganised or what-ever type, to get the best out of these two, really, and see where they connected. I was really trying to make sense of being between these two myself.

I had helped form the Independent Film Makers' Association,(IFA) but when the Independents organised themselves into a Guild and were asking for 25 per cent of the BBC's output, I opposed that because it had no cultural remit. The campaign for Channel 4 in the early '80s came partly out of this situation. The Channel 4 Campaign Group was a very strange alliance of Marxists, Surrealists, lunatics and entrepreneurs—the entrepreneurs using us, and us using the entre-preneurs. And it was very successful. We established Channel 4 in the way in which we wanted. A crucial ally was Willie Whitelaw, who as a Tory grandee, did not want Channel 4 to be vulgar, like an ITV2. Channel 4 was to be established in 1981 because of a whole series of conjunctions at the time.

It was an attempt to have an outlet for those who had no means of expres-sion on the other channels. That was really it. Of course that has changed a lot, completely in fact. The irony was that the campaign for Channel 4 was to become a kind of Trojan Horse for Thatcherism. But that is inevitable if you are not in power: you advance something, and, as William Morris says, it comes in a way that you had not envisaged. We had initially fought against the BBC using contracting out as a way of getting rid of their own staff and so on. But many independent film-makers started to lose their original *raison d'être*; they forgot why they wanted to be there in the first place and became entrepreneurs. This was when I learnt that when certain so-called Marxists are given capital they think it is really wonderful, and they start behaving even worse than the capitalists. There was such evidence of that. And there is now. People who would exploit unemployed 16 year olds, people who made shitty programmes just to go on making more programmes and more money. You have almost to freeze-frame those people and look at them hard for what they are. It is unbelieveable how they have really betrayed everything. It is a long story, which I don't want to go into, but it wasn't a shock, because I saw it in Nicaragua. I am always amazed, though, that people forget so soon.

When I was filming in Nicaragua, an electrician who had been a guerilla during the revolution lent us some cables and one so-called Marxist, who was in charge of cinema, brought him in to the office. I shall never forget it—this man, who had been a peasant, took off his hat and held it by his crutch, with his head down, while this guy had the temerity to lecture him. So I lost my rag; I just went completely apeshit; I could not believe it. I don't understand how that process happens and nor do I know how such people can live with themselves. I really do not. But they do.

I have got into huge arguments with people on the left especially in the Socialist Workers' Party about my films. I had a big fight with Jim Nichol for instance over *Night Cleaners*, and Paul Foot attacked *Utopias* at the memorial meeting after David Widgery's death, claiming the film portrayed him as a socialist dissident. I was so angry, furious. We were actually filming at the memorial at the time, and the technicians were just as incensed.

Then I got in terrible trouble with the series of Nicaraguan films that I did, from both the Nicaraguan authorities and the Nicaraguan Solidarity Committee because I did not portray leadership. I have never been too interested in leaders, which is a fault of mine, maybe, but I just don't like it very much, though I can see that a poor country does need heroes. I think it was true I didn't understand the poverty enough, nor that need—there was such an emphasis on leadership. Indeed when the leaders would go to the square and millions of people went to hear them, the slogan was, 'National Direction, give us our orders', which I just could not bear. I could not stomach it: it should have been the other way round. I saw too many instances of authoritarian bullying, stupidity and censorship, and not having confidence to say to the people what was happening. Even though the kids were coming back in coffins. I spent a lot of my time in the cemetery with the mothers of the dead, who were a bit like night cleaners: robust, warm, just amazing. They were like the waves of the revolution, you know, they really were. Some were market women, with massive arms, almost a sort of brutality. Their sons came back in coffins, and they went to maintain the graves, and every Sunday we would be with them. Fifteen year olds, fourteen year olds, getting killed in the Contra war.

If I went back now I know they would still be there. But Nicaragua will have forgotten completely. And what did they die for? That is a question one really has to ask. Those fifteen year olds. There were beautifully painted monuments built with streets named after them, but, Managua having the climate it has, the rain, sand and dust would soon pulverise them. Even after only three years you could see the change. Just before the elections when the Sandinista government was defeated, I returned to make the last film, *Scenes from a Revolution*, going back to the places to which I had gone. We filmed the change. Even then I was very aware that those boys would be forgotten, as indeed Nicaragua has been forgotten. No longer in the headlines, so why bother?

It is difficult. There has always been a desire to see yourself in the mirror: 'Who's the fairest of us all?' There is a sort of hunger, and certain films have a purchase on that. But I have always been very wary of films that move

people! It is the puritan in me. I resist it, especially if I feel I am being manipulated. And yet I like delirium; I think films should be delirium. But there is a
difference between delirium and being moved. I think it is to do with truth
telling, and I don't do enough of it in a sense, especially with Nicaragua. There
I left a lot of things out, though not in that final film, which is more brutal.

The Nicaraguan Revolution has been forgotten, but I see it not as a duty
but more a desire, my own and that of historians or whomever, to arrest those
moments, to freeze them, to look at them, to make them explode. I want to
surprise people through imagination—to give existence a sort of epic rendering because, be it the clown in the Nicaraguan state circus, or the night cleaner,
or Cliff Williams, we don't arrest our lives sufficiently to see how extraordinary
they are. I don't. But that is part of the beauty of film-making: you can do that.
I can stop the frame, and I can look, really, really look: this is a person who is
talking, someone alive. That was partly what *Utopias* was about, rendering the
epic nature of all this. The film that I have recently finished writing, which is
on Milton's *Paradise Lost*, is to do with that.

There is that line of Milton from the sonnet he writes about his blindness,
when he is asking if God really means him to go on as a poet. Suddenly he
realises the vanity of that question, and he says, 'They also serve who only
stand and wait.' Serve God in other words. Be you a ticket collector or a night
cleaner, you can serve God, just as well as a poet.

Milton wrote *Paradise Lost* out of the loss of the revolution. Twelve chap-
ters, separate books, each an average of 1000 lines: 12,000 lines, 40 composed
more or less every night, 20 dictated to his daughters in the morning. In
Paradise Lost, Milton's resolution to all this was a quietism, whereby paradise
has to be within you. The real issue now is that nobody has done a *Paradise
Lost* for our generation. It needs something of that epic nature. Nicaragua,
Cuba, you can talk about all the failures, all the betrayals, all the corruptions.
Nevertheless it is a hell of a period through which to be living, not just to have
lived. There is so much, but I can't bore everybody with it. There is a lot, a lot.
I think the main strands are here.

Marc Karlin interview
by Sheila
Rowbotham, 26
June 1998, edited by
Marc Karlin and
Sheila Rowbotham

12 Documentary Poet

Murray Martin

Murray Martin
studied art in Newcastle
before helping to set up
Amber Films in 1968.
The group have been
working in the North
East ever since. Their
films include *Seacoal*,
about Northumbrian
seacoalers, *In Fading
Light*, about North
Shields trawlermen and
their families, and
Dream On which was
created with a women's
darts team and writing
group.

HB How did you come to be in the North East?

MM I came here to university. I had been brought up in a working-class background in Stoke, where I lived with my grandparents, a mining family, and my parents, who worked in The Potteries. Very late on I got interested in art, and I had a sort of political awakening at school. My roots are absolutely traditional working class; there was no doubt you would be killed if you thought about voting anything other than Labour—you never questioned it— but you were encouraged to be independent in lots of ways. I think I was the first person who refused to join the Cadets at school, and I did so because the idea of wearing a uniform and marching up and down seemed ludicrous. I was made to clean the floor in front of the cadets. That didn't work, so they then put me on spoon bashing, cleaning all the cutlery after the school dinners. I had one teacher in tow, a French master, and eventually we got friendly, and he started to take me to the swimming baths instead, but once that got out, the next year there were about 50 kids, and after that the whole thing began to collapse. So that was a lesson for me, and it was echoed again when I was at university.

I came to do Fine Art and chose Newcastle because I thought it was a great working-class city. It was a contrast with Stoke, which is very much a series of terraced houses and connected small towns, six not five as Arnold Bennett had us believe. None the less I felt at home because of the terraced houses, and the city itself was grand—the river, the Victorian architecture, the quays, the bridges. In the first place it was the football team that drew me. I was quite a good footballer when I was a kid, and for me Newcastle was fantastic. It was the only place I applied to, and I got in on an entrance exam. But in my second year I became disillusioned with the politics, in which a few were selected as part of the elite and the rest were being left behind and dropped. I didn't like that at all, I don't know why, but it rankled with me. It wasn't a thought-out theory for me, I just thought it was wrong. Quite naively, I organised a protest where I asked everyone to write a criticism of the School, and 95 per cent did so. I asked them all to sign, which dropped it by at least half, but about 40 per cent still did. Then we faced a process of threats from the staff, which I had been through before at school, so it did not intimidate me one bit. This involved them telling me—two years before the end of the four-year course—I wouldn't get a degree.

The teaching and painting staff wouldn't speak to me after the second year, so I was basically sent to Coventry. However, the art historians didn't get involved, and one of the Marxists, Ron Davey, used to say, 'Go with the social political history behind the painting,' and that attracted me increasingly. I found the art historians criticised my paintings in interesting ways and would suggest that we 'go and look at such and such an image in Birmingham'. In the end I got a 2:2, and at the same time a job in the local art school. I think I was the only person who got a job, not just any job—a sought-after one as an art historian! The art historians recommended me for it, and soon after I started I became involved with a sort of radical theatre. A number of us at college had felt that we were in a sense being designed out of our background. It's a common experience for working-class people to become alienated and, up to a point, inevitable, because once you are at university your parents are already seeing you as better than them. They admire you, and they love you for it, but actually they are saying that you are not now of us. That troubled me I have to say. I have come across a number of people from working-class backgrounds who have become successful and are then, by definition, no longer working class save for their taste and ideology. But they couldn't find any way to reconnect. Even as a student I felt that we had been selected because we had this talent, this vision, this ability to do art, but then they would say, 'Forget all that, now we will tell you what art really is about, shape and line and colour and style.' You learn the language, and you are in through the door; if you don't, you're out. It did not ring true somehow. So some of us started painting, recording working-class subjects again, drawing what was on Tyneside—the ship-yards, the river, the docks, that sort of thing. I began to get interested in photography and in film-making, so while I was working as an art historian I decided to take a film course to learn the technique.

I chose a very technical film-making course at the Regent Street Polytechnic in London. I also taught two sessions a week there on the philosophy of aesthetics and earned myself a bit of money. At the end of the course I got together a group of people and said, 'Look, we've spent two years knowing each other, I think we should form a group and go and start documenting, making films about life in the UK.' We considered Bristol, Liverpool and Glasgow, but I always had Newcastle in mind. Eventually I went there with a number of these people. We chose to call ourselves Amber, because we were trying to think of a name that wouldn't tie or label us. The most anonymous drink that I knew then was Amber Ale, which was the women's drink, as the counterpoint of brown ale. Nowadays everybody thinks of precious stones when they hear Amber, but it was Amber Ale, a light-blue labelled brew, that we got our name from. We formed Amber Associates and Amber Films.

In the North East our first project was to document the Working Men's clubs and to try and make a film about them, and for this we did a lot of research. I don't know where it all is now, but I went around all the clubs with the Northumbria club secretary, a bloke called Jimmy Lineham. It was like an intro-duction to working-class cultures, and I felt that this is what we should be recording and documenting. We moved to live in Byker, which was still a working-class terraced area, in the late '60s already under the threat of redevelopment. We lived there because we liked the place, and eventually Sirkka Konttinen began to document Byker through photographs. For a while we had a studio in Raby Street in the centre of town. We swapped photographs: if one of the local people gave us a photo, in return we took one of them and gave it to them. So we began to record the area in this way.

We didn't have much money. Whenever we did jobs (we worked part-time in art schools or took on little jobs for the BBC, or whatever we could get), a percentage of the money always went back into work. There was Peter Roberts, who joined very early on, Sirkka who was there at the start, but our central character was Graham Denman. He left in the late '70s but still works in Newcastle in film. Then there was me, and Lorna Powell, someone I had known in Newcastle in the '60s, who had the administrative skills we needed. We pooled all the money and set up an egalitarian wage structure—a system we still maintain today. We didn't have much money for film, but we began to fund raise and get grants, and eventually initiated a policy of creative documentation of working-class life.

We went to pubs to record the singing. Occasionally I come across some of those reels of film stuck around the place. One of them has a performance of some old women singing, and that appeared in films we made. We made a film about Byker, and the text in it is as told to us in this early period and reproduced by actors. So it's not our text, but the people's voices. There is a sequence in this film, two or three scenes of pub singing, that were shot in the Balarat in North Shields. A lot of people were confused about that way of working, but taking stuff from our archive to make a film became part of our approach. One we did, *Tyne Lives*, wasn't brilliantly successful, because even though we couldn't raise the money to make the film we wanted, we said we would do something anyway, which was typical of us. It included three characters, a well-known local trade unionist, Jim Murray, a housewife (a character played by an actress and based on stories told to us) and a pigeon man. Its setting is a journey down the river on a boat that carried ash from the then Stella Power Station to dump it out at sea. As it went down the Tyne the film was intercut with their stories. You can look at it as a document of areas like Benwell and Scotswood or as a record of the protesters against factory closures, but it is also about life along a river.

We made films in quite a bizarre way depending on when we had money. I remember Sirkka, Pete and me were down at Wallsend when they were going to launch this giant tanker, and we thought, Why haven't we ever filmed this? So we approached the shipyards and built a relationship with the PR person there; eventually they let us in, and we had total freedom. Easy days compared with now! We'd done a job at the college, and I'd asked for film stock as payment. We had something like 2000 for 1000 product Kodak or Kodachrome 2, reversal stock, and we shot the film with that! It's one of the most successful we've ever done. After we shot it we never used it until the edit two years later. It's called *Launch*.

HB The result was beautiful. It was like an artwork.

MM There is a tradition within Amber that originates in the fact that its founder members all came from an art background. I did fine art and painting, Peter was employed as a graphic artist, and Sirkka's interest was really in art. In many senses, therefore, it was an artists' collective but with a commitment to the working class. You can see the strain within Amber's work in making creative documentaries, which takes you back to the tensions in the 1930s documentary tradition. In 1968 we made a film about the ferry. Edgar Anstey saw it, and he got in touch with me. He said he was shocked because it was exactly what they'd been trying to do 30 years earlier. He had been Chief Film Officer for the British Transport Film Unit that made *Night Mail* (1936). He'd also been responsible for *Terminus* (1961), a film that John Schlesinger made about Waterloo Station.

The difference between that constituency and us was that in many ways the 1930s' film-makers worked for the state, were employed by it and censored by it. Hence there are no images of unemployment from the 1930s or at least very few. Even John Grierson saw himself as working for the state, his Calvinist Scots social-worker background I suspect. Whereas, as you quite rightly say,

Seacoal, 1985 (Sirkka-Liisa Konttinen: Amber)

we came from an artistic background, but one with a political dimension. It is a different tangent and a much more independent one. We raised our own money and funded our own work.

We had a company, Lampton Visual Aids, which made educational slides that helped fund us. We used to spend nights photographing and copying slides. We carried cameras and made up sets. There is a huge archive here of those slides—terraced houses, pork butcher shops. We recorded anything and everything. The slides gained quite an international reputation, but nobody would really connect that with Amber. Similarly, later, very few people linked the Side Gallery and Amber. We have always been film-makers and photographers. We made one film, *Quayside*, which, if you look, you will see is a moving camera, a visual poem about the quayside they were going to knock down. It was made largely with me driving and Peter on the bonnet of the car. We bought a rear-drive Passat, took off the bonnet hood and put in the camera. The film is a continual movement along the quayside, and the stories on the soundtrack were collected from people who worked and lived there.

We made *Quayside* as part of a local campaign to save the area, which was successful. But our films mostly fall in a tradition of what I would call 'poetic documentaries', largely because we have never taken a didactic political line. The working class hate being talked down to, however inarticulate they feel sometimes. They don't like people who talk over their heads, and it's a real mistake to do that. And that's one of the problems of the documentary. Although people believe in it—believe it represents truth—they much prefer to get involved with people's emotional lives, which is why the power of soap operas is so great. They love the idea of a slice of life into which they can peep. So I was getting increasingly interested in the early 1970s with reconstructing situations. This had always been an instinct of ours and something that was true of the classic documentaries. It was really acting, using working-class people acting and saying what they wanted to. And this not only made them more poetic but also more emotionally accessible.

In the 1970s a bloke called Jeff Gillham was putting on plays as revolutionary propaganda in Working Men's clubs. I thought what he was doing was interesting, but the plays themselves were crass. I went to see one of them with Tom Hadderway, a local fishmonger who became a writer. Tom's work has that poetic quality and superb North East dialogue, which was quite special. Well, we went together to see this play. It was in a club in Ashington. There were six people in the audience including us two. Tom almost fell about laughing because he thought the play was so wooden. But I said, 'Yes, Tom, but the potential is there. We should think about doing plays like this in North Shields,' and he agreed. Tom had a play he was working on called *The Filleting Machine*, about a man whose wife wanted their children to better themselves. The man himself, a rather inarticulate but a skilled filleter, was keen that the kids, the son in particular, should follow him on to the fish quay. But the wife had other ideas and wanted the boy to go to grammar school, basically to get a job in an office somewhere.

It is a really beautiful, poetic play, written, as most of Tom's plays were, from his own experience and background. Though we could never get the money together to make it, he wrote another magical script for us, *The Pigeon Men*, about two men who work in a smokehouse. One of them is mentally retarded and in great fear of losing his job as a consequence. The other is frustratedly controlled by the boss and takes it out on the mentally retarded bloke, who always deflects him by talking about pigeons.

So, anyway, we began to see the potential of theatre connecting and having an interface with film. We combined a socio-political theatre group, a film company and a photography workshop, all documenting working-class life and based upon access to the community. It would go round by word of mouth that we had done a play, and we would find bookings no problem at all. The only theatre we played in town was the famous Bamburgh's Music Hall—people forget that we made it to Bamburgh's.

Groups from around the country began to come and see us. I remember being in East Morton one night, and this theatre group was on. It wasn't a big audience, but they were distinctly different. They had come from Leeds and were called Red Ladder. Well, Red Ladder had heard that we could crack the clubs, which they couldn't. And they couldn't because their theatre was didactic! I remember going to see *7:84* in the Boiler-Makers Club in Gateshead: a phenomenally successful play, audience in raptures. They did the same play a week later in Scotswood and were booed off. The first audience were politically educated and wanted to hear what was being said. But that was easy really. We didn't make plays and films that were didactic or directly political for that reason. We saw that political issues had to be presented in conjunction with other things.

When talking about Amber in the very early days it is important to say that we spent as much time socialising as working. In Byker in 1969 we paid 15 shillings a fortnight rent, which was quite low even then. If you cleared a fiver a week you were OK, so we were not pressured. And so we spent a lot of time on the move, observing, talking, enjoying ourselves, having a drink. We were doing enough work to survive, discussing with other photographers our thoughts about what structures held for the future, you know, politics. Amber was on a reasonable footing because of Lampton Visual Aid, though the theatre groups had no money. I remember the day they brought in job creation: I said to one of our Theatre group, 'Right, go and sign on at Hetton-le-Hole as an actor.' The next day we advertised for an actor at Hetton, and of course he got the job. Because he had signed on his wages were paid under the scheme. That changed the whole structure: we sacked everybody and took them all back on.

On a national level several of us, including Red Ladder, were involved in Equity. We said to them, 'Look, we are members, right? We belong to you, we are not funded, we are not waged, you know, but we are theatre workers. You are not doing anything for us, and we want an agreement.' So they wrote the Community Agreement, and that is where it came from. In turn they told the Arts Council, 'Here's the Community Agreement. Why are you not waging these community-theatre workers?' That's why the Arts Council started to get interested in community. At one time there was seven or eight community-theatre groups fully funded in Newcastle.

Having said this, I am not a theatre fan, and I don't go to the theatre very much. But theatre and Working Men's clubs was, I thought, terrific. I eventually split with live theatre, mainly because they wanted to develop a big permanent base and not tour. I considered touring, going out into communities, the whole point of the exercise. Anyway, the plays, like the photography, were a means of making direct connections and retrieving aspects of working-class experience.

At first film was too expensive for us, however, increasingly, as we became more successful as film-makers we got more opportunity. Throughout the 1970s, through the trade union, we also pushed the idea that there could be a radical form of film-making. When Channel 4 arrived in 1982, a workshop sector had become union policy. They financially and politically supported us, and Channel 4 gave us a percentage of their budget. For ten years, the workshops flourished, and this led to a lot of production around the UK. As well as us, there was Chapter in Cardiff, Sheffield Film Co-op, Leeds Animation, Trade, A19 in the North East, Edinburgh Film and several black groups, such as Black Audio Film Collective. Many others too. So there was a national movement of workshops predominantly making films and recording working-class experience.

HB At this time were you based in The Side?
MM About 1969 or 1970, very early on, yes. As you know we are situated in this very narrow alley. Initially we only rented the middle floor and the cottage (where I lived for £3 a week). On the left side of the alley there was a plumber's workshop on the top floor, which when the plumber left we rented for another £3 per week. We had long leases, and when the developers tried to kick us out they found they were in real trouble. That was an extremely important phase in our development. We were threatened with removal from the building, and we decided to fight, which led to us being involved in that campaign to save the Quayside. We won, and as a result we were able to buy the other side of the alley, which was all we wanted at the time. Ultimately we bought the building next door, where the café is now located. We bought it because we needed it as a fire exit for the cinema. We weren't property developers! Although we could have bought the Quayside actually because it was going for nothing at the time.

In the new space we were able to open up the gallery and cinema, and we ran a cinema here quite regularly between 1977 and 1982, in what I would call our 'exhibition phase'. And then, in 1982, Channel 4 came on stream, and we reverted to production as a priority because that was what we really wanted to do. When we got money as a Channel 4 workshop, although the gallery still operated, it took on less of a role within Amber. We were now in a position to be out in the community making films. The 1980s were dominated by this consistent relationship with Channel 4, making documentaries and dramas, some with directly political themes.

HB Was the relationship with Channel 4 a major change for the group?

MM As film-makers we always took the question of distribution and audience very seriously. Whenever we made a film we would organise a post-production distribution package, something we still do. In the 1970s we took them to pubs and projected them ourselves. From 1977 we owned our own cinema, which was quite a luxury, and we would show them there. The head of the region's transport authority happened to be at a gathering where we showed our ferry film, and he really liked it and asked if we would make a film for him. We ended up with a contract to document the Metro system that had been developed in Tyneside. So, for a while, it was quite a vibrant movement. We were in Working Men's clubs showing films because we had our work accepted as a second feature on the club circuit. We had linked in with their distribution man and told him that though we weren't going to make any money out of it, we'd love to have our films shown there. So when he had a feature that wasn't quite the right length, something like *Launch* would be a second feature. This was great, particularly in Tyneside and places like Wallsend. Don't forget there were 400 Working Men's clubs in the area, so our films began to follow the path of the theatre groups.

HB Was this film or video tape?

Film totally, no video. At that time, of course, internationally there was a growing interest in the working class, and so people would visit Newcastle and take films away with them. As a result, the festival circuit began to open up. But in the main we were organisers of our own stuff, distributors and exhibitors, and that's how we liked it. We saw that as part of the job really, and I think we did it fairly successfully. Sometimes we lost energy and didn't do it as well as we might, but broadly speaking that never inhibited us from making films. Often, of course, especially after we opened the gallery, though even before then, we had exhibitions that toured, showing the films in conjunction with exhibitions. This made absolute sense, of course, and increasingly still does. So if we did an exhibition on the dust bowl in America, of Russell Lee or Dorothea Lange, we would show *The Grapes of Wrath*. We had quite an integrated exhibition, production and distribution policy through the 1970s. But what we couldn't crack was television, until Channel 4 came along.

Channel 4 was a complicated issue. It was developed partly as a battering ram to destroy the trade unions. One of the problems with TV at the time was the rigidity of the unions, especially the guilds, which I would say included Equity and ACTT. We believed in the closed shop that allowed everybody in and then insisted that you join them. But you can't survive with the guildist position where you must have a job to get a ticket, but you have to have a ticket to get a job. This went against all my background—it is not generous. You were seen as a threat if you were on the outside and made a film as an independent. Those on the inside resented the idea that somebody could make a crazy film beyond their terrain. So it was a very difficult thing to get independent films shown on television. The closest thing we came to it was in the early 1970s when a man called Axleby ran BBC Newcastle. He thought the ferry film was terrific and said, 'I'll show the film except for one thing—you'll have to change the song, people won't understand it.' When I protested that it was a Geordie song he still wouldn't change his mind. So we didn't show it because we weren't prepared to make that compromise. We never got on TV after that!

We worked for it nevertheless. We sold our skills as crew to television to earn money, but we wouldn't make their films. That may have been an oddball position, but it says something about us. We wanted to make films we believed in. If TV wouldn't fund those, then it could do so through our making *The Money Programme*, or whatever we crewed. We learnt our skills that way, which was useful. We were developing our craft, but we were not compromising our ideals, and we never have.

HB But this changed with Channel 4 and the Workshops?

MM In 1982 Channel 4 opened up under Jeremy Isaacs. Alan Fountain had been on the BFI panel with Isaacs, and he got the job as Commissioning Editor for Independent Film and Video. I am not saying that was the only reason. Alan was part of the independent sector, which was lobbying for him to get the job, and Isaacs was the sort of person who would listen. Alan stayed for ten years; most people last three or four at the most. Throughout that time he was overseeing the independent sector, and as a result we got regular support from 1982 to about 1992. Alan, however, was never a great believer in workshops, and you had to twist his arm a lot. A committee was set up by ACTT, chaired by Roy Lockett, to represent the workshops, and I sat on it throughout that period. We were in negotiation constantly with Channel 4, and it wasn't easy. Alan Fountain subsequently employed Rod Stoneman and Caroline Spry to be in charge of workshops, but neither of them favoured workshops either. They didn't like the idea of their independence. It takes a very brave person to say, 'Yes, I will give you money-get on with it.' Their instinct is control, and as a result most workshops only got funding for a very short time. We were an exception at Amber. We constantly did something a bit surprising that made them feel unsure about us. At the inception of Channel 4 for example, Alan had said, 'You have a choice of £300,000 or £30,000.' I told him we'd opt for £30,000. Again we made the decision on the basis that we wouldn't compromise or do what they wanted us to do. In the end I was embarrassed because he upped it to £48,000. We didn't want accountants sitting on our backs while we were making other people's films. Virtually everybody took the big money, and they were destroyed by it.

HB So how did this work out for Amber?

MM We were perfectly happy to get £50,000; sometimes £100,000. We made features like *Seacoal* on £100,000 as well as another film, *Boxing for Hartlepool*. This shocked Channel 4. I remember Stoneman coming to see the film and asking, 'Where has this come from?' We explained that we were a workshop, and we shot stuff all the time. That we did not necessarily tell him what we did and were not obliged to do so under the agreement, which was to provide them annually with a certain 'minutage'. We were doing that and more. That was the way he worked. But they didn't like it. Nevertheless Channel 4 gave us stability. It also gave us credibility, and that was something we had always wanted. Television was, and is, the only way to reach two million people at one go. If you are used to showing to around 30 people around clubs in Durham, that's a lot of showings! There is something different about screening a film such as *The Scar* on television and reaching 2.5 million in one evening. We were very happy with that.

HB But The Scar was the BBC, wasn't it?

MM Yes. Channel 4 increasingly moved away from publishing and enabling towards 'The Commission'. You know the sort of thing: 'We'll do this series on sex, so put a good idea on sex to us, the more extreme the better, and we'll back it.' That's the way they came to operate, and we felt fairly uncomfortable about it. But in the mid-1990s Tessa Ross became the Commissioning Editor for the BBC and invited us to do some work for them. So it was perfect timing. *The Scar* was the first one we did for her.

HB What did you put out for Channel 4?

MM One of the positive things about Isaacs was that he was interested in acquiring material for television. He would say, 'Tell us what to buy, and we will buy anything as long as you are straight with us.' So they took all that stuff we had done in the 1970s: *Launch, That's Not Me* (a film about the comedian Tom Healey), *Quayside, The Filleting Machine* (which we had shot in two weeks in a flat in Walker on £7000), *The Last Shift* and *Bowes Line*. All that stuff went on television, a whole catalogue in a sense.

We had Workshop money, and we were obviously in dialogue with the commissioner. We valued our independence, but we knew that they wouldn't carry on supporting us if we didn't deliver something that helped their position. So in the mid-1980s, after we had done a series of documentaries, I clearly remember Alan saying to me: 'I'm in real trouble. Nobody is delivering any interesting drama.' So we said we would, and we went on and made *Seacoal*, and Isaacs loved it. Looking at it now I see it more and more as a documentary, and I think most of our films are documentaries, but 'dramatised' documentaries. *Seacoal* was, as was *In Fading Light*. We also had *Keeping Time* and *Byker* about the East End community. We were showing films every year, sometimes two, sometimes three, and we were doing quite a lot of production.

HB Did you find the move from strictly documentary to documentary drama difficult?

MM Not at all, no. If you look at *High Row*, a documentary we made about a drift mine at Alston, it is totally reconstructed. We wrote the script, and we talked with the men, then we rented the mine for the week, and there the men reconstructed their lives. So it was done as a documentary, but in fact it's a complete drama. One scene involves a man coming home from work, who throws a brick that almost hits a rabbit. They all laugh. Well, that was all classic Eisenstein montage stuff. One day we saw a rabbit, and I threw a brick at it and said to Pete, 'Focus on the rabbit.' We looked at the shot and saw that it was OK. Then we got one of the men to throw a brick and turn and smile, that's all he did, and we put the two together. Equally when we did *Last Shift*, about a brick-works, we thought we should do a little documentary about these men. We turned in one day, and the blokes we knew were not there. We asked the watch-man what had happened, and he said they'd all been given a minute's notice. It seemed the firm had been taken over a few months earlier, and it had closed down the factory. I asked him where everyone was, and he gave me their addresses, and so I went round and organised things. Those who had just signed on would get their unemployment benefit in a week or so's time. So, I said I would pay a week's wages, and we would open up the factory again and make a film! So that was obviously a total reconstruction, and if you then marry that with our experience of live theatre and doing realist plays and so on, you can see it all as part of the same thing. We shot the *Filleting Machine* as a drama; it's a play on film really. Even so we decided to record it because it was also important as a piece of record.

HB One of the themes in your work you have mentioned several times today is the problem of generations. The next generation may succeed, but success always involves a sense of loss. Could you talk about this? Is it something coincidental, or is it an intentional development within Amber?
MM A lot of film-making is autobiographical. If it isn't within your own history, it's very difficult, and I don't understand how people go in and invent a story. So I would say that it's not a conscious theme, but I would accept that in a 'psychiatrist's chair' you'd have to give it credit. What you hold on to and what you let go of, what you retain and where you move to are very important issues. This is a central problem in the current debate about the future of the coalfields. You have a whole generation of men who have done one job, followed by another generation of men who have been forced to do 20 jobs in order to retain the same level of income that they had in the mines. And now of course we have another generation who don't know anything about the mines because there has been a headlong rush to erase all evidence of that history. They have no reason to know where the pit was. The only thing you have left in most villages is half of a pit wheel stuck somewhere in a piece of concrete.

One of the themes that interests me is personal relationships and what responsibilities one generation has to the next—what you leave and how you retain that respect for history in a headlong pressure towards consumerism. Nowadays the advertisers have realised that young people hold the key to the future. Get them at seven, and you've got them for life. The film we are doing at the moment focuses on these issues. We have a man who is an ex-miner. He is bright and strong and clear about himself in his own way, but he has skeletons as everybody does, and he does not deal with them. He can't release

The Scar, 1998 (Amber)

the next generation until he unlocks those skeletons, which includes his treatment of his own son and his inability to accept that his son is doing his best in very difficult circumstances.

So families are important in a lot of our work. After *Seacoal* ten years later we did *Eden Valley* with the same family. It looks at what has happened to those people a decade on. There is a father-and-son story. *The Scar*, too, is about relations, about emotional connection, about whether people can cross the cultural divide. The woman is a former activist, but, like a lot of people, she is in crisis. She meets somebody whom she likes and gets on with, but he is 'the enemy' so she gives all that up. But can she?

HB She has a son too.

MM She has a son who gets a job in the strip mine. And, you know, going back to *The Filleting Machine*, it is the same sort of thing. You're right—there is a lot in our films about family and relationships and generations.

HB And because you are so firmly placed in this town, and in Tyneside and Northumberland, you are able to use the physicality of the place in addressing the issue of a working-class community. That was very clear in *Launch*, but in other films also. The buildings and the machinery become a critical part of your description of people's lives.

MM Absolutely, and I think that is right. As I said earlier, we come from a documentary tradition, so we want to record the culture. There are a number of different strands in our films. One is subject-matter led, in that you tell a story, but you record the physical, practical activity. I would say *Seacoal* is an example of that. We thought this was a really interesting context, people collecting coal after the horses and carts; that culture should be recorded before it disappears. The film that we made about harness racing was the same. It is a culture that is fragile and could go. Harness racing is very strong in Wales and in the North East, but they are the only two areas where it's so. So we felt that it was very important to record it in its detail.

We also wanted to do a film about fishing. To do that we went to Esbjerg in Norway and bought a fishing boat. You know, when I think about it now it's almost bizarre. Getting on a plane to Esbjerg, knowing nothing about boats; negotiating and buying a fishing boat because that was where they were cheapest and best, if you like, in quality. Asking two old men whom you meet that weekend to sail the boat over to North Shields. They turn up precisely on time on a Monday morning with a boat that all the fishermen admire. And that's what gets you—it's a brownie-points score—the respect you have to have in these things. For two years this boat centred around our making a film, *In Fading Light*. For me it is another film about work. Often the fishermen went to sea and didn't get paid at the end of it. They could go to sea for a fortnight and end up in debt because they borrowed money for food. Fishing can't be compared to what most of the world is about. But they clung to it. No trade unionism, no facilities—an horrific industry in many ways. But there was also a great macho-romantic tradition attached to it, in which there were heroes. The skippers were gods not for any other reason than that they delivered well for the men who worked for them.

So we bought a boat; we also bought a pub, which is the simplest thing to do, you know. We were at a bit of a loss in the group and thinking about our community base, and I said, 'Well, why don't we buy a pub?' If you want a community base that's the thing you do. So we went to Newcastle Breweries and persuaded them to sell us a freehold pub in North Shields for £23,000. We used that to shoot a lot of stuff. A whole sequence of *In Fading Light* for instance. So we record ways of life.

Our other strand is very much to do with what I call the *internal landscape*. *The Scar* is a good example of this. As is *Dream On*, another film that went to Channel 4, about women—wives of fishermen—left at home. What do these women in North Shields do? The film is about three of them. About the generation thing again, and about husbands (often repressed husbands) and wives.

HB We have been talking about events across the '60s, '70s, '80s and '90s, a time during which some remarkable changes have taken place. Are there problems now for film-makers and photographers trying to work without those established images and ideas of the working-class?

MM Absolutely, but not just for those reasons. The changes have made it more difficult; it is visually less interesting now. If you are talking about classic working-class imagery, the Metro shopping centre isn't that enthralling. People may go in their droves to shop there, but it isn't somewhere you want to spend a lot of time in—well, in any case, I don't now there is no more tradi-tional industry: steel is non-existent, ship-building virtually non-existent, coal non-existent. So those classic images have gone, which is probably why we are getting more and more dragged into the internal landscape, the residue of all that. However, the other problem is that documentary in the sense of recording and celebrating people's culture is very unfashionable at the moment. Like documentary photography it is not rated at all. Furthermore, if you are talk-ing about recording that culture it's very difficult still how to find the celebra-tory elements of it. In places like Horden it is a bit more like *Boys from the Blackstuff*. People are drinking hard, and they get into the drugs; there are teenage pregnancies. There is no work, and no leisure potential other than the clubs, and sex and drugs and rock'n'roll. Beer is expensive; you can get heroin as cheaply as beer. It can be quite depressing. So you tend to be dragged increasingly towards those people who are nostalgic and remember the past.

HB And this is what has moved you towards the internal landscape?
MM Absolutely. And this has many difficulties and more dilemmas. When we lived in Byker we didn't do any photography for two years until people started talking to us about outsiders, which indicated that we were let through the door. When you become part of a community you are treated quite differently from somebody who comes in as an anthropologist or observer. You have to build up that trust. And when they open up to you, you have to be responsible for that trust. That is not the great history of film-making, which is the opposite; it's all exploitation of trust for the most part. So we have to be very careful. And that's the other reason, by the way, why we reconstruct. Because people will tell you stories in great confidence and expose themselves in ways that it would be irresponsible to reveal publicly. In order to have the freedom to do so you have to reconstruct it. There was a very good documentary on televi-sion recently, where three young girls under ten were talking about their parents as drug-dealers. It was a remarkable study of kids, but I thought, God, what is this doing? What is it doing for the girls and for the parents, and where is it going to end up? I couldn't believe it could be ignored: they were talking about people coming to the door with packets of drugs. So I think if you enter into people's private lives you have to be very responsible.

I learnt that lesson very early on when our ferry film was shown at a public gathering. I was standing next to the son and daughter of the ferryman whose voice-over records his thoughts as he drives the ferry across the river at the mouth of the Tyne. I suddenly realised that he had started talking about the son, saying, 'I should never have put him to this painting and decorating, he should have learnt the electrical trade.' I thought, God, he may never have said this to the son. This is dangerous, dangerous ground. As I stood there I saw the son was really pleased, but he could have been the opposite. I was lucky, and it taught me a lesson.

Murray Martin interview by Huw Beynon, 10 September 1999

13 Revealing Desires

Isaac Julien

Isaac Julien studied art at Central St Martin's and then worked in the black film group Sankofa. His films include *Territories*, *Who Killed Colin Roach?*, *The Passion of Remembrance*, *Looking for Langston* and *Young Soul Rebels*. He has also lectured on film at several North American universities. He was shortlisted for the Turner Prize 2001.

Around 1976 I can remember being very influenced by certain cultural and political moments, one being punk rock, the other the image of the Soweto uprising in South Africa. I saw this picture in a newspaper of a young woman hugging her brother—that famous Sharpeville photograph. Trying to put these two images of Soweto and Sharpville together made me realise that black people were being represented in certain ways. I was also aware that reporting about a younger black generation was constructed from a very specific point of view. So I recognised that there was some kind of bias in the media before I really had any language to explain it.

At that time any sort of black representation on television would be terribly exciting because it was so rare, an important event that the whole family would watch. They could be doing anything, from being in a game show to *Top of the Pops*, but there was an awful amount of pressure on whatever the person was doing. Questions of race were initially introduced in comedy register, through television situation comedies such as ITV's *Love Thy Neighbour*.

I was involved in a number of political campaigns while I was at Dainford School for Boys, Bethnal Green, at the top of Brick Lane. There had been an influx of Asian immigrants into the area, and by 1976, the second generation from the Bengali community around there were starting to enter the school. There was a lot of racial violence because my school was situated between Old Street and Hoxton, which was a National Front stronghold—the Front had their headquarters there. Consequently Brick Lane literally became a battleground, and we had to organise, learning self-defence, forming vigilante groups, all those sorts of things. It became obvious that there was a political problem, and through all the anti-racist activities I got involved in various youth socialist organisations. In this period there was also the Anti-Nazi League and Rock Against Racism—we had a big march to Victoria Park. In youth culture punk rock was making the media a point of critique.

Images of different sorts of sexuality were everywhere then: one example is David Bowie, another is punk rock. New kinds of identifications were forcing their way into popular culture and were especially evident in the youth culture of the period. So there was this space where you could be quite cool and give yourself a bisexual identity or something. It was not something that was completely clear-cut, but there was a possibility for being different, a potential

Young Soul Rebels, 1991 (Sunil Gupta: BFI/Film Four/ Sankofa/La Sept/ Kinowelt/ iboamericana)

for non-conformity. When I look at it retrospectively I think that I was very interested in the space around self-representation.

My film *Young Soul Rebels*, which appeared in 1991, is loosely based on all this activity. It is not autobiographical and takes a completely different story that is not mapped as realist. However, the film samples real-life moments and reinvents them, as it were, into a storyline. It was an incisive time for me, during which I became interested in both art and politics, and in trying to put those two things together.

Of course none of this was an accident; at that time there were a number of radical cultural workshops based in the East End. One was the Newsreel Film Collective, which included Paul Morrison, Alan Hayling and Noreen MacDowell. Newsreel gave screenings, showing films about the revolution in Portugal and the anti-colonial struggles in Angola and Mozambique. Another was Camerawork, which produced a magazine and held exhibitions of radical photography. There were also left papers such as the *Leveller* and *Gay Left*, which were all talking about what would now be termed 'representation'. I read the men's group magazine *Achilles Heel* as well because I was interested in anything to do with sexual politics. I also appeared in *True Romance*, a film about the sexuality of lesbian and gay teenagers, which was directed by Joy Chamberlain. Among the local groups was the Kingsley Hall Action Group, which is where Richard Attenborough had filmed one part of *Gandhi*.

Of course there were formations such as *Race and Class*, but I didn't really like their approach to masculinity or the way in which they spoke about things.

Young Soul Rebels,
1991 (Sunil Gupta:
BFI/Film Four/
Sankofa/La Sept/
Kinowelt/
iboamericana)

There was a certain rigidity. I preferred the people connected to a libertarian left group, Big Flame, who were influenced by the Italian Lotta Continua and based in East London, organising around the Ford factory in Dagenham, where my father worked.

I was also involved in—well, not really involved, actually, but very much hounded by—the Workers' Revolutionary Party (WRP). I think by then I was seen as someone who could be an organiser of some kind in a youth group. The WRP had a newspaper that I used to find quite crude, because all the articles ended in the same thing: the working class would overcome. That was like propaganda, but equally, because it came out every day, there was a fresh perspective on the main news, which was quite interesting.

The WRP had a lot of people, like Vanessa Redgrave, involved in film. But the politics was too narrow. I thought it was important to have some relationship to the Labour Party, because you can't organise in a small group and be this almost counter voice. That seemed strategically hopeless. So while I was involved in working with the WRP, I didn't vote for them but for the Labour Party instead. Then when the Conservatives won in 1979, I decided that politically you had to organise differently, which led to a focus on the media.

So a combination of influences were getting me thinking about the politics of representation in art: photography, painting, and film. The media seemed to be a real area of power, the point of contestation, an important place where something could be done. I did an A-level in Communications, which meant that I read people like Raymond Williams and Stuart Hall, and I studied sociology and related concepts. By the time I went to art school, I had already decided I was very interested in film.

I went to St Martin's, where I was introduced to making film. The film course at St Martin's then was about experimental cinema, structuralist film they called it. People like Malcolm le Grice and William Raban taught us, and I remember looking at these films and thinking, What on earth! These were not the films that I was used to, not my idea of making films at all. I had seen lots of political documentaries, but I had never seen experimental films that completely destroyed your idea of viewing. However, the process became interesting; I realised that there wasn't just the possibility of making films that were going to be political, but also of challenging how people viewed film, and that this was also political. I discovered Eisenstein, the art of the Russian Revolution and photomontage. I could see how Peter Kennard was re-working that in his contemporary political art. There was some of that work, too, in left journals. Later on I saw films by Jean-Luc Godard, where you get a direct correlation between politics and image.

A non-narrative film I had made for the class at St Martin's got me into an argument with one of the teachers who said, 'Come on, Isaac, no one from a working-class background would be able to understand what you're doing.' I thought, OK. Then I made a documentary, Who Killed Colin Roach?, as a direct response really. It was about a young black man, Colin Roach, who was found dead at a police station, and was my re-entry, you could say, into the issues I saw as important. The camera would be situated in a political struggle, and you would read the film as a document, as an oppositional image against the dominant media.

Coming from a working-class background, I felt that there was a rigid or prescribed view, which resulted in a puritanical approach to how working-class people could be portrayed. We formed a film collective, Power and Control, and we held screenings in the so-called 'black communities', inviting friends and other people. As an exercise, the screening followed by a discussion came very much out of what Cinema Action, the Newsreel Collective, Camerawork and Four Corners had been doing.

We were very aware of the ethnographic framing in most anti-racist documentaries. Black people were always constructed in those films, in terms of a problem, which was the only time you would actually get interest. This was partly because of anxiety but also because the people who made the more radical documentaries were people who cared about 'social problems'. Their political commitment made them want some identification with those voices. There was not much humour in these sort of documentaries; it was very earnest.

There were just a few inspiring alternatives, the work of Horace Ove, for instance, and to some extent Menelik Shabazz. Their films were really important and constituted the first beginnings of the kind of black cinema that we wanted. They were about class and race, articulated at the frontline as political documents. They were mostly trying to document young black men's struggle with the state and with the police, and how this was affecting the community.

One of the most productive moments was during and immediately after the miners' strike of 1984 to '85 when all the film workshops had been shooting the different activities up and down the country. We tried to bring all these questions around policing together, showing the ways in which black people were being policed and how this got revisited on the population. The policing tactics used upon those mining communities were the ones that they had already employed against the black sections of society. It was like a turnaround: they were being treated like blacks. I feel this explains why there was a strong support for the miners' strike in many black areas.

In the early 1980s the film union was trying to recruit black members, yet, despite this, it remained a closed shop. You had to have people who signed you into the union, only then would you get employed. So it was very closed, and there was a lot of racism within it then. However, the London-based, left-dominated part of the union, where there was input from the independent film-makers, were conscious of this.

Then there was the GLC, which felt like a representation of aspects of Anti-Nazi League politics. People were identifying and seeking to relate to communities of interest, such as black people, women, gays and lesbians, a whole counter movement, which traditionally had not been seen as part of the left. This was occurring in an institutionalised context, which resulted in all sorts of problems. It was a very interesting moment, and one out of which came that hostile construction of the 'loony left'. This critique was easy to make partly because these categories were often taken in a peripheral sense. I felt that they had to be considered along with class, I didn't see them as separate.

I have to confess, that when the GLC closed down part of me felt very sad, although I did dislike the institutional politics. I never knew what an ethnic minority was until I walked into the GLC: I had never heard that sort of bureaucratic language. I found it very odd, and I was very suspicious of it. On the other hand the presence of the GLC created a base of sorts. For example, Sankofa, the film group I was in, got financed then, and we would never have been funded otherwise.

The name 'Sankofa' was given to us by our friend Kobena Mercer; it symbolised a bird flying into the future with its head turning back, looking at the past. That was the concept. Culturally there was a lot of support for there to be a black workshop, and the political will was there too: we knew we could organise ourselves. However, an argument took place between us and the Black Media Workers' Association, a group of organisers including presenters, who worked within the media. Diane Abbott was head of the organisation then, and she thought being a workshop was wrong, because it meant that we had marginalised ourselves and would therefore always remain on the periphery of the industry. She argued that we should get involved in the mainstream and go for the existing structures. We were not interested in doing this at all, because in the mainstream you ended up only doing journalistic things. We would have been interested in entering the mainstream through fiction or drama. That was really what we wanted to do.

By the mid-1980s I had come to the conclusion that on the whole working-class people don't really want or desire documentary in the same way as the middle class. Documentaries are very much made for the middle class about their relationship to the working class. On the whole, it seemed that working-class people were more interested in fantasy, in stories and narrative, in this way of talking about their experience, where they were not constructed as victims, in a didactic sense. So I did not want to make films that were going to be realist, or in any sense ethnographic.

The question of representation had become fairly complicated for me, because of thinking about class and about race and sexuality and gender, as well as knowing more about the history of film and representation and how these are all intertwined. I have kept searching for different ways of trying to answer those sorts of questions in my work. Making films such as *Who Killed Colin Roach?* (1983) and then *The Passion of Remembrance* (1986) was

Young Soul Rebels,
1991 (Sunil Gupta:
BFI/Film Four/
Sankofa/La Sept/
Kinowelt/
iboamericana)

almost the in-between. You tackle policing, but shift it from documentary to something that involves fiction. Obviously in *Young Soul Rebels* or *Who Killed Colin Roach?* I am dealing directly with social and political issues.

There have been times when I wanted to deal directly with these kinds of issues, and other times when I preferred to use fantasy. In 1989, after *The Passion of Remembrance* I made *Looking for Langston*, which to my mind is in many ways my most successful film. It comes out of the Harlem Renaissance cultural movement and looks at the black American writer Langston Hughes. I did a great deal of picture research with Mark Nash, and a lot of thought informs everything that gets reconstructed. In the 1920s and '30s, people were filmed, so if when you don't have written archives there could be a visual record. However, explicit answers about how people lived their personal lives are not going to be available to you because of certain repressive or self-censoring aspects of a culture, in this case because of race and attitudes towards sexuality. Then you have to reinvent things in some way. *Looking for Langston* is particularly influenced by Derek Jarman and Jean Cocteau as well as by early cinema.

In my experience, making films has been an attempt to try to bring out questions of desire, and these always seem to be located within fantasy, not in realism. Desire and conflict around desire is at the heart of cinema, and the cinema in which I am interested is the one that takes on these questions. Realising that the fantasy and psychic aspects of people's lives are so vital and influential has a lot to do with being involved in sexual politics.

I guess this is also because I feel conscious of the very narrow repertoire

Young Soul Rebels,
1991 (Sunil Gupta:
BFI/Film Four/
Sankofa/La Sept/
Kinowelt/
iboamericana)

of representation of blacks or gays. In a way one is working towards using the power of cinema where it is most strongly based, which for me is in the moment. Films that have a more ethnographic reference, which somehow represent working-class characters or experiences as 'the real', have a more programmatic relationship. I suppose that is an approach inherited from the left, with the left documentary tradition located in a very narrow genre. In contrast I am interested in stories that could locate experience in the Brechtian cinematic genre: fantasy, thrillers, film noir. Here you really have telling the story at the centre of the project and the mechanics of film are paid attention.

People like Hollywood cinema, for both these reasons: not only the technology but also narratives, certain of which are quite generic, boy meets girl, love story—we like the same stories to be repeated to us time and time again. I am also very aware that people are not interested in certain histories and stories, such as those involving black characters for example. Indeed black people themselves, when they go to the cinema, are not essentialist in how they view a film. Identification is a complicated process. As a spectator you forget your own self in the cinema, which is, of course, part of the experience. So the question of whether the characters are black or white, women or men, is important but not always crucial because if you are black you will identify throughout with the protagonist, whatever film you are following: identification can cross over. You can have the politics entwined in a film, but you have to find a strategy where the pleasure is foregrounded. That is really what people's relationship to the cinema is for now.

Take the success of *The Full Monty*. It is clearly not a film that completely involves fantasy, so I wouldn't say it works through its *mise-en-scène*, but rather through the script, the performances, and the fact that it is funny. A lot of working-class people identify with *The Full Monty*, because the characters are humorous and sardonic. They talk about people's relationships in the present and how they have been affected by the political crisis around joblessness and masculinity. But they do so in a way that expresses a lot of resistance through how the characters are drawn, which is quite complex. This is something that is really important.

There is a story behind *The Full Monty* that it was originally conceived as being largely about black characters. My friend Paul Bucknor, who I know from clubbing in London, used to come up to me all the time and say, 'Well, I'm a writer, Isaac, I'm making a film,' and I would dismiss him with a 'Yes—yes.' He is someone who is very much from my generation, a club organiser, entrepreneural, very astute. It was his idea, but the deal was that he gave up creative control. Though that did not rule out him having direct involvement in some drafts of the script, which was then passed on to Simon Beaufoy. So then Paul Barber as Horse becomes the only black character in the film: *The Missing Monty* as they call it. It's a fascinating story, which leads us back to the question, What would the film have been if it had been all black leads? Of course they could not have made it with all black leads. Well, they could have done so, but you have to consider whether it would have been the darling of the film industry. Would it have been as popular, and would it have performed in the way that it did?

This background to *The Full Monty* shows the impossibility of thinking about class without race. People like Tony Garnett, Ken Loach and Mike Leigh have continued to make films that look at class, and if they weren't doing those films I don't know where we would see that sort of representation. But there are real problems in how race is presented. Take Mike Leigh's *Secrets and Lies* for example, which was one of those

Looking for Langston, 1989 (Sunil Gupta: Channel 4)

films that get picked up. The story, the narrative of *Secret and Lies*, could never, ever be convincing for black audiences. In terms of what he is trying to tell I read it as allegorical. But there is always a certain appeasement, or dishonesty with those sorts of films. I feel similarly about some of Ken Loach's films. He does have black characters occasionally in his scripts, which I think is good, but at the same time they are there in a concessionary way, slightly expedient. They are not developed, not really integral to the plot. It is a way of saying: there is this other representation of class that is non-white. That is about as far as it goes, and it is not really developed.

Because class has shifted and changed, there has to be a different language, a new language in which to express this. It's a quite different moment. Of course there are still people all over the country, my family for instance, who are working class in the old sense, but there are all sorts of other issues. Take the incredible amount of homelessness or the whole underground scene for example. *Trainspotting* was really the first youth film that broke through and caught some of this, which was good because people had actually been quite prejudiced against youth films.

Within gay culture, too, there has been a huge explosion of what is really prostitution. But it is not seen in a negative moralistic sense, just as one of the different ways people survive, in this case through their bodies. The prevailing attitude to work is still to want to be paid highly, but the free-time aspect has become more central, and leisure industries are expanding as other things are not. This raises questions about masculinity and its relationship to work and the working class. The market now means that men's bodies, like women's, have been turned into commodities.

Moreover globalisation has resulted in a multiculturalism with good and bad effects. You get Ian Wright playing for England in the World Cup and the Spice Girls. I go to New York all the time, and I can see how Americanised London is becoming. There are aspects of London I like that are not at all American, in terms of social conditions and the degree of violence. England is in many ways the opposite of America, where there are a lot of black people in quite powerful positions, but where, on the other hand, the black working class have been devastated and decimated.

Chantal Mouffe recently described Tony Blair as Thatcher's final victory. Twenty years of Thatcherism have got to change things; under New Labour it is really just business as usual. I do feel that the shift taking place is unstoppable now, but more class divisions will be created. This will mean that there can only be more class problems in the future. I don't know how you are going to enable younger, working-class black people to enter into a certain space. It is a huge problem.

You get a fuller expression of these sorts of experiences in music. I don't want to use a word like authentic, but it really is—more 'there'. I guess *Young Soul Rebels* was about this. There has been a shift even since then; there is a taken-for-grantedness now. For instance younger white friends of my brother's in East London speak with a sort of cockney-black accent. Of course much of this depends on where you are, though it is certainly part and parcel of a London, or at least an urban experience. You can hear the change in music, but film falls at least ten to twenty years behind.

Institutionally there are huge problems with which films get made. Film culture has certainly changed. There is a consciousness of the need to be innovative, and certain film-makers have been able to make films in new ways, such as Peter Greenaway, Derek Jarman or Sally Potter. However, it is all still very much cut from the fabric of a certain middle-class imagination. None the less what they have been doing is interesting in terms of film politics.

However, it is worth considering whether if someone like Derek Jarman were still alive, he would still have an audience. It is partly a problem of venue for innovative films, films which are 'different'. Derek Jarman's *Wittgenstein*, (1993), was shown at the Institute of Contemporary Arts (ICA) cinema in London with a short I made called *The Attendant*. There was an audience for his film, but the ICA is very much an art house and therefore small release.

These films would have had some theatrical release in the country through the British Film Institutes rep cinemas. However, there is increasing pressure on the programmers there to show things that will actually make money, be box-office hits and put bums on seats. So, they don't want to show anything that is difficult and won't risk space for anything that is not going to be perceived as a hit. The whole concept of their role in film education has almost gone, and there is a danger that it will completely vanish.

As a consequence the marketing and distribution of innovative films has become more and more problematic. There has been a shift away from experimental film-making, and there is now a problem of audience in terms of how those films are perceived. There has been a decline in the cinemas where they can be shown. It is very complicated, partly a global effect of the dominance of Hollywood and its impact on tastes.

The old BFI is losing its former identity. Although it is too early to say, this could mean the end of certain types of film-making. There is not a mass audience, but public taste is partly constructed: you have to build an audience for your work. When I started there was no audience for the sort of films I made, but they have found people who are interested in my way of working. In this television has been critical. You can show something on TV, and it gets seen by a million people, so you don't have to rely on cinema. You can make that intervention, try a multi-faceted approach, with an independent film that is not completely commercial. That, of course, was an objective for which Marc Karlin was campaigning. It is amazing to think that someone like Marc continued to get his films shown, because these structures of broadcasting have become increasingly closed, and decisions are now all made secret. The reason his work is still screened is because he is seen as like the Chris Marker or the Jean-Luc Godard of the British independent scene. But he was more or less the only person representing that sort of voice, that sort of perspective. The campaign for that independent sector has been largely lost, along with any black voice within it. Everything has become so marginalised that I sometimes think we need to return to some explicit institutional recognition, which could enable women, black people, gays and lesbians to make their films again.

In the 1970s and '80s experimental films began to reach a more popular audience through television and cinema, but now they are really going different ways. A lot of experimentation in film, which is no longer possible in these areas, has shifted into the arts space, almost into the museum. On the one hand, this has meant it has been downgraded; and is no longer able to challenge the dominant cinema. On the other hand, however, well-known artists like Gillian Wearing or Douglas Gordon, who won the Turner Prize, are all working in this sort of area, but in the gallery. It is another quite different way of working. But it's a space anyway, and one that I think has to be taken up pragmatically. It is too early really to say how it will develop.

Another quite critical audience is opening up in universities. My films have all been distributed in the United States in this way, and there is already a lot of support for my work there, which is why I have a very strong relationship with America at the moment. I taught at New York City University and am teaching now at Harvard. Of course one would like to make a film that also breaks out of these academic spaces, but none the less it is an important constituency in the States.

On the whole audiences do want to see films that are more commercial, and you can't ignore that. With the computer age they relate more to the new technology: people have cameras and make their own images, which can be seen on the internet. Of course this applies only to a very specific part of the world and a specific group within it. None the less the possibilities are enormous, which is why I am quite excited about it. This is the moment when I hope we have reached the crossroads.

Capital and technology are located almost totally in advertising, so in that sense it has become the only space for young people to go. I am interested in utilising technology, especially the techniques used in certain rock promos, the visual language of which appeals to me. In a piece which I am making now, for instance, I am going to spend a couple of days on a flame, the special-effects technology used for a lot of advertising and rock promos.

What I would really like to do is to tell a story through film: something that is quite heavily storyboarded and has cinematic effects; something desirable to look at, an experience. So you could tell a story and arrive at some political statement, but in a very visually alluring way, which is what people like about cinema. This is a different strategy from Ken Loach or Mike Leigh, or even that of *The Full Monty*, all of which are much more upfront. I guess I don't see it as either/or. There should be narrative films that are populist in a way that people can understand as well as experimental work. I feel a commitment to both areas, but the question of visualisation should be considered as much in both.

I have been interested in trying to make different kinds of films for different sorts of audiences. For example *The Darker Side of Black* (1994) was made for the BBC's Arena programme and thus for a very specific audience, while *Looking for Langston* was for Channel 4's first lesbian and gay programme, another sort of audience. Then the portrait I made of Franz Fanon and his ideas, *Black Skin, White Masks*—the title is taken from his book—was theatrically released in 1997 at the ICA in London and reaches yet another.

In the future I would like to diversify. The film that I am editing at the moment, a dance piece, has a narrative aspect and will probably be 20 minutes long, a short film and installation project. There is *Bartering of Souls*, a film I am developing that is going to be shot in South Africa. My description of it is that it will be like *My Beautiful Laundrette* gone wrong. Then there is a project that we are trying to develop with television on the representation of angels: *Only Angels Have Wings*. In the age of telecommunications, it looks at the angel as a metaphor for how communication processes take place—by messenger,

aeroplane, the internet. The idea is that the angel is travelling around Europe, a subliminal way of talking about racism, though not in a didactic, upfront style. This could be a digital project.

My work will be a mix of films for television with film-installation for galleries. These are possibilities, but you have to be quite strategic. What I want to make in an art context is going to have to be very specific—you can't just make something and then think, Oh, it's going to go out. So that's my plan! It sounds good, but it tends to be complicated in actuality. It is never straightforward, but then no story is, is it?

Looking for Langston, 1989
(Sunil Gupta: Channel 4)

Isaac Julien, interview by Sheila Rowbotham, 5 July 1998, edited by Isaac Julien and Sheila Rowbotham

14 Struggle Not Submission

Gita Sahgal

I got into television by accident—when Bandung Productions was formed in the mid-1980s I managed to get a job there. Bandung was set up by Darcus Howe and Tariq Ali when Farrukh Dhondy was the multicultural commissioning editor at Channel 4. I always assumed it was a shotgun marriage because Darcus and Tariq came from very different political backgrounds. Tariq had been involved in Trotskyism, the International Marxist Group, nothing to do with the black left, whereas Darcus came out of the socialist part of the black-consciousness tradition.

Bandung was to be the first attempt on British television to combine an Asian and Afro-Caribbean programme. Its approach reflected the political orthodoxies of the time: radical Asians as well as people of African descent were calling themselves 'black'. As far as I know it was to be the only example of black and Asian programmes being tried within the same format.

Bandung's slot was supposed to be a programme for black people settled in Britain. But because of their political commitment, Tariq and Darcus always gave this a wide interpretation. For instance we ran something about South Africa nearly every week before the emergency and then during it got footage out from various radical film-makers who were working there whenever we could. There was always an international dimension to Bandung's work, cultural as well as political.

I came from a very similar background in India to Tariq's in Pakistan—upper middle-class progressive families. I had been at university in Britain and involved with student left politics during the mid- to late '70s, when there were a lot of anti-racist marches, campaigns against welfare cuts and the rises in overseas students' fees. Those were the last days of the Labour government, and how we hated Labour! The most right-wing thing in the union was the Labour Club! I was quite sceptical of feminist politics, though I remember Anna Davin speaking about working-class women in history at a meeting, and I was aware that groups were around, but this was only translated into any sort of political action when I went back to India in 1977. I really got politically active around feminism by taking part in the Indian women's movement campaigns of the late 1970s and early '80s around rape and dowry deaths. We were making our own agendas, taking what we wanted, where we wanted, and could afford to be politically eclectic in terms of radical feminist and socialist ideas, or whatever. I was also involved in voluntary organisations in India,

Gita Sahgal worked for Bandung from the early 1980s and her films included *Burned to Death* on dowry deaths in India and *Struggle or Submission?* about women and fundamentalism. In 1990 she directed *The Provoked Wife*, produced by Sylvia Stevens of Faction Films for Channel 4, and in 1995 *The War Crimes File* about the Bangladeshi war of 1971, also for Channel 4. She has written on fundamentalism, multiculturalism and feminism.

doing literacy and union work. These had initially had a Maoist inspiration, but after the emergency in India ended in '77, there was a decision to engage more with civil-rights struggles of various kinds.

When I returned to England in the mid-1980s the GLC was still around, and there was money going into the voluntary sector in London. It was the height of Thatcherism. By this period the left was incredibly fragmented, the old social-ist left demoralised both by Thatcher and by the internal arguments taking place in the left. In contrast, the women's group in which I got involved was very active and interesting. We called ourselves Southall Black Sisters, though we were predominantly Asian women and trying to make a very strong statement locally in the Southall community. We were raising feminist issues in the black women's movement where domestic violence, for instance, had not been discussed much, and we also felt it was very important to take a stand as black feminists in relation to the white women's movement.

My socialism I suppose would have been classified as 'white socialism'. I could understand the struggle for black autonomy, as well as women's auton-omy, and sympathise with the enormous sense of exclusion, but I never totally identified. I always felt myself to be somewhat outside that experience; for me ideas were always valid in themselves.

I found it a huge relief when I began working for Bandung, because, with Tariq especially, I was able to discuss how to approach researching films polit-ically. I had never really had ambitions as a 'film-maker' in mainstream televi-sion, but I was political and had journalistic ambitions. Bandung was the only place I think I could have gone. Over the four years I worked on the programme I must have done about 20 films. We shot each one in three or four days, all scrambled together, which was all the time we had, and then we would edit them over two or three weeks.

The programme had a news format when I joined as a presenter, but I did not want to be in front of the camera, I wanted to be doing research. As a researcher at Bandung you were able to have a considerable input because the directors tended not to know very much about the subjects of the programmes. They were very competent people, but they came out of the BBC mainstream tradition. They were not radical, nor were they hired by Bandung for their experimental film-making techniques. The black workshops, which were seen as Alan Fountain's domain, were very critical of Bandung's conservatism about form, but both Darcus and Tariq focused on what they wanted to say not on how it was done.

Bandung was unusual in allowing us to have people talking in their own voices with subtitles. I always preferred this to voice-overs because I assumed that there would be some part of the audience who would understand the orig-inal language anyway. But it is very unpopular, and you are virtually never allowed to use subtitles on television documentaries.

I begged Tariq for something as a researcher, and eventually I went off to India and researched *Burned to Death*, a film on dowry deaths, an issue about which I had campaigned in the women's movement in India. I also did one on sati there in 1988. This was the case of Roop Kanwar, a woman who was killed in late 1987, supposedly as a sati.

Both these films were for British audiences, and they were both about horrific subjects—about women burning, though in very different contexts. I felt no need to labour the horror, but to try and explain why it was happening to an audience who really had no handle on it. Usually programmes about these issues treated them as horrific survivals, some feudal remnant, or part of culture, tradition, whatever. While they can be read in those ways, I wanted to show there were very contemporary aspects too. Dowry, for instance, is an important form of capital formation in northern India, which helps explain why the deaths were so common. Of course dowries have always been given in India, but the particular form in which they have been demanded in recent years, the constant pressure to keep paying and the woman being actually killed if the family could not go on producing cash, rather than being divorced or discarded or abandoned in some other way, is quite modern.

Similarly satis were occurring in the context of a revivalist, religious cult. Although sati, the practice of burning widows on the funeral pyres of their husbands, has existed for hundreds of years, it had been a very different kind of practice, and the contemporary justifications were quite distinct. My film drew on the research of two Indian feminists, Sudesh Vaid and Kumkum Sangari, who had actually gone into the villages of Rajasthan where the satis had taken place and talked to people. They had detected a pattern emerging before it became a subject of great debate. The issue crystallised lots of arguments in India about culture and about tradition. Feminists fought not for the law to be changed, because obviously sati had already been outlawed, but for a ban on what was called its glorification. The government did actually forbid this, although they could not prevent sati happening.

I also did a film for Bandung on racism in employment, which is always very difficult to prove. I had written a report for the GLC on this in London and found that the law centres did not have very many cases on racial discrimination. It is very hard to make a case under the Race Relations Act when racism is structural in the working environment. How do you ascribe a racial cause to issues of promotion or lower wages? The whole casualisation process was occurring at this time, and through privatisation people were being employed in worse conditions in the same job, or the job itself was made harder.

There had, however, been a very big case at Heathrow Airport where Asian cleaners had actually gone to the Industrial Tribunal. A young lawyer, who we subsequently worked with a lot at Southall Black Sisters, had taken many case histories in order to build up the defence for the cleaners. These detailed statements about working conditions provided me with fantastic material for the GLC report and was the basis of the film I did about the impact of privatisation on a group of mainly Asian women workers at Heathrow.

Tariq thought it was a film about some little employment issue, until Channel 4 went absolutely bananas. The powers-that-be went nuts about the footage; the lawyers were very strict. You can make allegations about all sorts of people, but you can not name companies, even in juxtaposition, to suggest a hint of bad practice, unless you really can verify it. We did get across our main allegations, though we had to get rebuttals and include statements from the firms before Channel 4 allowed it to pass.

Then there was a lot of political hand-wringing about why we were talking about privatisation. I remember one of the commissioning editors saying to me, 'Surely the issue is about the jobs? There's the poor woman working sweeping the floor, and there's all these holiday travellers going off without a care in the world.' The message was, you could talk about race in terms of victimhood, but you were not supposed to connect it to political issues. We used a speech of Thatcher's about privatisation, and their response was that her policies had nothing to do with the women's working conditions. As far as they were concerned privatisation had already happened, but we were arguing more was being threatened, and that the result would be even worse conditions.

One of our great strength at Bandung was the extent of our contacts, which meant we could cover stories other crews could not. I remember going to Toxteth in Liverpool to do a story about policing when the violence was beginning to build up around 1988. The police were astonished that we had been able to go round Toxteth, but we had complete access and were totally safe. The kids were very interested, they knew where we had come from, and Darcus' daughter Tamara, our PA, was able to make all kinds of connections. We felt incredibly protected.

Bandung enabled me to tackle several controversial social conflicts. I did a programme on education, for instance, looking at the implications of parental choice in terms of race and class. There was a massive outcry in the newspapers and the media generally about white parents in Dewsbury, Yorkshire, who were quite racist. They had taken their children out of one Church of England school, which was predominantly Asian, to put them in another that was predominantly white. They had not been admitted to the school because they were outside the catchment area and were using a religious argument about being Christians and wanting their children to go to a Christian school, even though the original school was also a church school. A shift had occurred, making it respectable to express racism in religious or cultural terms, though not to support racial segregation by colour.

During this period of the late '80s the Tories tried to reinforce Christianity in the state schools by insisting on an act of Christian worship every day. They were also introducing so-called parental choice; some of the schools were going to be taken out of local council funding. Tariq asked me to do a film on the Muslim reaction to this. The Tories policies actually fuelled and legitimised the desire for separate Muslim schools, particularly girls' schools. I found that a lot of Asian parents were quite keen on sex segregation, but not necessarily on religious-based schools. These were issues with which people were not very comfortable, because there were certain orthodoxies about what kind of schooling there should be. Nobody was looking at the concept of separate Muslim schools, which exploded later, but at Bandung we did so quite early.

Again we did a film on Asian gangs in Southall. At that time there were two rival gangs, and the differences between them were largely cultural, in the sense that one was orientated more around hip-hop, and the other more around bhangra. They were largely made up of Sikh boys. The ugly side of it was that some people had been targeted by gangs: their houses were stoned, and they were turned into public scapegoats. Sometimes this was because of inter-gang rivalries, but they were also fixing on vulnerable people, specifically single women. Although everybody condemned the gangs, they also used them as a way of enforcing control over women. A husband might say to his wife, 'I'll set the gangs on you if you do this or that, or if you leave me.' That was always the threat, and it was not an empty one. Girls had been raped, and single women bringing up children on their own were targeted, lynched basically.

In the film we were not looking at the law-and-order side, the classic policing angle, but at how the gangs were a means of controlling women. These were arguments that we were making in Southall Black Sisters then, but they were deeply unpopular. The gangs had fought in the riots, boys had come out and fought the skinheads, and there was quite a romantic attachment to them because of that. This has changed: Southall has become much more communalised, and people who were sceptical of what we were saying as feminists are now campaigning against the division of gangs into Muslim and Hindu groups, or the Sikh and Muslim groups around Southall and Hounslow.

The gang fights are obviously very dangerous, and it is a young phenomenon, but this is not something just imported from the subcontinent. The police have tended to demonise the gangs as a peculiar alien phenomena, as if it were because they were not sufficiently British. Yet the gangs were acting in ways that are completely familiar within working-class British society, lads fighting over territory, culture, or their adopted cultural boundaries.

I was never bored doing that kind of work at Bandung because it was practically as well as theoretically challenging, and it made me develop ideas politically. Television often does not give you that opportunity. It usually deals with themes that are already in the public realm and kills ideas by popularising them. Generally you can't make the argument. One of the most formative films on which I worked on was on the Rushdie affair. *Satanic Verses* came out in '88, and after the book was burned in Bradford there was a lot of debate, about which we made a programme early in 1989.

It was as if all the politics I had been developing through Southall Black Sisters and with people at Bandung suddenly crystallised. The left was divided and quite unable to make a public statement about the fatwah against Rushdie; a lot of people felt completely silenced by the fact that it was a beleaguered minority who were being shat on from a great height by the media. Although I was really disgusted by how racist the media were, I believed we had to say something. Tariq was one of the few people in TV who had the courage to do that at that time. He was completely upfront. We made a film where we interviewed Salman, along with the leaders from Bradford and elsewhere. Quite fortuitously it was to come out on the night of the fatwah and was to be Rushdie's last public statement before he went underground.

At the time we did not look into the political origins of the attack on *Satanic Verses*. While it was evident that the movement was politically led, we were more concerned to understand how it was able to strike a chord in the hearts of many ordinary Muslims, a lot of young people, men and women living in Britain. We had to come to terms with that and analyse why that happened. It is very clear now that the leadership that originated from South Asia was politically organised and highly motivated, and came out of fundamentalist groups. It didn't arise just from people who were feeling oppressed in this country, as some of the left and anti-racist groups argued.

We were very careful to show that the attack on Rushdie came from one form of Islam. We never said all Muslims feel this way—although perhaps the majority did—or that Islam itself is fundamentalist. Instead in the programme we included Qawali popular songs, which are sung in shrines and religious settings, and often have a Sufi Muslim background. They express a close relationship with God, but quite a sceptical one as well, and the one we used criticised clerics for their hypocrisy. We juxtaposed it with other Muslim arguments, and with Rushdie's own, and tried to place him in a dissident tradition that has existed within Islam. Nobody was saying this in the media at that time. The assumption was that because some Muslims are fundamentalists, Islam was *ipso facto* fundamentalist, and all Muslims were presented as demanding Rushdie's death. Also newspapers such as the *Independent* were saying the trouble was that the opponents of Rushdie were not sufficiently British, as if the only British tradition was necessarily gentle and good and middle class. What about football hooliganism?

However, I also wanted to show that there were secular traditions among Asians, not simply religious identities. In the late 1980s Southall Black Sisters, along with various other women's groups, set up Women Against Fundamentalism. About 40 of us protested at the huge Muslim march through London that demanded the banning of *Satanic Verses*. We knew it would be filmed, which was one of the reasons for choosing to demonstrate. We felt it was important to make a statement, but it was extremely controversial. I remember lots of discussions, and some of our male socialist comrades, people for whom I have every respect, said, 'You mustn't do this, it will be seen as racist. It's not the right place to make a statement.' However, we decided that we must make it, because otherwise that demonstration would have gone unchallenged. We were not demonstrating as Muslims, although there were Muslim women among us, but as women from all sorts of backgrounds. We felt it very important to make that point. Because we came out of the left tradition and were very conscious that we would be called racist, we did not tell the police that we were going to demonstrate, as we felt we could not ask for their protection. We stood in one place without any barrier between us and the main march. I am sorry to say that on that demonstration I was bloody grateful for the British police who quickly formed a cordon around us.

At least three TV programmes made around that time mentioned our protest. One, for *Dispatches*, was supposedly from the 'Muslim' point of view. It followed one of the main leaders preparing for the demonstration and blamed the Women Against Fundamentalism demonstration for the violence that occurred later when young men fought the police on Westminster Bridge. Another was a *Heart of the Matter* programme on the BBC, which trod very much the same territory that I tried to cover in my film, *Struggle or Submission?*, but we handled it very differently. Although they did two moving interviews with Pragna Patel and another woman from the Women Against Fundamentalism group about the sources of inspiration in their lives and what had caused them to resist, the assumption behind the film was that people became more liberal, or more radical, more revolutionary, if they were more westernised. That was an attitude I was very concerned to blow apart in *Struggle or Submission?* Its title came from a slogan we had invented in the early '80s in Southall Black Sisters: 'Black women's tradition, struggle not submission'. In Women Against Fundamentalism, our banner said: *Our Tradition, Struggle Not Submission—* some people said, *Women's Tradition*, but I always felt that was too populist because, clearly, it wasn't all women's tradition. The slogan was also a play on the whole idea of Islam being a submission to God.

We wanted to show that there were differing interpretations among Muslim women. At that time very few Asian women had any voice in the media, and it was assumed that the veil was imposed on everyone who wore it. *Heart of the Matter* interviewed a woman who wore one because her father expected it. Smita Bhide, the writer who researched the Bandung film, found that some young women were choosing to wear a modern veil, which they called *hijab*. Moreover they were using impeccable feminist debate about the objectification of women to justify their choice: they argued that they did not want to be sexualised in the way that Western women were. They also invoked more traditional arguments in the Koran, which they allied to those arguments about the male gaze, saying that women were too precious to be exposed. However, a woman we interviewed from an Asian women's refuge referred to the same Koranic text but gave it a much more sensuous meaning. She said that we, too, have our dreams and desires; life is precious and we need to live it to the full. She was no feminist theologian, or somebody who was reinterpreting the Koran in an academic way. She had her own notion of the book, which led her obliquely to reject the fatwah against Rushdie. She was not christianised, nor English-speaking and considered herself to be a good Muslim, going later on a religious pilgrimage to Mecca. She had simply encountered huge resistance from her family because she wanted to divorce her husband, and the imam had refused to allow it. That struggle radicalised her, not a process of westernisation as such. I felt it was very important to reflect her views as well as those of the young *hijab*-wearing women who were, if anything, using western feminist arguments to justify their choice.

There are many ambiguities in how this notion of 'westernisation' has been used. It has also been seen and interpreted selectively by the media. There is a moment in *Struggle or Submission?* when the men on the Muslim march were asked by the researcher, 'Where are your wives?' They answered in broad northern accents that the women were at home making tea. To me these men were completely British. They had grown up here. They were Yorkshire boys, down for the day in London, who had left their wives behind to make the tea, as many Northern men would do! It was not the case that they had become Muslim fundamentalists because they had insufficiently imbibed British values, as the 'quality' press implied. It was rather that British values vary.

This class aspect was missed by the media; yet poor working-class communities were turning into an underclass, which might explain why the demonstration was so powerful, why so many people joined it, and why it became in fact a genuine popular movement. Although it was indeed led and organised by the Muslim right, it found an echo among a lot of people because there was nothing else, no other voice. A generation had been growing up to unemployment, to Thatcherism, to whole areas of the North that had been condemned to complete non-existence, because they were Labour majority areas. Their experience was never talked about, and unfortunately you can only glimpse this class dimension in the film. I was not able explicitly to discuss it in a 20-minute programme done under extreme time pressure, with very little editing time and so on. But that was what I was trying to reach towards.

Struggle or Submission? has been shown all over the place and has lasted, mainly because it deals with issues of identity. People do not usually want to discuss it in terms of the class issues that are implicit there, but they do want to talk about it in relation to identity: how you find yourself as Muslims, and what kind of interpretations you have of the Koran, for instance. A lot of universities have therefore shown it because it lends itself to such discussions. *Struggle or Submission?* was very important for me personally, though I never could have imagined that something knocked off in a few weeks would still be watched ten years later.

When we made the Rushdie programmes, Bandung had already done films about the Sikh and Hindu right. It wasn't as if Tariq had an anti-Muslim agenda because he came from a Muslim background. He certainly had a very clear anti-fundamentalist agenda, which was a great relief because a lot of other producers were too liberal to be as clear as he was about it, and many Asians did not want to handle something that was such a hot potato in their community. In contrast Darcus never talked about controversial religious issues: he is very conservative on that, though he is hard on policing and those were the only programmes on which he let me work.

I believe the Stephen Lawrence case really is a watershed. The tragedy is that it has taken such a long time. The same people, like Suresh Grover, for instance, in the Monitoring Group in Southall, have been working on policing and race issues for years. The Lawrence Enquiry was a culmination of many different local campaigns around racist murders, racist attacks, the actions of the police and instances of corruption. The Justice for Blair Peach Campaign has also been an incredibly long one. It has taken years for these local struggles to surface nationally as they have done over the Stephen Lawrence case.

Bandung was reflecting some of these experiences of policing, back in the 1980s, for example the rebellion that erupted against the police at Broadwater Farm estate in North London and the subsequent disputed arrests. Or the case of Trevor Monerville, a young man arrested and beaten in Hackney, on which I did a couple of stories. He had vanished—his grandparents had even phoned the police about him being missing—and his family eventually found him bruised and injured in prison. He had been in a coma and didn't know where he was or remember what had happened. The police and the prison both blamed each other for the injuries: no one would take responsibility.

It always strikes me how a lot of people of the old generation of Afro-Caribbeans were incredibly conservative: so many God-fearing, Christian, patriarchal figures, who just wanted to do a hard day's work and do well by their families. That was not recognised at all. Interestingly, I think a shift is occurring in how conservative English people see race. For instance Peregrine Worsthorne did a TV programme with Darcus Howe, examining ideas of Englishness by going around schools in predominantly black areas and country mansions in the Home Counties. In an article after the programme Peregrine Worsthorne wrote about how he had been a bit racist, but having met Darcus who speaks the Queen's English, knows Shakespeare and loves cricket, he had decided that Darcus, and Caribbeans in general, are basically good eggs.

When I read out the Worsthorne article to my friend Nira Yuval-Davies, who has written a lot on questions of identity and boundaries, she immediately asked whether he mentioned Muslims. Nira's work has challenged some of the orthodoxies on race because she has argued that racism is a matter of where you place the boundaries, rather than simply one of colour. Being Jewish has made her particularly aware that identities are defined differently in certain historical times and periods. I think she is right. The boundaries are being moved. We are living through a shift in who can be seen as acceptable and who is to be defined as alien, as 'the other'. The subtext is that it is now Muslims who are being regarded as intrinsically more 'foreign' than Afro-Caribbeans, because they are Muslim, have 'weird' customs and other loyalties that are much more powerful than any loyalty to Britain.

This presents those of us who have been trying to work critically around race and identity with a difficult dilemma. Women Against Fundamentalism and Southall Black Sisters have been accused of contributing to the hostile negative image of Islam because we criticised some of the political movements within it. We have been castigated as being part of the defamation process because we defended Rushdie's right to write. That was seen as disloyal.

The demonisation of Islam by the West is of course always selective. The Americans actually created some of the monsters they are now opposing. In Afghanistan, for instance, they backed Afghan fighters against the Russians and with their Pakistani allies are in part responsible for the Taliban. It is also remarkable the issues that are not addressed by the media in spite of satu-ration coverage. In 1995 I produced *The War Crimes File*, a film about the Bangladesh war of 1971, when the country was born. It was about paramili-tary death squads, Bengalis, who had helped the Pakistani military, killing under their orders and also on their own account. David Bergman did an enor-mous amount of work researching it with me, and the film was shown on *Dispatches* on Channel 4 in 1995. We named three of the people involved in genocide in Bangladesh who now live in Britain and argued that they should be tried for war crimes. These are people who are much younger than the Nazis who have been tried, who are not retired or leading quiet lives, who are still active politically. Unlike the Nazis, they had not changed their identities, and went under the same names, even their backgrounds were known, but they had never been investigated. It turned out that these political leaders had been active in the Rushdie affair here. When you think how masses of television time has been expended on the Rushdie story, it is remarkable that nobody had actually looked at who the political leaders opposing him were; that nobody had really tracked them or their political allegiances.

There are obvious similarities between the Bangladesh war and the discus-sions around the past in South Africa and Chile. Is justice only done when some accounting is made? When does this just become a political vendetta? However, much less attention has been paid to these questions regarding Bangladesh. The film got little publicity in Britain apart from the World Service, community and local radio, though it received enormous attention in South Asia.

David Bergman and I came across the information that led to *The War Crimes File* while working on a television proposal on the fatwah against Taslima Nasrin, a very popular writer in Bangladesh, who was quoted as saying—she denies she ever said it—that she thought the Koran ought to be updated. Our proposal was to be rejected, despite the fact that the Taslima Nasrin case received international coverage, on the grounds that the film would not be of sufficient interest to a mainstream audience.

This has been an attitude that has dogged us all the way through. They used to say, 'Send it to the Asians', and it has been argued that multicultural programmes marginalise issues. That might be the case, but when slots like Bandung's are closed down, then there is nothing. It is not as if anybody else feels impelled to take on issues of race in any depth: the discussion simply does not happen.

The representation of race has certainly changed in the sense that there is actually more visibility of Afro-Caribbean and Asian people on British screens in a range of different programmes—still not enough but we have a greater degree of visibility. However, though people may appear more, they are not discussed or situated. Just as class has become invisible, so in fact has race, and when the two coincide, the way in which they interact is not discussed either.

Sometimes this colour-blind approach is fine. You don't always need to dwell on class or racial aspects of a person's being, be they a school kid or mechanic, a car worker or battered wife. They are simply on television in a particular documentary connected for some reason with who or what they are. Their origin may not be relevant. On the other hand it may be. A real problem arises when this neutralised visibility is the only entry point to the media. I find it disturbing when I feel I am not getting the whole picture, because of the inability of the people making the film to comprehend the subject in a wider context. The issue now is really about a very limiting framework and the absence of any sense of history. The question of representation is not just about visibility but also about what can be included.

Although there is a celebration of Cool Britannia as multicultural and multiracial, this has led in my view to a new parochialism. You are OK if you are able somehow to break through into being trendy, then you are part of the same culture, a particular crowd. Television is always trying desperately to be cool. They put out tenders for independent producers and are constantly looking for different tribes or sub-cultures. The media wants to get into what young Asian people, for instance, are doing, not on tedious issues such as race but in music or theatre. Of course some of these are popular cultural topics and should have programmes made around them, but not at the expense of all other aspects of life. The parameters of what might be considered of interest have become increasingly restricted. There is an assumption, perhaps a fear because of the bid for ratings, that viewers are not going to be interested in unfamiliar areas of experience.

Unfortunately the tendency to eliminate and exclude becomes self-perpetuating. Because issues are not mentioned enough, they become unmentionable, and they do not get on. All the research shows that the less international coverage there is, the less people want it. The habit of being able to watch or engage with subjects that are not quickly accessible disappears. The situation we confront on the media now makes me think ruefully of all the times that the left criticised the old BBC, for its patronising Oxbridge-dominated culture. For that mission to educate did contain within it the idea that events have to be explained, and that it is good for people to understand things outside their immediate experience. Yet now there is a sense that if you can't apprehend something immediately, it's not worth it.

An example of how material is filtered is a film that I saw about Palestinian women, which did not receive funding from TV. The women not only talked about nationalism, and obviously about the struggle of the Palestinians, but also about being women and their relationship with their children. It was filmed very sensitively in their kitchens, setting them in their surroundings, an enclosed world, their internal world. The Channel 4 commissioning editor's response was, 'You can't imagine a British woman in Essex being able to relate to that.' But you think, Well, if she had an ounce of sympathy she probably could: a kitchen is a kitchen.

A consequence of course is that they erase the politics—I don't mean just in a flag-waving way. If you are blanking out the politics, it means you're blanking out the history and the context. For instance, when I did *Burned to Death* for Bandung, I included overt political statements by people who are activists.

They had done research on the issue and thus could be wearing both hats as participants and 'experts'. This was quite explicit in the film.

Television now will discuss similar issues of domestic violence but cut out the history of the feminist politics around it over the last 20 years. The accepted formula is for somebody to speak briefly from a particular political position, which is not examined, or to get an academic who has researched the topic to give an opinion. They tend not to use women who have been active in the women's movement, working in a refuge, who might have quite cogent things to say about the issue. There is an implicit feeling that if you are an activist, then you're banging a drum, and that this is illegitimate. Therefore the issues are presented powerfully, yet voyeuristically and horrifically, completely without context. This is happening more and more in television, and I see it as a very disturbing trend. It is often hard to argue with people in the industry who might be sympathetic politically but keep their politics outside what they do in terms of a programme. They say, 'Look, you can't do that, it's not part of the programme's duty to present alternatives.' When you explain that the problem does have alternatives, that it may not be solved, but there are people who have been working around the issue for years. Shouldn't they have a voice? But they claim they are just exposing the issue.

The implications came home to me when Channel 4 showed a programme that was a powerful critique of the police, the Crown Prosecution Service and the courts for not acting on domestic violence. The film confirmed what we had been saying for years in Southall Black Sisters. But when I talked to workers in Southall Black Sisters afterwards, they said women had rung up and cancelled appointments and said they did not want to go to court because they were so depressed by seeing the programme. It had made them think they would not win. Statistically, as the programme showed, the odds are stacked against women. What it did not say is that if you have good representation, if you have somebody working with you, if your confidence is built up, then you can go through with it and actually get somewhere. You are not necessarily sold down the river by the police and the Crown Prosecution Service. If you have somebody with you when you give your initial statement who can force the police to take cognisance of how serious the crime is and understand that this ought to be classified as grievous bodily harm and not just common assault or actual bodily harm, then the classification will be taken seriously later. If somebody has helped to do those kinds of things at the early stages, then you have got a better chance of success. But there was no voice on the programme saying that.

The film-makers were making a strong polemical argument: women are still getting a raw deal, even though things have changed, even though they are supposedly better. It's right and proper to say that. That is an argument worth stating very clearly on television. But if you don't show other possibilities the result can be that you actually discourage the very women the film is supposed to be defending. That's an appalling position to be in.

Cutting Edge on Channel 4 did a two-hour programme about a woman in

America who had killed her husband. The justification for putting aside two hours of screen time for one case was that they had access to the trial. She was a white English woman, being tried for killing a black man, but the fact that there could have been racial aspects to how the jury handled it or how it was viewed was not mentioned. The man's family refused to take part in the programme, so their viewpoint was never heard. I am not saying I felt sympathetic to him, but the film was silent on issues of race, which could have been relevant. Nobody said, 'Oh, he's bad because he is black', yet it was obvious that the woman was white and the man was black.

He had not been physically violent, and the issue was emotional violence. Leonora Walker, who developed theories of a battered women's syndrome, that have since been challenged, gave evidence on behalf of the accused woman. But the film made no reference to the fact that her ideas have been discredited. Nor was there any hint of the feminist debates about domestic violence.

I watched with a sense of *déjà vu*. The first film I directed after I left Bandung in 1989 was about women who murdered violent husbands. It was called *The Provoked Wife*, produced by Sylvia Stevens at Faction Films and shown on the *Dispatches* programme on Channel 4 in 1990. Yet from the *Cutting Edge* film you got no idea that debate on domestic violence among academic feminists is still raging. Even if you were to glimpse that a political discussion was happening in a programme now, it would not be dealt with explicitly or in any depth. That is one of the most dangerous things. It isn't that the politics goes away: the politics are buried, while the specific story is presented without any context. There is no sense of history or future, of where any opposing ideas have come from and where they might be going.

In the end you just end up with a titillating half-hour, hour, or, in this case, two hours of programme. You have been there at intimate moments of this woman's life—she discovers she's pregnant by the man that she killed, and she's standing trial for his murder; she already has a child by him, from whom she is terrified of being separated. You see them meet for the first time after months. There is a strong camera presence at these times, supposedly good television. You think, What is it all about? Why are we interested in these people's lives? What more do we learn, than, Oh, my God, what a tragic story. And, Oh, she seems so nice, I'm glad she got off. There is a deep-rooted reluctance to make broader connections. There is little space in television for really discussing subjects, and more could be allocated. At present, however, there is less and less debate getting through, and I am not sure that I want to make films within these terms. It is not only the quickly produced political films we made at Bandung that are now absent but also the more experimental ones.

When I left Bandung I learnt not to call myself a film-maker, but a television programme-maker, an altogether lower form of life. However, I became involved in a film directed by my partner, Ruchir Joshi, in India. Ruchir would see himself as a film-maker: he makes very political films, though not overtly so. Doing this film was a very good experience for me, though completely different from working at Bandung, from the kind of current-affairs work that I do. We were

Demonstration outside the Appeal Court in the Strand, London, in support of Kiranjit Ahluwalia and other Provoked Wives (Southall Black Sisters)

working on 16mm film rather than video, with very little money. There was no fixed budget, so we would raise money as we went along, buying a couple of rolls of stock and hiring a car to travel to villages. It turned into a long, sprawling film about Baul singers, a wandering religious sect, which like a lot of these little groups, had crossed religious boundaries, taking ideas from Buddhism, Hinduism and Islam. Some of their devotional songs are very old and have been handed down, but they also make up new ones. Rather like a court jester, they have a position as outsiders who can comment on society and the strangeness of modern life. Ruchir was interested in them through his own connections with music, from jazz to indi-pop, and the film was a critique of the kind of anthropological film-making that goes out and meets an exotic group of people and by the end of the film leaves you with the conviction that you know what they are about. He was challenging the idea that you could ever know. The standard of work was extraordinarily good and it was beautifully shot, on much less money than we had ever had to shoot at Bandung. It was very hard to get it made. Ruchir produced a trailer from the material he had shot on his own money, with friends, and, on the advice of another left-wing Indian film-maker, Anand Patwardhan, brought it to London and showed it to Alan Fountain, who was then commissioning for Channel 4. Alan Fountain not only gave him completion money to make it but also commissioned more work. Ruchir's films deal imaginatively with issues of identity, modernity and religion, and, although I didn't work in that mould myself, collaborating with him made me see there were other possibilities, different ways a film could be made. Film could try to say something more and still be funded by Channel 4's Independent Film and Video Department, and shown on British television at the end of the day!

I see nothing like that happening now. Those possibilities have closed down, and I don't feel at all optimistic about the future, though maybe it will find its own level and develop completely different forms. But, at the moment, I only hear people talking about newness, novelty and innovative forms, but they don't actually develop anything new. They are rehashing.

In contrast I remember sitting at home being a couch potato one night in 1989. I switched on the TV and was flicking through the channels when I found Isaac Julien's extraordinary *Looking for Langston*. What was doubly extraordinary was that I was not seeing it at the ICA and hadn't read a review or even a preview in the papers. I just found it on the box and was completely gripped by it. It was so beautiful. I knew who Langston Hughes was, I had read some of his poetry, because my family had his books on the shelves at home, and I had never heard him mentioned otherwise, nor had I read about him—it was a private sort of knowing. Then suddenly there was a beautiful, subversive film about him on television. It was wonderful to find it so unexpectedly. There was none of that sense of expectation you carry to the cinema to see some great piece of work. Nor anything portentous, as there often is about the places in which one goes to see art films or alternative cinema. If you just come across a film on TV, it possesses a very different kind of power, one that reaches out and grabs you. I think it unlikely that I would have that experience again.

Gita Sahgal interview by Sheila Rowbotham, 15 December 1998, edited by Gita Sahgal and Sheila Rowbotham

Section VI

ACCESS TO THE AIR WAVES

Sheila Rowbotham

By the late 1990s widespread criticism of British television was surfacing in the media; not in terms of how class could be presented, but as a protest against 'dumbing down'. The reasons for these changes in programming go back to the 1980s when Margaret Thatcher encouraged satellite and cable TV as a means of undermining the existing channels by allowing them to operate with fewer public-service obligations. Changes in taxation and the introduction of a competitive award system for ITV franchises made the commercial channels more dependent on advertising income. From the late 1980s the BBC was restructured. Internal markets and closer links to commercial cable and satellite corporations generated a mounting bureacracy of administrators and accountants and a shift from the public-service ethos.

So, while ITV has to please advertisers and increase ratings to secure them an improved share of the market, the BBC fears losing its income from the compulsory licence fee if it does not keep up high viewing figures. This preoccupation with ratings, along with cost-cutting, has affected the programmes shown.[1] It has also bred a conservative and ultimately uncreative inclination to play safe. As Kennith Trodd, a former BBC executive producer who, like Loach and Garnett, had begun working for the BBC in the early 1960s, remarked in June 1999, 'chancy innovation and risk-taking'[2] were in decline. Even Sir John Birt, who had instituted the restructuring, said, while making his final annual report as director general in 1999, that ratings should not be seen as the 'be-all and end-all'. The BBC had to remember what makes public-service channels 'different'. He also conceded that the BBC was failing young audiences and the 'less well off'.[3]

At Channel 4 Alan Fountain was able to show programmes that reached sizeable majorities. This was not only important in allowing for diversity of interest but also provided the space for innovation that is vital in a creative industry. This section begins with his account of the work of the Independent Film and Video Department.

Historically, change has frequently come from outside in terms of both form and in content. Kim Gordon notes examples of radical democratic initiatives in radio and TV devising new formats. Social forms of communication have thus contributed ways of broadcasting that have been subsequently adapted for commercial reasons. It is not then that 'the market' is in itself inventive, simply that it is adept in turning invention to profit.

As the documentary film-maker Roger Graef remarked in the *Guardian* in January 1998, 'There is no formula for success in creative television.' He goes on to say that while well-promoted, big-budget series have flopped, outside runners have struck a powerful chord of recognition with viewers: '*Our Friends in the North* is now cited by BBC executives as proof of their commitment to quality television. But it took 12 years to overcome internal resistance before the series reached the screen.'[4] In this section Huw Beynon looks at Peter Flannery's series about labour politics in Newcastle. He shows how it is both an account of the labour movement and a story about the choices and principles, compromises and defeats of two generations of working-class socialists.

Judith Williamson's point that there are two different projects involved in 'looking at class'—'labour' and the representation of working-class people in popular culture—is taken up by Jacquetta May, who acted in *EastEnders* as 'Rachel' during the early 1990s. She looks at how class, race and gender are depicted in a programme that has an audience of 20 million. British soaps, set in unglamorous working-class locations, abound in cosy invocations of community. Jacquetta May draws on feminist studies of soaps that have recognised the appeal of the drama of everyday life and demonstrates how *EastEnders* has given working-class-women characters significant roles. She brings her own practical knowledge to bear on how plots and parts are actually worked out.

The means of communication were being transformed once again in the late 1990s, this time by digital technology. Kim Gordon argues that radical social pressure needs to be reapplied in order to counter the dramatic concentration of ownership and control that is occurring in the media. Restructuring in the visual media has left viewers with less power to influence the content of TV than at any previous time. The concentration in ownership has been intensifying, even as the channels have been proliferating. Kim Gordon outlines the considerable obstacles to democratisation, but, echoing Tony Garnett, insists on the importance of engaging with the new technology Rejecting the narrowness of the 'Cultural Industries' approach, which focuses exclusively on the material aspects of communication, he insists that the key factor remains the will to communicate oppositional perspectives.

Kim Gordon's 'emancipatory moment' will require vision, combination and fierce tenacity. And, if a new generation is to create contrary images, reveal excluded experiences and realise the suppressed possibilities of other ways of seeing, they will need to scan in the wide-ranging dimensions of their rebellious inheritance—one aspect of which has been looking at class.

Notes

1. Thanks to Kim Gordon for background information on TV in the 1980s and '90s.
2. Kennith Trodd, quoted in M. Carter, 'Drama Unfolds behind the Scenes at the BBC', *The Times*, 4 June 1999.
3. Sir John Birt, quoted in J. Gibson, 'BBC Urged to Stay Clear of Ratings Games', *Guardian*, 24 June 1999.
4. R. Graef, 'The Flipside of Flop', *Guardian*, 5 January 1998.

15 Opening Channels: Channel 4 and After

Alan Fountain

Alan Fountain was Commissioning Editor for Independent Film and Video at Channel 4. He has worked as a film-maker, and was Head of the Northern Media School and consultant on various media projects. He is a co-founder with Sylvia Stevens of Mondial Online, a global media news project.

I became interested in European art cinema during the 1960s when I was in my teens. It was that great period of Antonioni, Godard and Fellini, when to be into European cinema was, for me, linked to being ferociously anti-Hollywood and anti-American. In my late twenties, I went to Nottingham University and did a degree in Philosophy. It was the mid-70s, when *Screen*'s intellectual influence was at its height and Marxist aesthetic criticism was being combined with psychoanalysis. A component within my curriculum was one of the first film courses, taught by Robin Wood, who came from *Movie* magazine and was completely opposed to all this *Screen* theory. We used to have terrible arguments, and I think his life was a misery faced as he was by a small group of students, including me, who completely bought the whole *Screen* approach.

I went to live in the Meadows, a run-down area in Nottingham, and started getting involved in housing activism and community politics. The conjunction of living in a working-class community for the first time in my life, studying Marxism at university during the day, and looking at culture and film in a different way made a big impact on me. Things all seemed to fit together in this period. After that I started doing a PhD—reading a lot but not writing. I got lost in it all really and learnt from it only in retrospect.

When I took a job as a film officer at East Midlands Arts, based in Loughborough, we began to put forward a coherent policy for developing independent film in the region around production, education and distribution. This was tied up with the idea of enabling more people to make films. I worked with teachers to try and introduce film and film theory into their curricula and ran weekend courses.

After about three years I decided I wanted to make films, and I started a documentary, informed by all this theory in my head, about my family and 'the Family'. This was the beginning of when discussions were being held with the film union, the ACTT, about what the incipient workshop movement was going to become. The idea evolved of unionisation of the independents and a wage structure that would create some sort of infrastructure throughout the country. When the Independent Film-makers Association (IFA) was founded I was drawn into that. My plan at that point was to leave the job that I was doing, get involved in the film workshop in Nottingham and start making stuff, which I did for a couple of years. But when the idea of Channel 4 came into being, and the possibility of joining the team came up, I felt torn. In the end I chose to go and work for Channel 4, starting in 1981. We were to begin broadcasting in 1982. I stayed for 14 years.

The atmosphere at the beginning was completely different from what it was to be even just five years later. In the early days of Thatcher, on the whole, the politics of the place were fairly progressive; the majority of people there were either left or centre left. In that climate, Jeremy Isaacs invited Rod Stoneman and me, and Caroline Spry, who joined the department later, to create our departmental policy. We were the Independent Film and Video Department, an oddity in the sense that all the other departments—sport, education, current affairs, feature films—were genre defined. Instead we were shaped according to areas of production, so we could do almost anything, within the limits of our budget, with anyone that we wanted to. We could do bits of fiction, of documentary, of experimentation. Part of the initial brief, and probably why I got the job initially, was to relate to the emerging workshop movement.

The basic ideas had been set out already by the independent workshops and the Independent Film-makers Association (IFA) before Channel 4 even existed. The IFA had produced the Foundation Document, calling for Channel 4 to give something like 10 per cent of its total budget, to an independent foundation that would operate outside Channel 4 and liaise, administer and give money to the workshops. The idea of the Foundation Document was to try nationally to build up a regionally based system of production, exhibition and distribution. The ACTT had agreed to recruit a lot of independent film-makers who had not been able to get into the film union because they did not necessarily fit any of the craft requirements. So they came into the ACTT, and the union embraced the idea of the workshop movement and created the Workshop Agreement that underpinned it, which was all about full-time employment. It was an extraordinary time really.

Looking for Langston, 1989 (Sunil Gupta: Channel 4)

My first task was to sit down with the ACTT—then a very strong union. I was then representing Channel 4 and involved, with the workshops and the union, in creating this new infrastructure that would finance the workshop movement. Other sources of finance were the British Film Institute (BFI), local authorities and European money, so the workshops got money from various places as well as from us. At its height, Channel 4 was financing something like 25 different workshops, by putting money into capital equipment and contributing to the Workshop Agreement, through which people had full-time jobs. Workshops would put forward a Programme of Work for a specific three-year period, and then we would sign them up for those years, and they got on with it. Channel 4 bought back the films we wanted to show from the workshop. So it was an incredible agreement.

The idea was that the workshops would be regionally based, and so they were formed in most cities: Belfast, Newcastle, Birmingham, Cardiff and Sheffield for instance. There were several in London, and some outside big cities. Part of the concept of the workshop was that its members would have close links to the communities in which they lived, something that supported the aim of enabling people who would never normally have had that possibility to be involved in the process of representation. The working class—whoever that might mean in each specific context—was obviously integral to the project. The idea was to work with trade unions and black communities as well, so there was a serious political agenda behind it all. Now how that all worked out—which workshops really were close to the community how successfully they were able to represent the people within it—is an interesting question, and to find the answer to it one would have to study different workshops. Obviously, Amber is a very good example, because their entire political ethos had taken them to Newcastle with that intention in the late '60s. How successful most of the regional workshops actually were in linking to local communities is a complicated issue, nevertheless that was the original ambition.

The other aspect of my department's work was the weekly slot, *The 11th Hour*. This became a programme into which a lot of the regional workshops' films were to go. We were also commissioning independents, which were not workshops, to produce films. But the criteria was similar, and our rule in the department was: 'We want to work with producers, and the people with whom they are working, to represent views, perspectives, analyses and opinions that aren't going to be represented anywhere else on British television.' That was always part of the test of any proposal that came to us. We felt that if another department could easily do it, then it was not something we should do. The idea was to enfranchise, a whole set of radical, alternative or different views that had not seen the light of day on television.

We were informed in broad terms by the radical ideas of the '70s. Our conception of 'alternative' included the radical element in the working-class and trade-union movement, the black community, women and feminism, gays and also internationalism, including the Third World. We started working with film-makers—both feature film and documentary film-makers—from Third World countries, doing Latin American or Indian seasons, Arab or Chinese cinema. We also linked up with quite a lot of film-makers in the USA whom we felt were offering another view of America, one that did not get much of an airing on television here and that we saw as a counter to the prevailing view of American society. Then we formed contacts with alternative European film-makers as well. So the department was involved in many different sorts of work, which loosely fitted into an overall framework. The programme we began to build up was not large in terms of money, but quite considerable in its international scope. There was a logic to the whole operation.

In the early '80s we hoped we were contributing towards real change in British TV, not only for the producers of films, but also for British audiences, opening up completely new areas and enabling them to see things they had not seen. This conception of putting another view on to TV was what the Independent Film and Video Department was really about. One aspect of this was being prepared during moments of crisis. The media invariably tends to lag behind what is actually happening. In my experience television is happy to finance and make films about struggles in retrospect. Once it is all finished, fine, let's make the movie. The problem always is making stuff at the point that it really matters. When the miners' strike occurred and later during the Gulf War, we were able to present programmes that otherwise would not have been there. That was partly because during the first few years this under-standing of our role was backed by Jeremy Isaacs. Although he did not neces-sarily agree with our perspective, he gave us a blank cheque—not a large blank cheque, but a small one—and a weekly slot. Consequently a lot of people who had not worked with TV before—had not made the breakthrough—were able to produce programmes. Some good things were achieved, though in retro-spect it is possible to see how that first generation, informed by '60s and '70s thinking in one way or another, arrived to create this alternative form of media just at the wrong moment historically.

The changes were to happen very gradually, though Isaacs' departure in the late '80s made a difference, because of his conception of what Channel 4 should be. For the first few years, the approach to television was very producer-orientated. Isaacs had an interesting, although slightly odd analysis of television, given that it is a mass medium. He would talk about the producer as a crafts person or someone with a vision, making a programme that was delivered to an individual viewer. This idea of communication in relation to a mass medium is at odds with how people on the left have tended to analyse television, yet it is an incredibly powerful approach when you are in the prac-tical world of television. It completely counters the 'What we've got to concen-trate on is audience levels' idea or 'Why don't we do another market survey?', the conception that was to take over subsequently at Channel 4.

The issue about fighting for market share was always there, of course, but after Isaacs went the emphasis was increasingly tilted towards it and justified by reference to the increasingly competitive age towards which TV was moving. When Michael Grade arrived he talked about the 'amateur' days of Jeremy

Isaacs and how the Channel needed 'professionalism.' Under the ideology of 'professionalism' all sorts of other things were introduced that ran counter to the Isaacs' ethos.

Obviously the point of making programmes is to reach an audience and communicate with people. One has to take note of audience, even just to keep the thing going economically. It is always a balancing act but it is then a matter of what becomes too important within that. The issue is: what predominates? I think that by now television is mainly understood as a market-driven system.

One of the problems we ran into was that the notion of what an acceptable audience level was began to change. It was crazy, really, because even very late at night, we were getting viewers of 400,000 to a million for Third World feature films, which is an incredible audience for that work. If you think of it in terms of cinema, distribution of the same work would get nowhere near that. But from the point of view of Channel 4 this was regarded as a terrible failure because the figures were too low. Michael Grade's view was: 'We are going towards this more and more competitive environment, and Channel 4 has got to build up its audience, because it's inevitably going to be knocked back.'

This perspective was arguable—one could make a case for it—but the result was to be that Channel 4 hardly ever now shows non-English language programming, and if they do it is very late at night. From an international perspective, British television has now reached a quite disgraceful level. One could argue that it was the Grade–Willis era that began the process of decline. If you want to see anything about Germany or France, there is almost nothing even produced by the Brits, or if you want to see French or German productions these are virtually non-existent. So even in terms of Europe, there is a complete crisis, let alone more problematic matters, such as the whole North–South issue. It is odd how we now have so many channels yet they are incapable of delivering; between them they have not really expanded choice at all.

One of the very weird things about Channel 4 is that it came into being at the very moment Thatcherism turned up. For the first few years, its thinking, the general political sense of the Channel was completely at odds with Thatcherism. However, looking back, ironically one can see that it was in tune with the Thatcherite economic model. Without anyone realising this at the time it was to be the battering ram that began to change the economics of television companies and independent film groups. In the long run, the independents fell into a terrible trap: they were thinking about widening the gates of television, whereas the structural implications of what they were doing was to contribute to a different economic model, so that television production became based on a small centre fed by hundreds of casualised producers.

From the aesthetic and political viewpoint, a new concept of TV was invented with ideas about greater access and new choices amid one of the biggest political upheavals of the century. Meanwhile an incredibly right-wing government was bringing about a complete reconception of what words such as 'choice'

and 'freedom' were held to mean. The fact that Channel 4 did some very interesting things in its first ten years was extraordinary in the face of the onslaught
upon the rest of society.

In my experience most people in television don't really have a political
perspective or any developed analysis of the business in which they operate
in. It always seems to me that the television industry is a very unconscious
and unreflective one. Even during the late '80s and early '90s, it was difficult
to have a political conversation in television about what was happening to the
media and the wider social effects of Thatcherism. Yet a lot of the decisions
that were driving Channel 4 were effectively a result of the Thatcherite process.
However, because there was no shared analysis or language, it became impossible to talk about this at all.

One of the ironic twists about the creation of Channel 4 was that it contributed
to the death of the movement of radical, independent film-makers that it was
supposed to support. Its advent brought with it the possibility of money, of doing
films and getting them on TV. It meant that suddenly people could be busy
making things, but that they also had to turn themselves into small businesses
to do it. Also, because Channel 4 seemed not perhaps the ultimate answer to
everyone's dreams, though good at the start, the sense of critique began to
drop away. Those of us working on the inside were acutely aware that all this
work was going on, that thousands of hours of television were being created
around the world, but there was hardly any discussion of it. I felt, as did the
film-makers, I suspect, that increasingly we were working in a critical vacuum.

No left critique ever emerged about how Channel 4 had begun, developed
and changed. There was a flurry of books at the beginning, but after that it
seemed not to exist any more. With the state of television criticism in the national
press so appalling, it never took place there either. The result is that there has
never been a full discussion or critique about the programme content of Channel
4. The whole movement in criticism that introduced Marxist ideas into literary
and film theories, which Screen represented in the '70s, had given a tremendous impetus to people to think about aesthetics and politics. Virtually any weekend there would be schools and events, screenings and discussions. Although
that created a lot of problems for film-makers, it was none the less an interesting, healthy time. Almost with the arrival of Channel 4 it collapsed overnight.

The production side continued to go its own way, relatively divorced from
criticism, while the theory side became an exclusively academic areas of interest, something on which you went and did a degree. In the process this theorising seemed to become increasingly detached from anything to do with active
political involvement. So what started out as being a potentially invigorating
situation, with practice and theory rooted in actual activity and real communities, disappeared into something else. Half of it vanished into the television
industry and half into the universities, and that was that. Who knows what the
effect will be. There are thousands of students engaged in film and media
degrees, who supposedly do leave armed with critical thought, but what appearance it ever makes subsequently, I am not at all sure.

Looking for Langston,
1989 (Sunil Gupta:
Channel 4)

One of the other problems we faced as radical people in the media was that from the '80s the trades-union movement was to go through a terrible battering. The meeting points between people working in film or video and radical parts of the labour movement were to be thrown into crisis as well. This change in the political climate makes it particularly difficult to think through and assess what the effect of Channel 4 has been, apart from the irony of its contribution to casualisation.

In the early days they actually ran a programme called *Trade Union World*. There was initially an absolute acceptance of the labour movement, and people at the top of the channel, such as Paul Bonner, were very keen that working-class life and people should be represented. One of our early slots was *People To People* involving quite a lot of discussion of working-class history and oral history. *People To People* was linked to a radical concept of history, and ran for quite a few years before it petered out because it became seen as irrelevant. Those ways of thinking about class and race or indeed history and society were categorised as 'old-fashioned'. A lot of the struggle in the late '80s and early '90s was couched in terms of fashionability versus 'old thinking', which of course is precisely what Tony Blair's done to the Labour Party. The gist of this approach is to define a whole category of thinking, which includes class or left politics, as 'out'.

I found myself being involved more and more in conversations with people saying to me, 'Don't you realise, Alan, that the world's changed, and the way you think is finished?' The dominant idea in television became: you have got to modernise, and thus 'old-fashioned' thoughts were dismissed as redundant. This attitude is to me a by-product of Thatcherism, now inherited by Blair.

It is interesting to consider the ways in which TV has changed and how these have constricted the manner in which the working class can be presented in terms of the kind of thinking that is deemed acceptable. It is not just that the definition of what it is permissible to show on television has shifted, but that the whole idea of trying to make anything analytical is completely off the agenda. Obviously the left's crucial concern is to analyse society, to try and understand what is going on, whereas now in television anyone who is attempting to make, say, a documentary that is aiming to be analytical would have very big problems getting it financed or commissioned: it would be seen as inappropriate and old-fashioned.

Detailed work would be needed to demonstrate exactly how TV has changed in terms of which ways of thinking are acceptable. In general terms, however, it would be reasonable to say that the working-class people on television tend to make an appearance as part of the spectacle rather than as active and engaged members of society with their own history and ideas. The working class is there to be a 'fly on the wall', or a participant in a game show.

In the '70s and early '80s there were certain conceptions about left culture in film and TV circles that no longer exist. There are some individuals who retain a left perspective, but there is no sense of a left critique. There is certainly no active group of producers who see themselves as representing a class-political view. There are those interested in dealing with environmental issues, or the development of the Third World but not many who are thinking in terms of trying to represent or work with working-class people or communities.

There are exceptions of course: Tony Garnett is one of the great survivors. He manages to keep going, retains some power and produces interesting work. Quite an achievement! Ken Loach has made a big comeback, too. He was trying to make films right through the '80s, during the miners' strike for instance, stuff that he knew was important to make. At one point in Channel 4 it was impossible for Ken to even meet people to talk about doing things, let alone do them.

There has been such an onslaught on the idea of class politics, or even of thinking about society and class, so it is difficult to know what to make of the '90s and understand where we have got to now. But it is a start at least to ask the question: where do all these changes leave those of us on the edge of it all ?

One of the difficulties of the whole modernist project that will not go away has been the audience question. There is a deep political-cultural issue around experimental work that queries the extent to which it can break through to audiences who are not already aware of the problematic out of which that work comes. When I was at Channel 4 I always felt that it was important to try and commission, and to buy a diversity of types of work or types of approach to issues. The left film and television culture in which I was involved prior to Channel 4, specifically the IFA, had included film-makers from lots of different traditions, from very experimental to very workerist. The IFA was an organisation that could combine people like Amber and someone like Marc Karlin at Lusia and very experimental people. That was one of its very great strengths, one of the things that was attractive and important about it.

It seemed to me that one had to acknowledge that there were very different sorts of radical film-makers. They ranged from people who were by conventional standards experimental in their approach, to these who had a conventional analysis of representation, who just felt putting a different view on to the screen in straightforward film-making terms was what they wanted to do. In my department we tried to recognise these approaches and aspirations and to cover a wide span. This was partly because in my job it was important to be open minded, but also because personally I believe this as well. In some areas of TV-making I might have definite ideas about what approach should be taken, but in relation to the work of left film-makers, I was convinced that diversity was vital. Creative work is a difficult and lonely path; in order to do it you have to be very convinced of your own 'rightness'. Often film-makers feel very passionately that their perspective is right, and other people are wrong. They do have to be relatively blinkered, because otherwise they probably would not be able to keep on. But someone else has to say, 'Well, this is fine, it should be included but it's not the only work to include, there must be a range.'

There are, furthermore, different moments for different types of work. When a real struggle was going on, say during the miners' strike or the Gulf War, I considered it important to screen programmes that were hopefully well made and effective, but were a reminder of a different viewpoint about this. They were showing that there were people in the world who have an opposing view or a differing experience from the one the dominant media was portraying. At points such as these, doing something that was probably aesthetically quite simple rather than tackling problems of representation, seemed to me to be vital. So I would commission these kinds of films alongside other work that was more problematising. That's why I wouldn't come down in any one camp or another. I wanted a range, within which experimental work would be respected. I don't really see it as one against the other. It's essential to have a wide span of aesthetic-political approaches. What I learnt most strongly was that when it was possible to show radical work there were a lot of people out there, of all ages and types, who wanted to see it. I hope that is still true. But it is an insufficiently large group for television to take seriously as an audience, or to make sense as an economic proposition.

I left Channel 4 in 1994. The original plan was to see if it were possible to create an alternative European outlet, a satellite channel. I had grown more and more interested in the international conception of television we had developed in the Independent Film and Video Department and so the idea was to try to create a channel that took globalism seriously. I knew from experience that there was a sizeable minority audience in Britain and other countries for international or experimental work. So I thought that it could be possible through a pan-European project to lock into these minority audiences, together adding up to a sizeable number of people. This is undoubtedly true. A channel like ARTE in France, a Franco-German enterprise, is already an example in Europe. They are beginning to get a reasonable audience in European countries and doing interesting work.

Through the group we set up called 'Mondial', Sylvia Stevens and I researched whether a European Channel was feasible and what it would cost. Basically we realised that it would be very difficult to finance, so we have been looking at what might be deliverable through the Internet or on some future version of it that has converged with television. We are going to start developing an Internet site that will provide services for producers internationally. It would make it possible to distribute work from around the world, with a lot of information about what is happening internationally in the media and so forth. We are also beginning to develop what we are calling a 'web channel'.

Where it will all go I'm not sure. There are interesting things you can do with the Net; it's a medium where you can get so far with no money. But if you are going to introduce new content and use the Internet in different ways, or make something that will survive financially, while you don't run into exactly the same problems as you do if you are trying to create television, you do run into some of the same problems, because you need money to do this sort of work. So, it is important to look at other medium. But at the moment everything pales into insignificance compared to television in terms of audience. That is the problem. It remains the main medium. Going back to the class issues, the difficulty is that the smaller, more specialist ways of showing or distributing work that have been proliferating in the second half of the 1990s tend not to touch working-class communities.

I don't know to what extent the left has in any way recovered on a cultural or intellectual level. It is not surprising, because not only did Thatcher arrive but there was the global context as well. There have been such huge changes. I remember, when I was a child in Chelmsford, at lunchtime you used to see thousands and thousands of people on bikes going home from the factory to have their lunch. Just seems an image now, and the main factory in Chelmsford where they all came from, one of the biggest that employed thousands, is being divided into lots.

I have just been doing a programme about Fidel Castro, loads of footage of him talking about his life and seeing how it has all changed since he started. To hear him talking now about his interglobal socialism and all that stuff is fine, but you think, Well, this really is a very big task, to say the least.

Alan Fountain
interview by Sheila
Rowbotham

16 The Social Side of Soap: *EastEnders*
Jacquetta May

Jacquetta May has acted in numerous TV productions and has appeared regularly in *EastEnders*, *Dangerfield* and *Cardiac Arrest*. Her most recent work includes the feature film *Get Real* and the TV series *Four Fathers*. She has also begun working as a television script writer.

As 'the opium of the masses', soaps are continually accused of preventing their audiences from taking part in real interaction and change. They never lack critics who see them as appealing to the lowest common denominator, harping on nostalgically and endlessly rehearsing a fixed format. Yet, in contrast to much TV, since it began in 1985 *EastEnders* has consistently represented working-class life, women, black and Asian characters and gay lifestyles. It also regularly presents its audience with controversial and contemporary issues. What interests me is how the conservatism and radicalism that are the tabloid perception of *EastEnders*, run hand in hand, and are actually vital, if unlikely, bedfellows. I want to look at the treatment of working-class women, race and social issues in this light.

The UK urban soap tradition demands a working-class set-up and a commitment to realism. Middle-class lifestyle is too private and career-based to create a realistic sense of community. And community, both actual and felt, is the lifeblood of *EastEnders*. Middle-class characters do occasionally become regulars (as 'Rachel' I was one myself between 1990 and 1992), but they are useful only as toffee-nosed baddies or positive liberal influences. Once these jobs have been done they become a bit redundant because, as professionals, their work and lifestyle make them difficult to integrate into the Square. This has become increasingly true. A current script-editor told me that, by 1997, middle-class regulars were perceived as too problematic, and that liberal or non-liberal characters were used instead.

EastEnders is also working class because it is aimed at a working-class audience. The programme was created as the BBC's response to pressures from ITV and Channel 4, who were taking up the majority of this audience share. Julia Smith, its co-creator, explicitly assumed that the audience would be working class. She imagined them watching it on television around tea-time before going out to the bingo or the pub.

The British soap format has also consistently put women at the centre of the drama. Moreover, soaps have traditionally appealed to women, and, despite changes to the programme, this continues to be the case with *EastEnders*. No one knows the actual percentage of male viewers because men tend not to admit to watching it. I suspect the figures might be larger than is often assumed because of how frequently taxi-drivers and shop-keepers said to

Eastenders, 1985
(BBC)

me, 'I know who you are—you're off *EastEnders*. 'Course, I don't watch the programme myself, but the wife has it on when we're having tea.'

It is not surprising that women watch. Compared to most male-dominated TV, *EastEnders* has a fantastic range of female characters, a healthy cross-section from schoolchildren to older women, from black and Asian to Turkish women, from daughters and wives to grandmas. A healthy cross-section. But does this mean they reflect any sort of 'true' experience? Are they in fact realistic portrayals? Take Cathy Beale for example. Surely no woman's life could contain such a catalogue of disasters: a slum childhood, two rapes, a drug-taking daughter—the product of the first rape, who eventually tops herself, a broken marriage and disastrous affairs, all followed by an alcoholic husband who endangered their son's life. Or Pat Butcher, who used to be a prostitute. She 'trapped' Pete Beale into marrying her when he thought she was pregnant but continued to play the field and had two sons by another man called Brian Wickes. Pete and Pat have a messy divorce, and Pat marries Brian, who knocks her about. And that is all before she has appeared on the Square. When she does, she meets Frank Butcher who it turns out had taken her virginity many years before. Pat divorces Brian who demands a car in return, and she marries Frank, inheriting two step-children. Frank eventually goes doolally, torches the car lot to get the insurance money and leaves. By the late 1990s she is with Roy, and things get a bit quieter.

The stereotypes are obvious in these two brief biographies. Cathy is the Good Woman, the victim, while Pat is the Tart. Other soap fixtures include the Gossip, the Mother-in-law, and the Bossy Old Grandma figure. So with the combination of melodramatic storylines and stereotypic portrayals, where exactly is the realism? Can *EastEnder* women characters be seen as reflecting or enhancing the image of actual working-class women? Or are they mere adjuncts to a male-defined space, just as they are in action drama?

To me the realism and the endorsement of female ability lie not in the big stories, dramatic reversals or amazing coincidences but in their fall-out. It is in the process of resolving dilemmas, in the day-to-day working through of problems that arise among the families and in the community that women are vital. In this area the Walford women shine.

Women are structurally indispensable because all UK soaps centre round family. Christine Geraghty points this out in her excellent study, *Women and Soap Opera*, and also shows how British and American soap dramas differ. In contrast to JR in *Dallas* for instance, she argues that most British soaps represent a matriarchal tradition.[1] At the inception of *EastEnders* the Fowler/Beale families nexus was the gravitational centre of the Square—four generations of it—and at the hub of this grouping was the mother. Over the years *EastEnders* mothers continued to take the major responsibility for the family, sheltering its members from the trials and tribulations of the world and absorbing their rebellions and conflicts. Pauline and Arthur Fowler represent another typical set-up, that of the strong woman/weak man. Arthur was only sporadically employed, often behaved like a little boy and had suffered a breakdown. It was Pauline who had to make the difficult decisions and keep the family together and functioning in the face of outside threats, such as poverty and unemployment, and internal ones, such as teenage pregnancy and depression.

There are frequent references to the strength and importance of family ties in the programme. 'But we're family' is a much overused phrase that means blood ties come first. Grant and Phil Mitchell endlessly fall out, come together, get drunk and say, 'I love you, bruv,' in a manly sort of way. Loyalty to clan is highly valued. On the other hand this does not mean that *EastEnders* is necessarily in the business of promoting *Daily Mail* 'family values'. We are not presented with exclusively traditional family images. There have been single mothers (Michelle had Vicky at sixteen), and single fathers (Clyde and Kofi), along with mixed-race relationships and gay and lesbian partnerships. Neither is family life, however traditional, ever represented as a bed of roses—it is hard graft and problematic.

Instead the value placed on family arises from the sense of belonging it provides and the need for roots and identity that it satisfies. And this idea extends outwards and encompasses the whole square. As Christine Geraghty observes community is seen as a sort of troubled family, prey to upsets and conflict but at the end of the day all pulling in the same direction, all in the same boat.[2] Community as family is not just an analogy, it is also a near reality. There are so many nephews and nieces, brothers and mother-in-laws, ex-wives and stepchildren that the majority of the characters are interrelated by blood or marriage. The incestuous atmosphere is constantly maintained, because unlike reality family members never move on and away—they always move to just round the corner. And if by any chance they are not there now you can bet your bottom dollar they will be turning up, long lost and full of dramatic potential.

This obsessive concern with family frequently threatens the programme's commitment to realism, but the over-representation makes obvious dramatic sense. Connection and interconnection are crucial in *EastEnders*, as is an intimate knowledge of fellow characters. The drama is generated on the basis of the most fierce and close bonds, for the deeper the knowledge, the more terrible the secret; the more wicked the rumour, the more awful the betrayal and the more cataclysmic the falling out. The denouement then is the shared triumph and the big celebration at the Vic.

So there the family is, and at the centre of it is a woman, who frequently plays a crucial role in the resolution of the drama. It is hardly contentious to say that more often than not working-class women still carry the burden of responsibility for family life, if not financially, often practically and nearly always emotionally. In *EastEnders* this job is never underestimated; on the contrary it is examined in quotidian detail, recognised as vital and the qualities needed to deal with such problems are consistently celebrated. There are big action stories, but the meat and veg of the series is in the talking needed to sort out personal relationship problems—marital, family or otherwise—and the examining of feelings that emanate from them. The traditional feminine qualities of emotional intelligence, perception and the desire to understand and negotiate are highlighted, and women are seen to deal with difficult decisions with care and concern. We always get the woman's point of view and are regularly shown how women can act competently and come up with solutions.

The talk is often between women: Michelle and Sharon discussing Grant, or Ruth and Gita talking about money problems and family. Confiding female friends are obviously useful to a soap because of the amount of information that can plausibly be divulged. But there is more than this—there is often reflection: the past is examined, regrets are expressed, and support and home-grown wisdom is offered. In action-led drama such as police or medical series, there is seldom time for this. 'Cut to the chase' is a common script-editing term—it means cut 'the bunny'—too much talking—and get on with the action. But reflective, confiding scenes have never been stinted on in *EastEnders*. Consequently female solidarity is recognised as necessary and fulfilling in a woman's life.

A clear example is an episode from 1997 where Phil Mitchell went to AA counselling while his wife Cathy chewed over past failures and emotional problems with Pat Butcher. It highlights the ever popular soap theme of the different male and female attitudes to life, clearly coming down on the 'women's side' in endorsing a traditional female approach. Phil's alcoholism has ruined his business and broken up the family; Cathy has overcome his resistance and persuaded him to go to counselling. The East End boy is put in an essentially alien and distasteful arena, where men are forced to talk about their problems and exhibit vulnerability: an affront to masculinity. Meanwhile Cathy and Pat re-examine past mistakes, and agree that life's hell, but you've got to keep struggling: tackle a power failure and mend the electrics ('Wait for a man to do a job, and you'll wait for ever,' says Pat) and have a laugh. Cathy's persistence is rewarded because after only one counselling session Phil is able to reveal the core of his problem: his father had beaten him as a kid, and Phil is deeply fearful that he will practise the same abuse on his son. The episode blames his drinking and destructiveness on the preferred male approach to failure and self-hate that Phil's father chose: violence. It says that unless such problems are understood and worked through (the female method), such abuse will re-present itself generation after generation.

While there is space for supportive female relationships, male/female relationships are the bread and butter of soap, and when women get together they nearly always talk about men.

Moreover, although women are rewarded for their dogged and intelligent approach to life, they are still carrying the burden of emotional responsibility and reacting to men. They are more likely to be congratulated for being long-suffering than acting on their own initiative. By and large it is the men that torch the Vic and the car lot or kill a publican (that is create the big action stories), while the women help pick up the pieces afterwards.

However, a stereotypical role in which women are highly active in terms of pushing the plot is as 'the Tart'. The tart cheats on her husband without remorse, seeks sexual satisfaction in an aggressive manner and is prepared to trample on female solidarity in order to achieve her aims. Interestingly, her sexuality is often connected to money and laziness. She is a woman who likes fast cars and expensive clothes and does not want to do a day's work in her life. Pat Butcher's early rampant sexuality was closely linked in the back story to her past as a prostitute. According to the conventions of *EastEnders* money debases desire. The tart figure might be manipulative and greedy and bad, but she is vital. Indeed the *EastEnders* audience ratings reached a high point in 1996–7 as a direct result of the Cindy/David Wickes storm. Cindy is a 'tart' who has a secret and stormy passion with David. Eventually Cindy hires a hit man to kill her husband, Ian. Figures built throughout the affair, hitting 23 million the day Ian Beale got shot. It was front page on the *Daily Mirror*, a soap triumph.

In 1997, talking to an *EastEnders* script-editor. I mentioned Frankie, the new tart on the programme. 'Oh, but she's a pathological tart,' he said. When I asked him if by that he meant she was a 'nymphomaniac' he replied, 'No, she's got, like, an illness where you break up marriages and move on. You always want something you're not allowed to have…er, it's called…Butterfly Syndrome.' To me, this verges on pathologising female sexuality: after all, who has heard of butterfly syndrome? They wanted that storyline badly enough to search through some obscure psychological tomes to find it. They wanted to push the limits of the character, and lacking plausible psychological and emotional motivation they had found an illness to give behaviour credibility. Frankie's actions are determined by a pathology, which is the modern gloss on being driven by an external evil force, or demon possession.

The tart is also vital because the contrast with her badness defines female goodness and the acceptable norm. It is not that other 'good' women can't have affairs, but more that when they do so they show love and get caught out.

However, if you are seen actively to pursue sex with no modesty and ulterior motive you become a tart and a villainess. The distinction is important, because without it the whole family structure would be threatened and by extension the community itself. In order for the tart to become a regular key figure she must first be 'made better'.

The reformation of the tart is one of the points where the general commitment to making characters behave consistently frequently breaks down. In an internal guide for *EastEnders* writers and script-writers, Michael Ferguson, an ex-producer laid out the ideal. 'The integrity of the character's personalities is never violated. No character's logic is ever distorted to serve an awkward plot. Their biographies are never adjusted retrospectively.'[3] In practice, however, with long-running programmes this is extremely difficult to maintain, and character is repeatedly sacrificed to plot. For instance Pat Butcher, notorious tart, nasty bitch and ex-pro, went through a radical and sudden character change when the programme decided to make her landlady of the Vic. She settled down, married Frank, took on stepchildren and mellowed, becoming bosom pals with Cathy and a great supporter of female solidarity. But in order for her to take on this central community role it was deemed necessary to make her into 'a good type', and none too subtly either.

Another area where Walford women exhibit self-motivation and independent activity is in work and careers, though the type of work they do is circumscribed by soap conventions. As Christine Geraghty notes, soaps focus on work in terms of personal relationships.[4] In *EastEnders* day-to-day life on the Square is full of people working—in the market, in shops, as mechanics and second-hand car dealers—but no one works in a factory, a large multinational organisation or a commercial office block. Big buildings would ruin the cosy nineteenth-century traditional geography of the Square. Characters could quite plausibly travel to work in such places, and very occasionally we see someone do so, but location shooting is costly, and a large office block requires complicated camera set-ups, time and a plethora of extras. Also work in large organisations is impersonal and to represent characters as cogs in a machine is anathema to the soap. In order for its world to function, work must be all about personal contacts. And indeed it is because as long as you meet the right person as you cross the Square you can pick up a job quite easily. Work at the laundrette is passed around and handed on in a highly ad hoc manner. Conveniently, its owner, a Mr Oppodopolous, only exists in name, so there have been no complaints.

Most importantly, places of work are meeting places on *EastEnders*. They are public arenas, where private concerns are aired and shared, where stories interweave and where information is swapped, as in the pub, where celebration of the community takes place. The reality of work and business concerns will always take second place to this. They are backdrops to the human drama. *EastEnders* does not show repetitive work, alienation or exploitation, the forces of capitalism at play or collective action. In its array of small-business concerns it tends to represent the rise and fall of the self-made man/woman, inclining to conservatism in its political approach to labour. On the other hand it does regularly represent unemployment, struggling to make ends meet, casual and part-time work.

As a consequence women are well represented among the Walford grafters. They are to be seen working in shops, in the pub, the café, and the laundrette; they own and run market stalls and cab companies and have shares in the car lot and the café. However, a successful career is more of a problem for Walford women—indeed Lorraine, Grant Mitchell's girlfriend, had a good job as a cosmetic saleswoman taken away from her. She had a house in Bolton, a car and money, but in order to get involved with Grant she had to lose everything so that she could plausibly take on a bar job at the Vic and romance could flourish.

The problem is that a key female regular with a successful career is not going to be hanging round the market or in the laundrette chatting during the day. She is going to be working elsewhere, and that is dramatically useless. Does this mean that any kind of educational or career development is impossible within the confines of the soap? No. An example is Michelle Fowler who, in 1990, was a bright and capable 24 year old who would realistically have been stretching her wings and moving on. Enter Rachel, a middle-class liberal who teaches women studies at the local poly, brought in to influence Michelle and to encourage her educationally, to augment her self-belief and challenge traditional work and life expectations. When Rachel bought a house on the Square, Michelle became her lodger, so the *Educating Rita* story could happen right there in the living room.

However, once that storyline had run dry, what was to be done with Rachel, whose lecturing job meant that she was away at college? The solution was to make her redundant and give her a bric-a-brac stall to integrate her more completely in the Square: a silly development of the narrative and highly unlikely and one that did not work. Michelle meanwhile completes her education and moves on to more professional jobs illustrating how it is only by leaving the programme that you get promotion. Eventually Rachel moves to Leeds to work in publishing, and Michelle to Miami to become a research assistant at the university there.

So although Walford women are well represented, and the female viewpoint consistently endorsed, although *EastEnders* champions women's work, emotionally and practically, boundaries and stereotypes are an inevitable part of the soap dramatic format.

Indeed one perspective on *EastEnders* is that it is fundamentally conservative and deadening, a cynical fictional consolation for the unhappy tedium of everyday life. There is no doubt that the open-ended continuity of the series, its endlessness, offers a kind of parallel world that the viewer can always pop into. For years on Mondays, Tuesdays and Thursdays at 7.30 or 8pm, those familiar characters will be going about their business on the Square. How reassuring! How comforting to know that the same storylines will come round again and again, that the same stereotypes, even archetypes, will repeatedly appear. With its nostalgic architecture, its references to the old days and people always popping in for a cup of tea, Walford is a safe haven and a refuge.

A common accusation of soaps is that they prevent a sense of real community by keeping its (largely female) audience in their seats, isolated in the privacy of their sitting rooms, absorbing personal interaction rather than practising it. I can't say that I wholly disagree with this criticism, although this reading of the soap format as fundamentally conservative does not do justice to *EastEnders* consistent attempts to tackle modern social problems and include different viewpoints. It has, for instance, made some effort to include black and Asian regulars. Obviously, East End demography demands that it should do so if the programme is to maintain its claim to realism. However, Manchester and Liverpool also have multicultural populations, and yet *Coronation Street* has an appalling history of representing black characters, while *Brookside* does not do much better. In soap terms then, *EastEnders* tries. The programme opened in 1985 with a black family already *in situ*. When I was in the series in 1990–92 the Tavernier family lived on the Square, and by 1997 there were six black regulars, one mixed race and an Asian couple, whose mother had just appeared.

The sheer number of these black or Asian regulars on *EastEnders* is very important because an isolated black or Asian character would appear mainly as 'different' from the white norm. Their 'difference' will then inevitably be used as story material, and although a liberal viewpoint might be espoused in the treatment of the story, the black character is nearly always forced to represent the race issue, becoming a cypher rather than a rounded personality who takes an active part in major storylines. So the range and number of characters is a plus point for *EastEnders* in terms of presenting race in more complex terms. The possibility of diversity is also more challenging for black actors who are not then restricted to playing stereotypical victims.

There is none the less an opposing pitfall, which is the not-mentioning-it-at-all trap. In an attempt at liberal inclusivity, the character's blackness is totally ignored. A case in point is Alan Jackson, husband of Carol (who is white) and father of Billy Jackson. The thinking was, Here is a woman who has had kids by various different men, and now she is with a black man. Full stop. This serves the liberal agenda of the programme very well. It says first that personality is more important than colour, and second, and very importantly, that the Square's residents are colour blind, that this working-class community is fundamentally liberal, unbigotted and untainted with racism. It doesn't mean that racism is not portrayed at all. 'Bad' characters and traditional old gossips can show prejudice—but if they do so, they will get their comeuppance. While short-term, visiting characters can be violently racist, which is fine because soon they will be gone and have merely served to show how exemplary and right-minded the permanent community is. Racists are outside the community, not within it.

By 1997 there was just one black writer on *EastEnders*, so it was a case of white programme-makers implicitly telling black audiences that because they have chosen not to think about 'colour', therefore problems of race don't exist.

A consequence of this colour-blind approach is that the contemporary impact of endemic, day-to-day racism simply can not be shown. While compared to other soaps, *EastEnders* does try hard on representation, it is not so hot on examining the experience of black *EastEnders* around race.

There are other areas to look at too. How about contemporary comment on what are called in soap terms 'issues'? Switch on the Sunday omnibus, and you are bound to bump into one or two—from male impotence and infertility, to drugs and homelessness, and of course, the butterfly syndrome! From the tabloids and Mary Whitehouse who regularly complain that *EastEnders* is attacking the moral fabric of our society, one could be forgiven for thinking that the programme saw itself as the radical campaigning arm of the BBC.

Take the HIV/AIDS story and its emergence, which was the issue with which I was most closely involved when I was in the programme. It had tragic roots in the fact that the original actor who played Mark Fowler at the start of the series took his own life. So in the programme the fictional Mark leaves the Square, never to return. After two or three years it was mooted they should bring him back using another actor. The BBC approached the family of the original actor, who had no objection to such a fictional resurrection. That was fine. Storywise, however, *EastEnders* had a problem—why had Mark been away so long and made no contact with his family? Mark had to be in pretty big trouble. The HIV/AIDS story fitted the bill perfectly. It was highly contemporary and plausible. It contained secrets, revelations, shock value and tragedy. How would Mark cope with this problem and how would his family and the community react? The ripples and repercussions were dynamite, and as long as there were still people on the Square who did not know Mark's secret the story could run and run and run.

Indeed years later it was to be used again. After a delicious set of rumours and coincidences, Peggy Mitchell, landlady of the Vic, overhears that Mark Fowler is HIV positive. She mounts a hate campaign, whipping up fear and prejudice until one day Mark returns home to find AIDS SCUM scrawled over the walls of his house. Good story—but now the programme has a problem with Peggy Mitchell: a key figure of the community has exhibited pigheaded ignorance and appalling prejudice. She must be punished and brought back from the edge. Enter—the breast cancer story. Peggy the malicious gossip and bigot herself becomes the victim of a life-threatening medical condition. At Christmas they run a Christian forgiveness story. Peggy calls on Mark and tells him she now knows what it's like to suffer as he has. Her apology underlies one of the basic tenets of the programme: underneath the skin we are all the same. We are all human and vulnerable, and our recognition of this should unite and not divide us.

The rather obvious point I am making here is that all issues are story material. The more contemporary and controversial, the more dynamic and exciting the story. I am not saying that once the character or plot has been served, that these socio-medical issues are not well researched and treated with a certain amount of responsibility. This is the public-service channel, after all.

And indeed one should never underestimate the educational value of the programme. For instance, a Terence Higgins education officer was overjoyed with the HIV/AIDS story. He said that, after years of campaigning in schools and youth groups, a hard and thankless task, Mark Fowler's revelation had initiated a rise in young people's awareness and tolerance, that was beyond his wildest dream. This was partly because the actor, Todd Carty, was already a youth hero from *Grange Hill* and *Tuckers Luck*, as well as being in our sitting rooms every week. Conversely, the breast-cancer story had generated complaints and a Right to Reply, but the issue had been raised on prime-time TV, and public discussion had ensued. Nevertheless, although *EastEnders* endlessly repeats a fairly conservative format, and although all issues and images are there first and foremost to feed the great hungry story beast, its positive by-products can not be denied.

EastEnders has changed since I appeared in it during the early 1990s. Among the practical influences on soap-making, the pressure of audience ratings is of key importance. When *Coronation Street* went three-times-a-week it was inevitable, despite a big back-stage fight, that *EastEnders* would too. A script-writer friend tells me that going three-times-a-week has necessitated a more plot-based, pacier format and has tended to squeeze out episodes where colour and character detail predominate. Consequently this has affected the women characters. She says it has reduced the reflective scenes where women just talk together. So the episode in 1997 where Cathy and Pat review their pasts was a 'special'; it was no longer run of the mill.

Moreover by the late 1990s the look of the series has shifted. There are far more night scenes, with an all-night cafe and a club. There are also many more young people and younger storylines. This is presumably to do with a conscious policy of capturing or building on youth audience figures—it makes sense to get them addicted young. The programme must change, and such changes militate against it becoming too cosy and old-fashioned. *EastEnders* has never been hermetically sealed like *Coronation Street* was until very recently. Two characteristics have, however, persisted since its inception. Controversial issues are still the lifeblood of the programme and its setting—the imagined working-class neighbourhood—foregrounds family and community. As long as this continues women will not lose their central role.

Jacquetta May, lecture at 'Images of Labour', edited by Jacquetta May and Sheila Rowbotham

Notes

1. See Geraghty, *Women and Soap Opera*, pp.62–83. I have also drawn more generally on Geraghty's study.
2. *Ibid.*, p.84.
3. Michael Ferguson. *EastEnders* internal memo, unpublished manuscript, *c.* 1989.
4. See Geraghty, *Women and Soap Opera*, pp.52–9.

17 *Our Friends in the North*

Huw Beynon

Towards the end of the seventh episode of *Our Friends in the North*, Felix, redundant from Swan Hunters, beaten up and savaged by a Rottweiler, now in the early stages of Alzheimer's, searches for his dead father. The camera pulls back to reveal this broken man, alone and confused, surrounded on all sides by tarmac and high-rise flats: the reconstructed, modernised North. This powerful image, symbolic of a disinherited generation, was one of several that made nine on Monday night compulsive viewing. As such, the series stands firm alongside other classics of television drama such as *Cathy Come Home* and *The Big Flame*, *The Party* and *The Boys from the Black Stuff*, *A Very British Coup* and *The Singing Detective*, *GBH* and so on, which over the past thirty years have related, in a compelling way, aspects of change in working-class life and politics.

In some respects, *Our Friends* compares unfavourably with the others. The characterisation is weaker, and occasionally the writing lacks the deftness of touch of, say, Alan Bleasdale, Trevor Griffiths or Dennis Potter. This weakness, however, stems from the bravery of the project and Peter Flannery's concern to thread a biographical narrative across thirty years of social and political history. It was the way in which the drama connected fictional lives with the television presentations of major historical events that the series was most innovative and forceful. Viewers of a certain age relived their own lives through the drama as they followed the events of the three-day week, the miners' strike and the hurricane. From this viewpoint, *Our Friends* can be seen not only as an intriguing television drama but also as a serious and original attempt at creatively interpreting social change. At its deepest level it raises questions about the political achievements of the generation that grew up in the 1960s. Born in the late forties, they experienced the post-war boom, and the welfare state; it was this generation that became equated with radical politics and an equally radical change in lifestyle; it was the era of 'sex, drugs and rock and roll', of fashion and style. This is the era of Flannery's four main characters ('our friends') and it is appropriate that their progress through the three decades is signalled through changes in hair styles, dress code and popular music.

In different ways, each of 'our friends' comes from the working class: Mary and Nicky's parents are manual workers, Tosker's mother runs a pub. We know less about Geordie, but in 1964 he was working in the pits. Mary and Nicky do well at school, but neither complete their university education: he drops

Our Friends in the North, 1996
(BBC)

out to join 'the movement'; she because she is pregnant with Tosker's baby. Tosker himself works as a factory machinist whilst attempting to break into the club scene as a singer. While none of their lives turn out as expected, three of them 'get on'. Mary enters the 1990s as a successful lawyer and labour politician, Nicky as a failed politician but successful documentary photographer, Tosker, having experienced the bitterness of redundancy, ends up as a rich man and owner of a new and exclusive floating night club on the Tyne. In contrast, Geordie, after adventurous years in London, ends up sleeping rough ('it was a bad time; the worst time I've had—so far') having escaped from his second period in prison. In spite of the acclaimed and redemptive final episode it is hard to escape the view of a socially mobile generation, self-absorbed to the point of obsession. Only Geordie seems capable of any sense of irony or humour; it is through his life that the series expresses the most profound expressions of the emotions of love and hate. We end with him, walking across Tyne bridge in the new suit provided by Tosker. We watch him and listen to the words of Oasis: 'Don't look back in anger.'

But these aren't our only friends. One of the irresistible features of the series lies in the relationships it portrays between the generations. This 'bond between our future and our past' is a strong characteristic of Tyneside. It was made explicit in Jimmy Nail's song about the river. It is seen most poignantly in Nicky's relationship with his father, Felix, and Mary's with her son, Anthony. Grappling with his illness, Felix is obsessed with his own past: 'He was a hard man, me father; there was no love in the hoose.' Nicky, having relived his father's journey through militancy to disillusionment, cries, 'I only wanted you to hold me and tell me that you loved me.' Tosker was also unable to express his love for his children and was despised by his son. Anthony in his turn feels deep love for his mother ('Hurt her again, and I'll break your neck') but feels the pain of her broken marriage, her political involvement and her unhappiness ('I didn't have a mother, I had a martyr'). As a policeman, he deals daily with the anguish of everyday life on the housing estates. He despises his mother's New Labour politics with its emphasis on the family and family values. The family, you feel, has a lot to answer for.

Most of the drama takes place in and around Newcastle-upon-Tyne. This is where you end up if you follow the signs that lead you along the A1 to 'the North'. This is Jack Common's 'canny toon'; the river city with its bridges across the Tyne, a place built around its shipyards and engineering works; the hub of the great northern coalfields of Durham and Northumberland and the coal-and-steel economy that emanated from it. A working-class city, made famous by its music halls, its pubs and clubs and its football team. The city of Alan Price and the Animals and the context of their single 'We've Gotta Get Out of This Place'. The city where Sting grew up and worked as a teacher. A hard place, too, with its history of crime and gang feuds as illustrated in the classic film noir, *Get Carter*. This side of the town is masked by Flannery who chooses to represent its homeliness as a way of heightening the contrasts with London: another river city, but the political capital and the driving force behind many of the cultural changes in the sixties and seventies.

It is to London that Geordie flees, escaping the consequences of casual sex. Here, his life is transformed in the expanding pornographic trade and his involvement with Benny Barrett. Barrett is skilfully played by Macolm McDowell who, some twenty years earlier, in *O Lucky Man!*, had mocked the political corruption of the north of England. Here, he reminds us of the ingrained and incestuous corruption that has characterised the Metropolitan Police Force since the Second World War. While lacking the power of the first two series of *Between the Lines*, the well-researched storyline details their skilful and cynical handling of the 'honest cop' from the North. It revealed how skilfully the Met survived to remain as a vital political force throughout the eighties. It was its officers with their white shirts and their brutal anti-provincialism who were most disliked by the miners during their epic strike. This compelling account was viewed by 'real-life' inspector Frank Williamson in his home in Macclesfield. He commented: 'I regret to say that the content is strictly accurate.' In the *Guardian*, 22 January 1996, Flannery added, revealingly: 'Those incidents did take place. I think it's valuable if people watch it and understand the possibility of the situation getting out of hand again.' At this point drama and documentary become as one; at others the fit is less well matched.

The idea of personal and political corruption is an enduring theme of *Our Friends*. While Geordie is involved in the seamy side of life in Soho, Nicky has dropped out of university to follow a nobler calling as Austin Donaghue's assistant in City Hall. Austin is transparently modelled on T. Dan Smith, the man who ran Newcastle Labour politics in the sixties before ending up in jail along with John Poulson, the builder Alderman, Andrew Cunningham and a number of other local Labour councillors. While Cunningham does not appear in *Our Friends* (in fact no trade unionists do), his role was an important one. He was regional secretary of the General and Municipal Workers Union, and leader of the Labour Group in County Durham, where he also sat as chair of the police committee. Between them, Smith and Cunningham controlled two powerful political machines: but they were different characters. Cunningham's political career was traced through the union bureaucracy and was firmly on the right of the Labour Party. Smith had no equivalent trade-union base: he was a phenomenal political organiser who had come to power through Marxism and involvement in the far left. Their contrasting styles were made clear on release from prison: Cunningham retired to his bungalow in Chester-le-Street to be visited by the then Prime Minister, James Callaghan; Smith gave a television interview in the Haymarket in Newcastle, asking people to appreciate his achievements though the reconstructed city that surrounded him. This sense of the political man is well captured in the characterisation of Austin, and it should be viewed alongside Amber's cogent documentary of T. Dan Smith himself.

Austin and Felix had been politically active together in the 1930s; both were committed militants with Felix having the edge (it is never clear how this ties up with Felix's role in the Jarrow March—a bipartisan 'crusade' that distinguished itself from the 'hunger marches' organised by the Communist Party). Both men had become deeply disillusioned with Labour politics. While Felix turns his back on it, to dig the allotment and make model boats, Austin decides to take over the machine and modernise it for the good of the people. His passion for modernisation is intense and reflects the powerful emphasis given to newness throughout the North East at that time. It gelled well with Harold Wilson's programme, and the role it gave to new technology. Importantly, and in contrast with the current modernisers, it was linked with a strong regional and class rhetoric. This came through powerfully in the ways in which his northern television consortium involved the trade unions.

Austin is played by Alan Armstrong, and during the scenes in Austin's office he successfully recreates these complex dimensions of the Labour boss; they also capture the man's sense of fun and the deep contempt he had for the people who surrounded him. He had to deal with them, and (to misappropriate Nye Bevan) he would fill their mouths with gold. Unfortunately, he also filled his own pockets. For Austin, the ends justified the means. He had enormous gall, and he thought he was flame-proof. Even after a change of government, he believed that the complicity of the Tory home secretary would rescue him. The exposure of this affair was one of the most sustained campaigns waged by *Private Eye* in the early 1970s, and the sordid relationship between the Home Secretary and Poulson is ably captured in Flannery's drama. What it leaves us with is a worrying sense of a shadowy malevolent state meshing with the disintegrating forces of 'Old Labour'.

This sense of corruption and disintegration is the main political thrust of the drama. It is reinforced by its treatment of the left, where the drama focuses upon the way the Labour machine on Tyneside is challenged first by Eddie, the third representative of Felix's generation, and then by Nicky. Eddie runs as an independent against the official party candidate. The key to his success (as depicted in the scene in the market) lies in his close personal involvement with his constituents. The personal involvement is turned into political support in the traditional way. In contrast, Nicky (after an unlikely involvement with the Angry Brigade) becomes a local tenant activist and fights a by-election as a Militant-backed candidate. The campaign founders on the incompetence of his supporters and his lack of any personal warmth. Unlike Felix, who campaigned for Eddie, he has lost any capacity to relate to the people on the street. The political severity he brings to daily life neutralises any advantage he hoped to gain from living locally. All this is played upon ruthlessly by the dirty tricks of the opposition.

These episodes were intriguing and mark the point in the series where the dramatical plot moves most clearly away from the documentary form. Eddie's election mirrors Eddie Milne's political struggles in Blyth, although later he seems to accumulate some of the biographical details of Dennis Skinner. In Nicky's case, however, there was no parallel election; certainly none of the safe northern seats were lost as a consequence of Militant's involvement. What did take place, however, relates to the right wing of the Party and the formation of the SDP. Three of the critical defectors (Rogers, Wrigglesworth and Thomas) were northern MPs, the latter in central Newcastle. Flannery chose not to develop these themes. What he does instead is accurately to portray a new kind of northern Tory MP—well represented by Piers Merchant in Newcastle North and Michael Fallon in Darlington. These were Thatcherite ideologues who held the Labourist machinery of Party and union in utmost contempt. It was their hope that this arrangement could be unbuckled and the North transformed from an old Labour heartland to a thriving enterprise economy in which the Conservative Party would play a critical political role. To this extent they were upstaged by New Labour, portrayed in *Our Friends* by Mary, first as leader on the Labour group in the City, then as a successful Labour MP. Here, the comparison with the politics of both Austin and Nicky is a powerful one; more poignant is the contrast with Eddie. In parliament Eddie serves as a left MP, and his death in the middle of the hurricane, his papers blowing around him, is symbolic of the ending and destruction of an important part of England.

There is much to be admired in all this, and it raises worrying doubts about the political contribution of the sixties generation to British political and social life. However, the smell of decay is occasionally overwhelming, and this is exacerbated by the silences in the account. While many of these social changes are finely textured (for example, in areas of gender and ethnicity) and difficult to demonstrate dramatically, they could have been integrated into the narrative in a different way. This could have been achieved through a more complex treatment of the miners' strike.

T. Dan Smith, 1987
(Amber)

This strike is commonly understood to have marked a watershed in the politics of labour in Britain in the eighties. The role of the police and the courts has been well documented, as has that of the Tory right in setting up the Union of Democratic Mineworkers (UDM) and building a bridgehead into the miners' union. These are the events that dominate the episodes of *Our Friends*; they are authentic and rather depressing. Undoubtedly miners were shocked by their experience of the criminalising process. Essentially law abiding and separated from the inner cities, they had little experience of being 'fitted up', of being stopped and searched for no good reason. As one of them put it: 'At the end of this strike the miners and the blacks will know about the state: but nobody else'.[1] But the strike also produced important links between the miners and other groups (groups of different ethnicities, cultures, sexualities, politics) beyond the coalfields. This was one of its significant features, as was the independent involvement of the women. In leaving these relationships unexplored, Flannery misses an opportunity to extend the analysis of political failure and relate it more clearly and positively to broader social changes.

Where these changes are dealt with in *Our Friends* they overwhelmingly emphasise the moral decay of elements within the working class. Accounts of the Meadowell Estate in East Newcastle became reasonably well known after the estate broke into riot, and the activities of the young men as 'ram-raiders' and car thieves became widely publicised. Within the logic of *Our Friends*, this development is most often comprehended as a consequence of poor parenting. Divorce, violence and disruption regularly accompany our visits to the lives of these people. Ironically, it is left to Anthony the policeman (and the next generation) to argue that the problem is not with the people but with the places where they live.

There was the double-edged flaw in Austin's modernising agenda. The slums may be cleared, but the replacements may not improve matters greatly. This was certainly the case with some of the high-rise and flat-roof accommodation. Moreover, the social relationships on these estates (when combined with an overheated property market and a pressurised housing-management policy) soon disassemble—all the faster when local labour markets collapse and fail to sustain high-wage employment.

In the North, the job markets for skilled engineers, shipyard and chemical workers, and coal miners collapsed in the eighties. Yet, none of 'our friends' were factory or office workers, or activists involved in the reform of trade unions and resistance to restructuring in the seventies. In fact, the reorganisation of public-sector unions, the national role played by Tyneside shop-steward committees and the creative role of local CDPs are all quite absent.

In spite of the much heralded 'New North' (as represented by Tosker and Mary), it has remained depressed. While the football club expands, and a new middle class enjoys the elaborated new shopping facilities of the Metro Centre, many of the post-war generation experience ill-health and declining living standards. Perhaps Felix's fate (demented and degraded in an underfunded health service) is theirs; perhaps they still have the capacity to press for social changes far beyond the manifesto of New Labour.

Note

1. Quote in Huw Beynon 'Introduction' to Huw Beynon (ed.), *Digging Deeper: Issues in the Coal Miners' Strike*, Verso, 1985.

18 Digital Television
An Emancipatory Moment in Waiting?
Kim Gordon

Technological innovations in communications have aroused high hopes. Video camcorders, for instance, are simple to use as well as cheap and portable. From 1965, when the first lightweight video recorder was introduced, it was believed that video would become a truly democratic technology, one that could help to wrest control of the televisual image from the professionals and the corporations for which they work. Ordinary people would no longer be passive objects to be directed and produced, interviewed and portrayed, but the makers of their own TV. Furthermore it was expecteded that the new video technology would make it easier for a wider range of ideas and views to be communicated. In the United States, particularly, many attempts have been made to gain access to the airwaves for radical and alternative ideas.[1] In the 1990s further advances in television computerisation, digital video-editing and the prospect of thousands of digital channels have meant that making TV programmes has become even easier. The argument for opening up access to the 'airwaves' is consequently more compelling than ever.

So, how have broadcasters made use of video's 'democratic' potential? With this question in mind a debate about the future of digital TV and its use as anything other than a money spinner for commercial broadcasters is now timely. I shall start it here with some initial thoughts on the viability of reclaiming channels from the vast wasteland that is multi-channel digital TV for a form of radical/ alternative-community/access TV.

Political Economy of TV

It is ironic that as television has become increasingly open to the possibilities of more democratic uses it has simultaneously slipped further out of the grip of any control by public authority, in a process of accelerating commercialisation that reaches into every nook and cranny of broadcasting.

In the UK, broadcasting has always been one of the most tightly regulated and controlled media, because of its almost universal reach and its supposed influence on listeners and viewers. Nearly all aspects of programming (BBC or commercial broadcasters) have been directly or indirectly regulated by public authority, which ensured that not everything in the broadcasting world was driven by commercial considerations—a duty to the broader social good was explicitly contained in the need for the BBC to Inform, Educate and Entertain. Within the regulated duopoly ITV also laboured under these programming

Kim Gordon has been active in socialist and black politics and worked on *Union World, Ebony, Free for All* and *Newsnight.* He is now a senior lecturer in broadcasting at the University of Westminster, London.

objectives, which ensured that television in the UK provided a relatively wide range of views and programme styles, and included transmission of a certain amount of critical and challenging drama and current affairs. But the victory of Margaret Thatcher with her free market belief in the value of competition began to unravel this unique and complex broadcasting mosaic. As a matter of government policy the BBC/ITV duopoly was undermined by a lightly regulated cable-and-satellite television sector, which was set up in competition with BBC/ITV but with few public-service programming obligations.

Furthermore greater competition was introduced into the ITV system with the auctioning of its franchises to the highest bidder. The federal ITV system also became less organisationally diverse. By 1999, ten of Britain's fifteen independent ITV companies were owned and controlled by three media groups, and it is expected that eventually only one or two companies will control all of ITV. The system is also facing stiffer competition from 'upmarket' Channel 4—which since 1993 stopped working with ITV and started selling its own advertising—and from Channel 5 with its explicit programming policy of sport, soft porn and imported drama, or 'football, fucking and films' as its programme controller described it. The BBC itself has been pressured to become more commercial, opening its internal production processes to external competition, setting itself up as a quasi-commercial broadcaster in the US and UK cable-and-satellite television market and adopting a centralised management culture that emphasises 'value for money' and efficiency.

As all broadcasters have become more responsive to competition, programme makers and schedulers have evolved a parallel concern with maximising audiences. Research conducted for the Campaign for Quality Television shows that over the past ten years the drive for ratings has had a serious effect on drama and current affairs. Serious current affairs has declined on the mass channels (BBC1 and ITV), with ITV producing almost no political, foreign or economic current-affairs programming.[2] In the words of the BBC's own John Humphries, the pursuit of ratings has led to a 'conscious and deliberate fusing of journalism and entertainment'.[3] The BBC's drama output has also been lambasted by its own. BBC TV's successful writing duo Laurence Marks and Maurice Gran have called BBC1 'the most mimsy and restrictive of all networks…Things you could say ten years ago you can't say now.'[4] The Campaign for Quality Television research found that TV drama as a whole was now ever more formulaic. They concluded that 'there was more caution and less room for experimentation with new ideas, new talent or different techniques.'[5]

Both main terrestrial networks, ITV and BBC, in addition to competition from Channels 4 and 5 also now feel the hot breath of the hyper populist satellite-and-cable networks on their necks. According to the ratings agency Taylor Nelson Sofres viewers with cable and satellite now spend 37 per cent of the viewing time on these new channels. Before the arrival of multi-channel television BBC and ITV would have commanded 100 per cent of viewer's time.[6] The role of the BBC as the sole non-commercial broadcaster is of concern as viewers with multi-channel TV begin to desert it, and the projections are that while only 28 per cent of homes now have multi-channel TV, some digital form of it is expected to be in the majority of homes by 2006–10 when the existing free-to-air analogue version is due to be switched off. In this new digital world, most viewers are expected to receive one of the following: either the 36 digital-terrestrial channels or the 140–200 digital-satellite channels or the 400-plus digital-cable channels.[7]

Animation by 4l Limited for *The Serpent*, 1997 (Lusia)

But how far will this enormous channel capacity represent an opening up of the air waves and wider viewer choice? Two things have happened to undermine the vision of greater diversity in programming. Not only has the level of diversity in ownership that existed in the early years of multichannel TV, such as ITV, been rapidly reduced but also the early hopes of programme diversity have fallen victim to the needs of the new channels to maximise audiences as fast as possible.

Consolidation and Concentration

In 1993 the cable-TV system was owned by a collection of 24 mainly North American communications/telecom companies. But by the late 1990s just three—NTL, Telewest and BSkyB—had control of the infrastructure (and this is expected to reduce to two). All three are controlled by US or Australian/US communication and media corporations. The economics of multi-channel TV has also meant that only the largest media organisations such as Time Warner, Flextech, Disney, Sony and News Corporation have the finances to invest in and produce the high volume of low-cost programming that cable and satellite demand. Within the UK only the BBC and the two biggest ITV companies (Granada Media Group and Carlton Communications) can play the multi-channel game on any meaningful scale. The prospect then is for control of distribution in this new corporate-digital world to lie in the hands of just four large companies (a super cable Multiple Systems Operator (MSO), a super ITV company, BSkyB and the BBC) while content will be dominated by the transnational, UK or US media conglomerates.

During most of the 1990s as cable and satellite has begun to take off in the UK the main concern of the cable and satellite operators has been to find programming that has the widest appeal to drive market penetration. Although most homes in urban areas are passed by cable, 70-plus per cent do not connect up to it because too little of the content is either original, relevant or well produced enough to inspire most householders. The channels that have driven cable and satellite are BSkyB's mass-entertainment generalist channels (those that cater to viewers with many interests like Sky1) and the themed channels (sport, porn, films, cartoons, lifestyle, pop music). In the pre-digital world of analogue TV, the more minority-oriented niche channels have found it difficult to survive. Channels aimed at Afro-Caribbean and Spanish viewers for example have been dropped by the cable operators, while the independent Chinese News and Entertainment channel on BSkyB was taken over by a News Corporation subsidary.[8]

However, it could be argued that the dominance of mass-entertainment channels is only a temporary phenomenon, resulting from the economic pressures in an analogue world where channel capacity is still restrained and where cable and satellite are still attempting to enter the majority of homes. As multi-channel digital TV finds a stable and large subscriber base, a new programming policy could emerge. The promise not of dozens but hundreds if not thousands of digital channels means satellite and cable operators are likely to be increasingly needful of channels catering for special-interest and minority audiences.[9]

Certainly the prospect of digital has seen increased activity among those wanting to provide minority-audience TV. Listed below are just some of the ideas for new niche channels that emerged in 1998/99:[10]

- The Community Channel. Aimed at the voluntary sector or those interested in related social issues. £1 million raised towards start-up costs from National Lottery. Gained three years free carriage on BSkyB as part of self-interested corporate 'social marketing' policy. BSkyB's Elizabeth Murdoch quoted as saying: 'Everyone thinks bad stuff about Sky. But we have to give things back to the community.' 2000 launch.
- Jewish TV. Aimed at Jewish viewers, 2000 launch.
- Mine TV. Aimed at black viewers; 2000 launch.
- Rainbow TV network. Aimed at the gay and lesbian community, seeking investors.
- .tv. The technology channel that includes the programme *Which On Air*. Already broadcasting on BSkyB.
- Sony Entertainment TV (SETV). General entertainment channel in Hindi aimed at UK's Asian community. Launched 1998.

New Digital Broadcasting: New Opportunities?

The new broadcast technology has significantly altered the way television can be made. It has made it cheaper and easier to produce high-quality images and sound, so eroding some of the advantages of the large broadcasters with their deep pockets and corps of highly skilled professionals. Furthermore, digital broadcasting means the end of channel scarcity and one major justification for rationing broadcasting channels. In one sense then the technology has uses that are potentially democratising, 'inherently democratic and challenging', according to Jon Dovey, a videographer since the 1970s. Or provide a 'revolutionary heartland technology' that, according to political theorist John Keane, will enable citizens to communicate in previously unthinkable ways.[11]

From the moment portable video technology was introduced in 1965, users, both the mainstream commercial broad-casters and radical and community activists, have been exploring the 'unthinkable'. During the 1960s and 1970s the notion of greater access to the media via video led to the creation of access-TV movements in a number of countries—in the UK alone more than 100 projects existed. A new mode of working with the medium developed around the notion of collaborative production, professionals and local people together producing video. Out of this a new aesthetic has developed,

Animation by 4I Limited for *The Serpent*, 1997 (Lusia)

which has infiltrated the mainstream. In Britain the establishment of the BBC's Community Programme Unit by radical video- and film-makers in 1972 started the process with the innovative *Open Space* series with its express objective of giving voice to the voiceless. This programme began to institutionalise the more democratic production practice of television professionals working under the supervision of campaigning groups.[12]

In later years producers of *Video Diaries* (1991, BBC) and *Free For All* (1991, Channel 4) worked more with ordinary individual members of the public. The programming legacy in the UK of this new way of operating can be seen in Channel 4's *Undercover* series, BBC's *Video Nation* and new forms of camcorder drama that pushed the use of low-gauge video into the super high-cost area of TV drama. The boundaries of creativity have been further stretched by independent-production companies Hi8tus (Maverick Television APT), who directly tap the writing and acting potential of ordinary people working with them *in situ*, for example young people in Belfast ghettos, black youths on the streets of Coventry or young offenders inside Hull prison.[13]

Not all experimental uses of video have been so concerned with its democ-ratising potential. Faced with the need since the early 1980s to fill large numbers of extra hours of television at ever lower cost—television income being more related to the rate of growth in the economy than growth of TV output[14]—main-stream television has used the new aesthetic and work practices for purely commercial reasons. Jon Dovey argues: 'Every new stylistic development which video technologies suggested has been eagerly seized and recycled to further increase profit margins and audience ratings.'[15] This is not to say that commercial broadcasters have not been innovative: the introduction of multi-skilled video journalists on Channel One, the *Daily Mail* newspaper group's London-wide cable-TV news service, is an example of radical working prac-tices that took advantage of video technology. The advantages of digital edit-ing and transmission technology also meant that the *Daily Mirror* group's cable channel, Live TV, could be staffed by a high ratio of new entrants to television.

However, the lower cost structures of both channels failed to ensure their survival. Live TV with its grotesque programming (topless female darts players, stripping female newscasters and fluffy bunnies who guided viewers through the 'happy' news items of the day) closed down in November 1999, while Channel One had already closed in 1998 after four years operation.

The camcorder or Reality TV programmes such as *Holidays from Hell* or *You've Been Framed* —whose unambitious content has been described by the *Financial Times* as 'cheap and lazy cringe tv'—are examples of more 'successful' recycling of the new stylistic developments to come out of access video.[16] A more imaginative use of the technology is arguably the docusoap genre, in which the lives, loves and struggles of selected working people (motorway workers, airport staff, traffic wardens, driving instructors, hotel employees) are endlessly videoed, the rough edges filed off, storylines straightened and repackaged as weekly soap opera. This genre with its ability to deliver insights into ordinary life has become a cornerstone of the peaktime BBC and ITV schedule as it achieved extraordinarily high ratings for significantly lower cost than the soaps and drama that would otherwise fill those timeslots.[17]

Is There a Radical/Alternative TV Niche Market?

How far then is it now possible to build on the techniques and developing production styles of this 'revolutionary heartland technology'? Can these be used alongside conventional production techniques to take advantage of the abundance of broadcasting capacity and create a new cable channel that is both challenging, radical and popular? At one level digital TV provides the opportunity. The capacity and the distribution networks exist. But can sufficiently engaging content be created on the tight budgets available to minority channels to entice a large enough audience, and will the MSOs and satellite corporations carry such a channel, or be forced to do so?

In terms of creating an audience, as programming on the mainstream networks becomes more homogenised and averse to taking risks, it could be argued that dissatisfaction among viewers in general will rise. It may be reasonable to assume some of them would support a channel dedicated to the non-commercial spirit embodied in the public-service mantra of seeking to Inform, Educate and Entertain.

Those on the political left might certainly be interested in more stylistically and politically challenging content. This could constitute a significant audience. According to a 1987 MORI poll it was estimated that 2.4 million voters identified themselves as being to the left of the Labour Party. In the introduction to this volume Huw Beynon and Sheila Rowbotham cite a 1995 Gallup Poll showing a large majority of the population still think in terms of class.

An indication of the total number of viewers needed for viability of any alternative channel can be gleaned from the relatively low viewing figures of the most successful broad-interest channels. For example BSkyB's top rated generalist channel (Sky1) is usually watched by between 50,000 and 300,000 viewers.[18] Moreover the start-up costs for a small-scale broadcaster need not necessarily be enormous. A new 24-hour local service on the Isle of Wight,

TV12 broadcasting, employing 17 staff and broadcasting to 500,000 people had start up costs of £250,000.[19] Even some of the most ambitious new cable-channel programme suppliers can have moderate costs. For example Rapture—an innovative production company aimed at 12–18 year olds producing original programming—had start-up costs of £2.5 million.[20] This sort of investment has to be compared with the £6.5 million invested by trades unions and others in the short-lived socialist weekly *News On Sunday* in 1987.[21]

Animation by 4I Limited
for *The Serpent*, 1997
(Lusia)

The Power and Poverty of Imagination

The question of content is crucial to success in the creative industries, but developing ideas and turning them into watchable television requires resources and imagination, a point that emerged in the very earliest days of radical/alternative television. One documented case from France points up the dilemmas and difficulties any alternative TV project would face. The 1973 'critical/revolutionary' cable television initiative on an estate in Grenoble started out full of revolutionary zeal: 'A community which can watch its life from day to day cannot but change,' argued the channel's Daniel Populus. For three years radicals attempted to bring their ideals to life with programming that included the work of local singers, musicians, theatre and immigrant cultural groups. But, after that, as the channel faced closure Populus admitted it had largely preached to the converted, having produced a mix of rather 'morbid' political and social programming.[22]

We have to look for something else, something more entertaining without being trivial. We must ask ourselves whether there are popular forms of entertaining that can be televised inexpensively.... We must have more time and more money to be able to innovate in this area. I have to admit this is a major stumbling block and that we have found no solution to it.

Whereas Populus *et al.* may not have found a solution to the problem of creativity, later examples of low-gauge practice that tapped the people, the politics, the spirit of community/alternative television have proved it is possible to develop great innovative ideas. It could be argued that the very irreverence and youthfulness, non-professionalism, and underfunding—the very counter action of alternative TV—has been crucial to creativity.

Since 1981 New York's left-wing Paper Tiger collective has been critiquing the US media on cable television in an engaging way for $300 an hour. The desire by Paper Tiger not to ape the US network studio style meant that Paper Tiger's weekly 30-minute studio show developed and invented its own unique format, a non-hierarchical, non-technological 'handmade' one that says low budget. It evolved techniques that demystified the production, such as showing the studio crew in action and revealing the handcranked credit roller with graphics, deliberately held up with fingers in shot.[23] Years later and on the other side of the Atlantic this style of studio presentation appeared on Channel 4's morning slot, *Big Breakfast*, where it became a signifier of youthful anarchism.

Paper Tiger's radical approach to TV grew out of a long tradition in the United States of radical broadcasting stations, starting with the Chicago-based labour radio station of 1926 to the pacifist FM radio station KPFA in Berkeley, California, that began after the Second World War. Like Paper Tiger they relied heavily on volunteers, were keen to involve listeners and made major efforts to demystify the production process and introduce highly innovative programme formats and styles. For example KPFA ran programmes without scheduled ends (an idea that reappeared on Channel 4 with the *After Dark* series during the late 1980s) and started using phone-ins as a form of talk radio, declaring, 'We are the streets.'[24]

The sense that the non-professional can be a significant resource rather than a burden is now also finding recognition within the commercial mainstream. It is recognised that the development of cheap and innovative ideas is no longer entirely a function of professional experience or age. First Granada TV and now LWT (two of the largest ITV franchise holders) have introduced special low-cost production teams, where new entrants to the industry are hired (at a third to a half of the ordinary rate) to devise and produce low-budget high-volume programming.[25] Meanwhile BBC TV's light-entertainment department has recruited five amateurs—including a media-studies graduate, garden-centre worker, data inputter and assistant theatre director, all described as 'novices with ideas, ideas, ideas'—to develop fresh programme concepts.

Hurdles to New 'Democratic Technics'

However, the obstacles to gaining greater access to multi-channel digital TV for the new 'democratic technics' remain considerable.[26] The control exercised by the private oligopolies over Britain's multi-channel TV systems now means that the public actually has less power or influence over the shape and uses of the broadcasting medium than at any previous time. The extra capacity has not led to any diminution in control, which is exerted not simply by determining those channels that are carried but in which packages or bundles they are sold. Those sold in bundles or packages that include high-rating premium channels (sport, popular new films and so on) will find their way into more homes than those that are not. In the digital world while there may be more packages closely targeted at minority viewers, the power over minority channels remains with the platform owners.[27]

So gaining access, in the right bundle/package, on the right digital platform, at the right price, will be no easy task for a more progressive and radical, non-commercialised channel, the content of which might not appeal to advertisers or the political sensibilities of the controlling transnational media conglomerates. Currently there is no regulatory mechanism to ensure provision for minori-

ties or those wanting any form of alternative service (as required of Channel
4 by the ITC, for example). Or guarantee that cable's 130-plus franchises
must provide local programming (as
required of them in the early days or as
is still required of ITV companies by the
Independent Television Commission
(ITC)).The public, through the ITC, only
has the power to license cable and
satellite channels to ensure they
conform to the standard requirements
of taste and decency, avoid incitement
to crime and offer political balance.

Animation by 4I Limited
for *The Serpent*, 1997
(Lusia)

Faced with such powerful forces and weak public control how would an alternative channel come into being? In the USA there has been some success in
prising channels for educational/community or non-commercial broadcasting
out of the grip of the powerful commercial operators. Battles during the 1930s
first raged over radio and then in the 1970s and 1980s over cable TV. While
the Broadcast Reform Movement was effectively defeated in the 1930s, the
Community Access Movement of the 1970s and '80s won a temporary victory
in 1972 when the federal government gave powers to local authorities only to
grant cable franchises to those companies that reserved some channels for
non-commercial purposes. For a period the new cable companies supported
community cable (as in the UK it was regarded as a popular and cheap form
of programming that could drive market penetration). However, as demand
deepened the cable corporations sought to overturn the 1972 ruling, which they
eventually succeeded in doing. Despite this 2000 access channels still remain
on cable TV, producing 15,000 hours per week of original programming.[28]
Thus the powerful communications companies of the United States have for
self-interested reasons welcomed minimal non-commercial use of cable during
one period, only to become vociferous opponents of non-commercial multi-
channel TV later. In the UK we have seen BSkyB, perhaps the most commercially astute and agressive of the multi-channel broadcasters, offer free carriage
to the Community Channel as part of its own marketing strategy.

The television that most of us currently receive is becoming the victim of
commercial pressures that have led to a 'dumbing-down' of content. But the
new multi-channel era of digital at least holds out the hope of a different world
in that the capacity now exists for those who want to produce challenging and
thought-provoking TV. Digital video, editing and transmission technology also
means that the non-professional with a little training and guidance can themselves produce transmittable TV. While the mainstream networks have taken
advantage of these new technologies to strengthen their own bottom lines
they have adopted many of the techniques and ideas that originated with the
advocates of low-gauge people-based TV. There is now a convergence

between the practice of TV in the mainstream and that in the low-gauge world. But while cable and satellite owners have the capacity and possibly the motive to see new, minority or niche-market uses for digital TV channels, the US experience shows these huge media conglomerates can be fickle. The only guarantee is for public authority to insist that this huge communications resource is not left entirely in the hands of private media companies and is opened up for others. So far there has been no real challenge to the media conglomerates—little or no debate has taken place on the uses of either digital terrestrial, cable or satellite for no-commercial purposes.[29]

However, digital multi-channel TV constitutes a technology that could have an extraordinary social and cultural potential. It presents opportunities for spreading radical ideas, developing alternative images of subordinated groups of people and strengthening grassroots or community values. It remains an emancipatory moment waiting to be realised.[30]

Notes

1. Boddy, 'Alternative Television in the United States'; Janine Marchessault, 'Reflections on the Dispossed: Video and the Challenge for Change Experiment', *Screen*, 36:2, summer 1995; Dovey, *Fractal Dreams*, and 'Old Dogs and New Tricks: Access Television in the UK' in T. Dowmunt (ed.), *Channels of Resistance: Global Television and Local Empowerment*, BFI, London; Engelman, *Public Radio and Television in America*; Douglas Kellner, 'Intellectuals and New Technologies', *Media Culture and Society*, 17, 1995, pp.427–8.

2. See 'A Shrinking Iceberg Travelling South: Changing Trends in British Television', *CQTV*, October 1999.

3. John Humphries, 'Do We Want a World of Infotainment Journalism', quoted in *The Times*, 15 October 1999.

4. Laurence Marks and Maurice Gran, quoted in the *Guardian*, Media, 20 September 1999.

5. See 'A Shrinking Iceberg Travelling South'.

6. See *TV International*, 19 April 1999, p.3.

7. The attraction of cheap telephony, super-fast interactivity and super-fast internet access is likely to lead to the eventual domination of digital cable. With its greater compression technology it is expected eventually to have the capacity for thousands of channels.

8. CNE was taken over by the News Corporation controlled by Pheonix] Television. CNE was launched on 3 September 1999.

9. See 'Finding Your Niche', *Cable and Satellite Europe*, May 1999.

10. 'See 'Maggie Brown's Diary', *Guardian*, Media, 8 November 1999, p.5; 'Charity TV Must Prove It is Worth Investing In', *PR Week*, 18 June 1999;, 'Do-gooders' TV? That is Historic', *Observer*, 14 November 1999;, 'Sony to Launch Asian Pay Channel', *Broadcast*, 30 January 1998, p.3; 'Finding Your Niche'; 'Mind the Gap', Cable and Satellite Europe, October 1998; 'It's Kosher: The Jewish Mother of All Game Shows', *The Times*, 20 March 1998.

11. Jon Dovey, 'Revelation of Unguessed Worlds' in Dovey (ed.), *Fractal Dreams*,

pp.110, 117; Keane, *The Media and Democracy*, p.160.

12. Jon Dovey, 'Old Dogs and New Tricks', in Dowmunt, *Channels of Resistance*, p.165.

13. See Andy Porter, Hi8tus TV, 1998.

14. See Rod Allen, 'This is not Television' in J. Steemers (ed.), *Changing Channels: The Prospect for Television in a Digital World*, University of Luton Press, 1998, p.65.

15. Dovey, *Fractal Dreams*, p.131.

16. See 'More Channels Equals More Rubbish', *Financial Times*, 2 June 1999.

17. See 'Pop Fact Fabulous', *Broadcast*, 9 October 1998.

18. See 'Why Sky is the Real Threat to ITV', *Broadcast*, 10 October 1997.

19. 'The Wight Stuff', *Television*, August/September 1999. TV12 is one of the first new local quasi-commercial broadcasters granted Restricted Service Licences to use ordinary over-air frequencies for up to four years by the Independent Television Commission (ITC). TV12 will be supported by regional advertising. Currently four areas in the UK have these new, ultra-local services.

20. 'Teen Commandments', *Creation*, June 1998.

21. B. McNair, *News and Journalism in the UK*, Routledge, London, 1999, p.158.

22. Populus, quoted in Mattelart and Piemme, 'New Means of Communication: New Questions for the Left', *Media Culture and Society*, 2, 1980, p.323.

23. Engleman, *Public Radio and Television in America*, p.261.

24. Engleman, *Public Radio and Television in America*, pp.29, 49.

25. See 'The Channels that Hope to Grow and Grow', *Financial Times*, 26 January 1998, and 'LWT Launches Lab for Low-cost Shows', *Broadcast*, 30 October 1998. 'Will Youth Triumph over the Suits?', *The Times*, 14 May 1999.

26. Lewis Mumford, quoted in Keane, *The Media and Democracy*, p.160.

27. See 'Finding Your Niche'.

28. Engleman, *Public Radio and Television in America,* p.260.

29. As Peter Goodwin points out in *Television under the Tories* (BFI, London, 1998, p.6), the debate on UK television policy has in general been confined to elite circles. The organisation of television has not featured as a General Election issue in any campaign in the 1970s, '80s or '90s.

30. I am adapting the ideas and words (as quoted in Engelman, *Public Radio and Television in America*, pp.261–2) of one of the United States' leading video activists, Dee Dee Halleck, who argues that while public-access cable TV in the USA may only occasionally carry dissident voices it has great potential for the dissemination of progressive ideas. 'The American left has largely ignored the cable potential', she argues.

SELECT BIBLIOGRAPHY

Aitken, Ian, *The Documentary Film Movement: An Anthology*, Edinburgh University Press, 1998.

Alexander, Sally, 'The Night Cleaners: An Assessment of the Campaign', in Alexander, Sally (ed.) *Becoming a Woman and Other Essays in 19th- and 20th-century Feminist History*, Virago, London, 1994.

Basinger, Jeanine, *A Woman's View: How Hollywood Spoke to Women 1930–1960*, Chatto & Windus, London, 1993.

Baxandall, Lee, and Morawski, Stefan, *Karl Marx, Frederick Engels on Literature and Art*, International General, New York, 1973.

Berger, John, *Ways of Seeing*, Penguin, London, 1972.

Beynon, Huw, and Austrin, Terry, *Masters and Servants: Class and Patronage in the Making of a Labour Organisation*, Rivers Oram, London, 1994.

Beynon, Huw, and Glavanis, Pandeli (eds), *Patterns of Social Inequality*, Longman, London, 1999.

Beynon, Huw, Hudson, Ray, and Sadler, David, *A Place Called Teeside: A Locality in a Global Economy*, Edinburgh University Press, 1994.

Boddy, William, 'Alternative Television in the United States', *Screen*, 31:1, spring 1990.

Burton, Alan, *The People's Cinema: Film and the Co-operative Movement*, BFI, London, 1994.

Campbell, Beatrix, *Wigan Pier Revisited*, Virago, London, 1984.

—*Goliath: Britain's Dangerous Places*, Methuen, London, 1993.

Caughie, John, and Rockett, Kevin, *The Companion to British and Irish Cinema*, BFI, London, 1996.

Chambers, Colin, *The Story of Unity Theatre*, Lawrence & Wishart, London, 1989.

Cook, John R., *Dennis Potter: A Life on Screen*, Manchester University Press, 1996.

Cook, Pam (ed.) *The Cinema Book*, BFI, London, 1987.

Cook, Pam, and Dodd, Philip, *Women and Film: A Sight and Sound Reader*, London, Scarlet, c. 1993.

Coole, Diana, 'Is Class a Difference that Makes a Difference?', *Radical Philosophy*, 77, May/June 1996.

Corner, John, *The Art of Record: A Critical Introduction to Documentary*, Manchester University Press, 1996.

Dickinson, Margaret, *Rogue Reels: Oppositional Film in Britain 1945–90*, BFI, London, 1999.

Dickinson, Margaret, Cottringer, Anne, and Petley, Julien, 'Workshops: A Dossier',

Vertigo, 1, spring 1993.

Dovey, Jon (ed.), *Fractal Dreams: New Media in Social Context*, Lawrence & Wishart, London, 1996.

Eagleton, Terry, *The Illusions of Postmodernism*, Blackwell, London, 1996.

Engelman, Ralph, *Public Radio and Television in America: A Political History*, Sage, Thousand Oaks, CA, 1996.

Evans, Jessica (ed.) *The Camerawork Essays: Context and Meaning in Photography*, Rivers Oram, London, 1997.

Forsyth, Scott, 'Marxism, Film and Theory: From the Barricades to Postmodernism' in Leo Panitch (ed.), *Socialist Register*, Merlin, London, 1997.

Fountain, Nigel, *Underground: The London Alternative Press, 1966–74*, Comedia, London, 1988.

Fuller, Graham, *Loach on Loach*, Faber & Faber, London, 1998.

Geraghty, Christine, *Women and Soap Opera: A Study of Prime Time Soaps*, Polity, Oxford, 1991.

Gilroy, Paul, 'Black and White?', *Vertigo*, 2, summer/autumn 1993.

Glendinning, Caroline, and Millar, Jane, *Women and Poverty in Britain in the 1990s*, Harvester Wheatsheaf, Hemel Hempstead, Herts, 1992.

Griffiths, Trevor R., and Llewellyn-Jones, Margaret, *British Women Dramatists: A Critical Handbook*, Open University Press, Buckingham, 1993.

Hall, Stuart, *The Hard Road to Renewal: Thatcherism and the Crisis of the Left*, Verso, London, 1988.

Hewison, Robert, *In Anger: 1945–1960*, Methuen, London, 1981.

—*Too Much: 1960–1975*, Methuen, London, 1986.

Higson, Andrew, *Waving the Flag: Constructing a New National Cinema in Britain*, Oxford University Press, 1995.

Hill, John, *Sex, Class and Realism: British Cinema, 1956–1963*, BFI, London, 1985.

—*British Cinema in the 1980s: Issues and Themes*, Clarendon, Oxford, 1999.

—'Every Fuckin' Choice Stinks', *Sight and Sound*, 8:11, November 1998.

Hogenkamp, Bert, 'The Sunshine of Socialism: The CPGB and Film in the 1950s' in Croft, Andy (ed.), *A Weapon in the Struggle: The Cultural History of the Communist Party in Britain*, Pluto, London, 1998.

Hogenkamp, Bert, *Deadly Parallels: Film and the Left in Britain, 1929–1939*, Lawrence & Wishart, London, 1986.

Hudson, Ray, and Williams, Alan M., *Divided Britain*, Belhaven, London, 1989.

James, David E., and Berg, Rick, *The Hidden Foundation: Cinema and the Question of Class*, University of Minnesota, Minneapolis, 1996.

Jancovich, Mark, *Rational Fears: American Horror in the 1950s*, Manchester University Press, 1996.

Keane, John, *The Media and Democracy*, Polity, 1991.

Kuhn, Annette, *The Power of the Image: Essays on Representation and Sexuality*, Routledge & Kegan Paul, London, 1985.

Laing, Stuart, *Representations of Working Class Life 1957–64*, Macmillan, London, 1986.

Lovell, Terry, *Pictures of Reality: Aesthetics, Politics and Pleasure*, BFI, London, 1980.

Lukács, Georg, *The Meaning of Contemporary Realism*, Merlin, London, 1963.

Macdonald, Kevin and Cousins, Mark (eds) *Imagining Reality: The Faber Book of Documentary*, Faber and Faber, London, 1996.

McKnight, George, *Agent of Challenge and Defiance: The Films of Ken Loach*, Flicks, Trowbridge, Wilts, 1997.

McRobbie, Angela, *Back to Reality? Social Experience and Cultural Studies*, Manchester University Press, 1997.

Maschler, Tom (ed.), *Declaration*, MacGibbon & Kee, London, 1957.

Mitchell, Carla, 'How Not to Disappear from That Choice: Four Corners, 1972–1985', *Filmwaves*, 4, spring 1998.

Murphy, Robert, *Sixties British Cinema*, BFI, London, 1992.

—(ed.), *The British Cinema Book*, BFI, London, 1997.

Neve, Brian, *Film and Politics in America: A Social Tradition*, Routledge, London, 1992.

Nightingale, Virginia, *Studying Audiences: The Shock of the Real*, Routledge, London, 1996.

Norris, Christopher, *New Idols of the Cave*, Manchester University Press, 1997.

O'Morgan, Kenneth, *The People's Peace: British History since 1945*, Oxford University Press, 1998.

Paget, Derek, *No Other Way to Tell It: Dramadoc/Docudrama on Television*, Manchester University Press, 1998.

Philips, Deborah, and Haywood, Ian, *Brave New Causes: Women in Post-war British Fictions*, Leicester University Press, London, 1998.

Philo, Greg, and Miller, David (eds), *Market Killing: What the Free Market Does and What Social Scientists Can Do about It*, Longman, London, 2000.

Pilger, John, *Hidden Agendas*, Vintage, London, 1998.

Pines, Jim (ed.), *Black and White in Colour: Black People in British Television since 1936*, BFI, London, 1992.

Pines, Jim and Willemen, Paul, *Questions of Third Cinema*, BFI, London, 1991.

Raban, William, 'Lifting Traces', *Filmwaves*, 4, spring 1998.

Rees, A. L., *A History of Experimental Film and Video: From the Canonical Avant-garde to Contemporary British Practice*, BFI, London, 1999.

Richards, Jeffrey, *Films and British Identity: From Dickens to Dad's Army*, Manchester University Press, 1997.

Richards, Jeffrey, and Sheridan, Dorothy, *Mass Observation at the Movies*, Routledge & Kegan Paul, London, 1987.

Roberts, John, *The Art of Interruption: Realism, Photography and the Everyday*, Manchester University Press, 1998.

Roberts, John, 'Philosophising the Everyday: The Philosophy of Praxis and the Fate of Cultural Studies', *Radical Philosophy: A Journal of Socialist and Feminist Philosophy*, 98, November/December 1999.

Rowbotham, Sheila, *A Century of Women: The History of Women in Britain and the United States*, Penguin, London, 1997.

Rowbotham, Sheila, and Mitter, Swasti, *Dignity and Daily Bread: New Forms of Economic Organisation among Poor Women in the Third World and the First*, Routledge, London, 1994.

Savage, Mike, and Miles, Andrew, *The Remaking of the British Working-class, 1840–1940*, Routledge, London 1994.

Segal, Lynne, *Why Feminism? Gender, Psychology, Politics*, Polity, Oxford, 1999.

Schnitzer, Luda, and Jean, and Martin, Marcel (eds), *Cinema in Revolution: The Heroic Age of the Soviet Film*, Secker & Warburg, London, 1973.

Spender, Humphrey, *Worktown People: Photographs from Northern England, 1937–38*, Falling Wall, Bristol, 1982.

Stacey, Jackie, *Star Gazing: Hollywood Cinema and Female Spectatorship*, Routledge, London, 1994.

Stead, Peter, *Film and the Working Class: The Feature Film in British and American Society*, Routledge, London, 1989.

Thompson, E. P., *The Poverty of Theory*, Merlin, London, 1978.

Thompson, Kristin, and Bordwell, David, *Film History: An Introduction*, McGraw Hill, New York, 1994.

Voloshinov, V. N., *Marxism and the Philosophy of Language*, Harvard University Press, Cambridge, MA, 1986.

Williams, Raymond, *Marxism and Literature*, Oxford University Press, 1977.

Williamson, Judith, *Deadline at Dawn: Film Criticism, 1980–1990*, Marion Boyars, London, 1993.

Wollen, Peter (ed.), *Raiding the Icebox: Reflections on Twentieth-century Culture*, Verso, London, 1993.

Wood, Ellen Meiksins, *Democracy against Capitalism: Renewing Historical Materialism*, Cambridge University Press, 1996.

Worpole, Ken, 'Oppositional Culture: Yesterday, Today and Tomorrow', *Camerawork*, 11, September 1978.

Youngblood, Denise J., *Movies for the Masses: Popular Cinema and Soviet Society in the 1920s*, Cambridge University Press, New York, 1992.

INDEX